What's In A Name? - And Other Pieces Of My Mind

WHAT'S IN A NAME? - AND OTHER PIECES OF MY MIND

THE POWER OF NOMENCLATURE

Stephen Pearl

ISBN-13: 9781542697620
ISBN-10: 154269762X
Library of Congress Control Number: 2017900980
CreateSpace Independent Publishing Platform
North Charleston, South Carolina

Cover Illustration by Dominique Andréassier

TABLE OF (DIS)CONTENTS

For Brigitte, helpmeet extraordinary and plenipotentiary

FOREWORD

———◆———

IN THE DAYS BEFORE COMPUTERS came on the scene and changed things beyond recognition, people kept notes in files and placed those files in filing cabinets; that is to say, some people did—namely, those with a purpose in doing so.

I was not one of them. When thoughts occurred to me that I wanted to retain, I scrawled them on whatever piece of paper happened to be at hand. I kept these papers—unsorted, mostly undated, and always without context—in bags and shoe boxes, and with no clear, or even foggy notion of an ultimate purpose.

Then came computers. I am always late in adopting new technology; I was one of the last to give up my wooden-frame tennis racket for one with a metal frame, and I succumbed to fashion only to discover that I was already behind it. Steel had by then given way to aluminum and then to carbon fiber and then fiberglass, and rackets had grown bigger heads. But by this time, the first of my God-given hips had given way to plastic and cobalt chrome and the second, eleven years later, to ceramic, and active sports had become limited to the Exercycle.

EXODUS
Computers brought with them programs such as Squarenote, suggestively subtitled "The Ideas Library," and stimulated me to organize my scraps of paper. Many had to be discarded, either because they lacked enough context to be usable or because the handwriting was indecipherable. The remainder posed

the taxing and taxonomic problem of sorting them into meaningful categories, especially since many of them fell into more than one.

The Promised Land

So it was with Squarenote, which worked only in something called DOS and took me only as far as Windows, that my poor filing habits were superseded. There I was, stranded by the side of the road with a broken-down vehicle—indeed, one beyond repair until, after hitching successive rides with passing vehicles, I was finally set down at what I dearly hoped was my final destination—Evernote.

"Be Fruitful and Multiply"

Over the years, multiplication has proceeded apace, and the individual "shreds and patches" have been sorted and amalgamated into the various pieces in the pages that follow, and constitute an attempt at fruition.

Something that caught me unawares—and only very gradually over the years—was the fact that a substantial number of the pieces, although differing in theme and title, appeared to be organically linked with the effects of "nomenclature." I have placed them under the umbrella category "What's in a Name?"

The other pieces may not appear on the surface—at least to the author—to have any one thematic link in common, but if there is (as is likely, since they are all the products of one and the same network of neurons), it may well be more apparent to an outsider looking in.

Other groupings of pieces have gradually emerged, including, notably, one related to the society, lifestyle, politics, idiosyncrasies, personalities, and events of the country where I have now spent most of my life. These are grouped under the heading "Americana."

Another group of subjects, which over time gradually came to appear to belong under the same umbrella, is titled "The Sexes." I decided against the title "The Genders" in case readers of my own generation might—and commendably—take it for a treatise on grammar and for fear that readers of their grandchildren's generation might take it for a TV family sitcom.

The remaining pieces were too recalcitrant to be driven kicking and screaming under a one-size-fits-none umbrella.

WHERE ARE YOU COMING FROM?

"FULL DISCLOSURE"

It has been my experience that very often when issues are controversial and freighted with history, interlocutors, rather than listening to what other parties are actually saying, simply focus on determining "where they are coming from" or which side of the particular fence—my side or the other side—they are on. In my own case, "where I am coming from" is, among other things, from *outside* the United States, the country where I live and where I arrived fully equipped with the culture, history, values, and traditions of the country where I was born, raised, and educated—the United Kingdom.

Winston Churchill is famously reported to have quipped that the British and the Americans are two nations divided by the same language. That same language, however, has the effect of obscuring or blurring differences in national temperament, outlook, and values, which can be just as great as those between Americans and other European nations with whom they do not share a common language.

My sensitivity to the differentness of American phenomena was very sharp when I arrived, and while it has no doubt been blunted by years of residence, it still remains.

One result of expatriation is that it has lent distance to my view of the old country and, with that distance, a measure of *outsider* detachment in looking back at it.

There is an old saying that "the spectator sees more of the game." There may be some truth in this, although decidedly not in the case of American football, which is best watched through the lens of the TV cameraman.

I first saw American football being played live at the old New York Giants stadium in the Bronx. I came armed with typical British scorn for what appeared to be a grotesque, spasmodic, and unfathomable travesty of rugby. Over the years, without intending or trying to, I have become a zealous convert to what I believe to be the world's most compelling spectator sport since the Roman gladiatorial shows—especially now that you can fast-forward through the commercials. Its unique charm is that you don't have to be a fan or supporter of either team in order to find it entertaining, and even gripping, although there are one or two rules I would change to make it even more so.

But when it came to American language, life, and culture, no one old enough to have lived in Britain through the Second World War and well beyond it before coming to the United States could have been anything other than well primed.

Before the advent of television, the cinema was far and away the most popular mass entertainment in my youth, an entertainment consisting almost exclusively of Hollywood films depicting American life and culture—however glamorized—with American actors speaking their own language. For school-age children, there were even special showings on Saturday mornings for, if memory serves, the modest sum of six pence. My whole cohort and I grew up with Mickey Rooney, Judy Garland, Abbott and Costello, the Marx Brothers, and somewhat later, the "Road" films, with Bob Hope, Bing Crosby, and Dorothy Lamour.

In the latter stages of the war, I lived through the friendly occupation of the country by GIs—"overpaid, oversexed, and over here!" as the saying went.

Later still, during my national service in the Royal Air Force, when British youths and maidens converged in droves on "dance halls" on Saturday nights, we new recruits were allowed out of our barracks and descended on the nearby town of Warrington, Lancashire. Our pay was fourteen shillings a week, and we were hopelessly outmatched by the vastly better-paid "licentious American soldiery" from neighboring US bases in their slick gabardine uniforms, who spoke in the glamorous accents of the Hollywood movies. We were relegated to the one-shilling dance hall at the YMCA, undoubtedly not frequented by the cream of Warrington's young womanhood.

My second year in the RAF was spent in Cambridge, lodged in a private hotel that could well have served as the setting for the film *Separate Tables*, based on the Terrence Rattigan play. It was located in Newnham Terrace, very close to Newnham College, one of the two women's colleges of Cambridge University at the time. The same "licentious soldiery" were still with us, and they were to be seen "walking *our* babies back home" every evening before the college's curfew. (The song "Walking My Baby Back Home," sung by Nat King Cole, was very popular at the time.)

Finally, it is my hope that readers of these pieces might be interested, amused, entertained, influenced, piqued, or even mildly provoked, but above all, what I hope for is a reaction that I assume any author might aspire to elicit— that some readers will say to themselves, "I never thought of it like that!" or "I had never made that connection!"

Stephen Pearl

WHAT'S IN A NAME?
THE POWER OF NOMENCLATURE

———◆———

Juliet: "What's in a name? That which we call a rose
By any other name would smell as sweet."

If it's possible to answer a rhetorical question, then the answer is a hell of a lot more than even Shakespeare envisaged.

The following fifteen pieces, in one way or another, all reflect the power of nomenclature to influence attitudes and events—and ultimately behavior.

TOPIC 1

ENGLAND/(GREAT) BRITAIN/UNITED KINGDOM? WHO ARE WE, AND WHERE DO WE COME FROM?

IN THEIR TWO-MAN LONDON REVUE, *At the Drop of a Hat*, performed in the 1950s, Michael Flanders and Donald Swann composed an "English National Song."

It was designed, according to Flanders in his introduction, to fill the gap so tenuously occupied by "Jerusalem" and to get back at the "three unfriendly powers": the Irish, Scots, and Welsh, who shared the British Isles with those Johnny-come-lately Anglo-Saxon immigrants and who each had their own national songs in their own languages, which in all likelihood contained rude remarks about the English. Michael Flanders scratched the surface of a serious and deep-lying discomfort when he pointed out that "when we've won, the newspapers write "Great Britain wins," but when we lose, it's "England loses again."

The French, *en revanche*, to name but one of the more fortunate nations, lead lives of enviable and unequivocal noncomplexity. They never have the slightest doubt or hesitation (well, unless they are unsure of their gender or number) about who they are—"français(e)(s)"—and where they come from—France.

Early on in my career at the United Nations in New York, we were lined up and presented to then secretary general U Thant. When my turn came, the chief of my service told U Thant my name and that I was from the United Kingdom. U Thant asked me, "You are British?" I assented. I doubt he could have gotten away with quite such an economical expenditure of his scarce conversational resources if I had been, for example, French. Having been told I was from France, even he might have felt that it was a touch threadbare to content himself by asking if I was French.

Since then, I have always envied the advantages enjoyed by the French over the inhabitants of the British Isles in terms of national nomenclature. Their country is known unambiguously and unequivocally by a single name; it is a name, moreover, which is immediately more or less recognizable on the lips of speakers of most of the world's languages. It consists of a single word—nay, a single syllable—with all the economy of time and effort that affords; it can be used, except perhaps by one or two disaffected Basques and Bretons, without let, hindrance, qualm, or misgiving, by all its citizens.

When the French are writing home, they don't have to wrestle with second thoughts about whether they may be offending the delicate sensibilities of friends in different parts of the country, as I do when I am addressing envelopes to people in Edinburgh, Cardiff, or Belfast. Should it be "Edinburgh, Scotland"; "Edinburgh, Scotland, UK"; or "Edinburgh, UK"? I even suffer a twinge of guilt when I address an envelope to "London, England," *tout court*, and usually end up adding "UK" for a little affirmative action.

When people in the United States, as they so often do, ask me "Where are you from?" I usually take evasive action by replying "London," hoping against hope, if I am too near the Canadian border at the time, that they will not follow up with the supplementary "London, Ontario?" and force me to specify the name of the country where my London happens to be situated.

When I am writing from abroad, I never quite know how to address the envelope, especially to correspondents in Cardiff or Edinburgh. Should it be "Wales" or "Scotland," and should I leave it at that, with all its *independentista* implications? Or should it be "Wales" or "Scotland" followed by "(Gt.) Britain" or "UK," with the condescending and disobliging implication that the Albanian or Mexican postal service wouldn't know where on earth Wales or Scotland was otherwise? Or, on the third hand, should I leave it at "Wales/Scotland" *tout court* because of my uneasy awareness that if I were writing to "England" it would never occur to me to add "(Gt.) Britain" or "UK," thus ascribing an invidious and overweening primacy to one member of the union?

All this is complicated by the fact that people in many foreign countries actually mean (Great) Britain or the United Kingdom when they use what appears to be their word for "England" or "English," a usage at which the Scots, Welsh, and Irish, understandably but wrongly, tend to take umbrage, since no offense is willfully intended. The Russians do this with *Anglia* and *Anglisky*. When they issued a postage stamp in honor of G. B. Shaw, they described him as "The Great Anglisky Writer." The French really have no choice, since the same misplaced *amour propre* that makes them call the English Channel "The Sleeve" precludes their calling us "*Grande* Bretagne," especially since General de Gaulle, on behalf of his countrymen, reserved it for their use, as in *la vocation de grandeur de la France*. This leaves only "Bretagne," which is already spoken for by their own skittish province of that name.

I have to say that in recent years I have taken to writing "UK" in the space provided for both "citizenship" and "country of origin" in innumerable landing cards and immigration forms around the world, but only because the extreme brevity of this option has saved me many man-hours of scribal effort. The core issue remains unresolved.

Attentive readers will have noted that I can only bring myself to put the "Great" or "Gt." in "Great Britain" in parentheses. This is a true reflection of my discomfort with the immodesty and increasing inappropriateness of the apparent claim to "greatness," which, as we have seen, de Gaulle has preempted.

T.—or should it be A.?—Blair may very well succeed in dragging us kicking and screaming into "modernity" by attempting to strip us of all those institutions and features, such as ermine-clad peers in the House of Lords, that make Britain, while not exactly great, shall we say, distinctive and interesting, at least in the eyes of foreigners. However, except for Greenwich Mean Time and being the terrors of the terraces at football grounds around the world, there is really not enough primacy left to warrant the use of the word "great" in its nonterritorial sense. Paradoxically, the comparative form of the adjective, as in "Greater" London, seems to convey a lesser degree of *braggadocio* or chest thumping than "great" itself.

In international organizations and meetings around the world, countries are entirely free to call themselves whatever they like—and they frequently do—and not only in their own language! "Cote d'Ivoire" and—at least at the time of writing—"The Libyan Arab Jamahariya" are both the official English names of those two countries.

Now, as far as I can determine, the official name of the country we are talking about seems to be "The United Kingdom of Great Britain and Northern

Ireland," which, now that I come to think of it, makes us the world title holder not only in length and grandiosity of nomenclature but also in the unwieldiness of the acronym it generates—TUKGBNI.

In international bodies, countries sit in (usually English) alphabetical order. However, instead of taking their proper places among the Ts, along with Thailand, Tanzania, and the like, "British" representatives choose to sit behind nameplates marked "UK." However, perhaps this is because they like to cozy up to their immediate neighbors and "special relations" from the "US"—although on the other hand, it used to mean sitting next to the USSR. Of course, this played "right" into their hands since it gave them the—frequently exploited—opportunity of referring waggishly to "my neighbor on the *left*."

This disquisition would not be complete without extending my sympathies to those who share the territory of the British Isles with the "English," for the discomfiture to which they must be continually exposed when they are traveling "abroad" (a term that itself must give them—or at least a good many of them—pause).

"Where are you from?" they will be asked by friendly natives of "abroad," or worse, Englishness will be assumed and thrust upon them, whereupon they must strive to disabuse those friendly natives of this objectionable misidentification good-humoredly, coolly, testily, indignantly, or even with outrage, as the spirit moves them.

TOPIC 2

PROPAGANDA BY NAMING: "A ROSE BY ANY OTHER NAME SMELLS AS SWEET"

———◆———

WELL, NOT QUITE! IF IT did "smell as sweet," the proabortionists would not have called themselves "pro-choice," and the antiabortionists would not have chosen the title "pro-life"! Significantly, the former would not have balked at describing themselves as "pro-life," nor the latter at "pro-choice"—at least not before these catchphrases had come to be identified irrevocably with the causes they find anathema.

Shakespeare is, of course, referring to a *tabula rasa* "state of nature" before words had been chosen to represent things and concepts in the various languages and had not yet acquired non-onomatopoeic associations.

Take "family planning." This title seriously misrepresents what the subject is really about—namely, the freedom to have sex without fear of pregnancy and its consequences through the use of contraception. It would be quite a stretch to claim that unmarried adolescents who use contraception do so in order to plan a family. When they don't use it, and the female partner falls pregnant, the traditional telltale formula for describing this misfortune used to be that she was "in the family way." The result may have been "unplanned" but cannot be described as a "family."

But spouses are equally free to "plan their families" without contraception, by abstaining from sex if they don't want children and indulging in it freely if they do as well as by staggering their episodes according to their "family plan." This, of course, is not the kind of "family planning" or "choice" that raises the hackles of the "pro-life" camp, whose hackles are perversely left conspicuously unraised when it comes to the inevitable loss of life in such events as the "shock and awe" bombing of Baghdad in 2003, which took the lives of thousands of civilians. The number is disputed by the bombing side, but the fact is not. In the course of the "just cause" US invasion of Panama in 1989, the estimate of the loss of civilian lives varied between three hundred and six hundred, but once again, the fact was not in dispute and left "pro-lifers" equally unmoved.

For the "family planning" supporters, coming straight out with it means proclaiming that they are in favor of what has become, or has been made to appear, an ugly-sounding process. For the other side, "telling it like it is" would mean coming straight out and proclaiming that their campaign is in a negative cause, and what is even more damaging, losing the public relations benefits of the implication that theirs is a positive campaign that allows them to pose simply as champions of life itself, something that everyone is in favor of—except, of course, ISIS, Al-Qaeda, and, by implication, their "pro-choice" adversaries. There are, doubtless, pro-lifers who have nothing against capital punishment or killing their enemies—that is to say, against going blithely about their business while others do the killing for them.

Thus, the abortion debate is one in which what it is really *about* is tendentiously represented, misrepresented, or suppressed by the names chosen by the pro and anti movements.

TOPIC 3

A FALSE PARALLEL

———◆———

IN HER JANUARY 5, 1997, letter to the *New York Times*, titled "But Some of My Best Friends Are…" Polly S. Browder wrote, "Why is it that WASP is the only ethnic slur that is still considered to be politically correct?"

"Sticks and stones can hurt my bones, but names will never hurt me." So goes the old children's chant. But saying it doesn't make it true—unless, of course, you are a "WASP."

As a rule, when people start by saying "Why is it that?" they are not actually seeking enlightenment so much as giving vent to indignation, but if it *is* a question, then this is the answer.

Relations between groups in a society, especially between what are conventionally known as minorities and majorities, are not necessarily reciprocal or mirror images. The ability to wound by name-calling is, in fact, one-way traffic—from the majority to the minority. There is a sense in which WASP is neither ethnic nor a slur. "Whitey" and "honky" are only superficially or formally equivalent to the opprobrious epithets whites can use to wound and "put down" blacks and other "undesirables." When such epithets as "honky" are used to or about whites as a way of hitting back, although the intent may be to wound, the effect is not. In the days when the sitcom *The Jeffersons* was prime-time entertainment, there was no groundswell of outrage on the part of the predominantly white viewing public or indeed on the part of the white characters who were its targets in reaction to the endless antiwhite racial invective uttered by George Jefferson. This was because neither the white characters nor the white viewers felt particularly wounded or ethnically slurred.

9

"Down to up" opprobrium has never worked. Short people can never really "put down" and get back at tall people, no matter how ingenious and inventive their range of invective may be, for the humiliation the tall can inflict on the short by mere name-calling. "You big...!" can never make up for the humiliation inflicted by "you little...!" Most recently, in March 2016, during the campaign for the Republican nomination for the US presidency, Donald Trump had frequent resort to the use of the word "little" to humiliate a distinctly shorter rival, Marco Rubio. Rubio's rather desperate and contrived efforts to retaliate were ineffectual—for something like the same reasons that Jefferson's "honkies" fizzled out like damp squibs.

WASP, unlike the real ethnic slurs reserved for minorities, is not associated with, or a probable precursor to, a history, a likelihood, or a fear of actual persecution. Furthermore, when a member of a majority uses an offensive epithet to or about a minority or one of its members, he or she is also reminding him or her of all the derogatory and inferiority stereotypes it implies—stereotypes that are not only purveyed by the majority but have also seeped into the consciousness of the targeted minorities themselves. That is why pseudocompliments like "blacks are fast runners" or "blacks have rhythm" are, in fact, offensive. The movie *White Men Can't Jump* got a totally free ride and passed without comment, while Jimmy the Greek (a cognomen, which ironically might itself well have passed for an ethnic slur), a well-known sportscaster for CBS, was fired for publicly claiming precisely that "blacks can jump higher."

The principal stereotype shared by all minorities in a society about the majority is that of invulnerably superior or privileged status. When, for example, did a white American ever try to "pass for" black—except for a stunt? This stereotype of the majority conveys nothing of the lacerating contempt inherent in bona-fide slurs where even the very nomenclature of the target group is itself a slur—nigger, kike, wop, take your "spick," terms that have now been outlawed from polite society and that if used by those in the public eye can cost people their jobs. An extreme but illuminating case was the innocent use of "denigrate" in a public forum, which cost the user his position. If "honky" were indeed a true and equivalent slur, everyone connected with the sitcom *The Jeffersons* would have been fired—indeed, it would never have been uttered in the first place.

The hatred may be mutual, but not, alas, the contempt—a weapon that can only be wielded effectively by the stronger party against the weaker, whether the parties are individuals or groups.

EIN VOLK, EIN REICH, EIN FÜHRER! HISTORY'S MOST TRAGIC MISUNDERSTANDING

———◆———

IT HAS BEEN REPORTED THAT Adolf Hitler's ambition was to be a painter. Frustrated in that goal, the story goes, he took it out on the Jews and every European country within reach.

The reason why the real truth has been withheld from the general public for so long is that it was only recently that I happened to learn the real meaning of the word "führer"—which is, of course, what A. H. fervently wished to become if he could not be a painter. It was while I was in Vienna idly thumbing through a guidebook to the city that I noticed the word "führer" recurring frequently in the text. Alarmed by what appeared to be clear evidence of a recrudescence of Nazism, I hastened to consult reliable German-speaking sources. The unequivocal consensus was that, in fact, the word means nothing more dire or sinister than "tour guide," a perfectly harmless and respectable vocation and one often exercised by artists-in-waiting as a stopgap until such time as their artistry is duly recognized and rewarded. Suddenly all the pieces of the puzzle fell into place, and it became clear what had actually happened.

Except for Christopher Isherwood and one or two other decadents, Weimar Germany was not a major tourist Mecca, and any decline in tourism always hits hardest those on the front lines of the industry—tour guides, among others.

Wandering disconsolately around Munich one day at that time, young Adolf must have fallen in with a friendly bunch of brown-shirted individuals, who somehow gave him to understand in the course of conversation that they were looking for a führer and that if he happened to be interested in trying out for the job, he would have to come down to the beer hall to be interviewed.

Down at the beer hall, he was told that when his name was called, he would be taken in to meet the search committee and that the audition would take the form of an off-the-cuff, stand-up, raving and ranting routine. Many of the candidates gave excellent accounts of themselves as ranters or ravers, but young Adolf alone impressed the committee with his performance in both departments.

He got the job, and although it turned out not to be at all the tour-guide position he had aspired to, with the job market as difficult as it was, he could not afford to be too choosy. Later on, when the slogan "Ein Volk, Ein Reich, Ein Führer" became the order of the day and A. H. had secured a firm monopoly over the führer business, all the other tour guides in the Third Reich, if they wanted to stay in business, probably had to do so under another title, and if I had done my homework properly, I would, of course, have let you know what it was. But except for that, the rest is history.

NATURE, NURTURE, OR NOMENCLATURE? NO MORE BABY TALK!

———◆———

SOMETIMES, USING CERTAIN WORDS FOR certain things (rather than other available alternatives) is of great social significance in terms of both cause and effect. By way of example, here is a sneak preview of one of the provisions from the Nomenclature Revision Act 2084.

WHEREAS: people, particularly women, as the parties primarily concerned, are always talking about having "babies",

WHEREAS: babies are particularly cuddly, innocent, helpless, small, large-headed, and big-eyed, which traits have been shown by analysis of the proportions of Mickey Mouse and other Disney cartoon figures to be congenitally disarming, appealing, and endearing,

WHEREAS: no woman, or man, for that matter, can be reasonably expected to resist the "triple threat" of being disarmed, appealed to, and endeared all at once—not to mention the milky, talcumy body odor that babies keep in reserve to wipe out any lingering pockets of resistance,

WHEREAS: with an average life expectancy of more than seventy years for the US population, babies can not only be expected to turn into "people" at some point, but, depending on where the transition is thought to occur—First Communion, bar mitzvah, high school graduation, menarche, pogonarche—can also be expected to stay that way for a good 70 percent of their existence,

WHEREAS: further, there is the intervening period of "childhood," when most former babies, along with the scaling down of head and eye size and the consequent ebbing of innocence, cuddliness, and the other built-in neonatal charms, have also developed individual characteristics ranging from hard-to-live-with to actively repellent, such as the capacity for forming and expressing judgments—often uncomplimentary—about their erstwhile absolute rulers,

WHEREAS: this cuts down even further the proportion of their lives that "people" spend as "babies" to about 3 percent at the outside,

WHEREAS: on top of it all, with the particularly long life expectancy of women, the would-be mother who was so eager to come home with a "baby" may very well end up as the mother of a person who is him- or herself a middle-aged frump, bore, shrew, slattern, drunk, failure, or snob in a state of unappealing physical decrepitude, and this may last for six or seven times as long as she was the mother of the corresponding "baby," and furthermore, as is conclusively borne out by fleeting, secondhand, casual, sporadic, and impressionistic observations and other such compelling scientific data, this sad, overweight, over-mortgaged, divorced, frustrated, balding, and geographically distant "child," who somehow never made it to law school or medical school and has chosen a hopelessly unsuitable mate, in eight and a half cases out of ten is, moreover, liable to be ungrateful for everything she, the mother, has done for him or her,

WHEREAS: the careful fostering and inculcating of the notion that what in fact women give birth to in maternity hospitals are *people*, who happen to spend an insignificant, temporary, short, and swiftly vanishing portion of their lives in cuddly-hood, can only exert a sobering and moderating influence on the rush to motherhood, and anything that helps people toward a more precise recognition of what they are in for must be better for society as a whole—hence all the pressure for truth in advertising,

IT IS HEREBY DECREED: that throughout this republic—and any others that have the good sense to know a good law when they see one, or all others that have the good fortune to be in receipt of foreign aid from this republic, aid that can easily be cut off if they do not shape up—the use of the word "baby" shall be prohibited in all formal, professional, medical, and public documents and utterances in connection with childbirth, maternity, child welfare, and the care and nurture of the human person in infancy. It shall be a federal offense for the post office and wire, cable, and telegram companies to accept the word for transmission and for it to be printed, aired, or posted publicly on TV, on the radio, on the Internet, and in print media. All advertising of goods and services in connection with pre-, post-, and perinatal processes and events shall replace the word "baby" with "person."

In all graphic material depicting parents and neonates, equal and proportionate exposure shall be given to all the chronological phases of parenthood so that the image of the aged mother with her bald, sagging, grizzled, bifocal, and curmudgeonly son shall be as common as that of the young mother with the tender-skinned, appetizing, milky, and dimpled proto-person cradled at her breast.

After all, of Shakespeare's seven ages of man, there are likely to be five during which you are the child of some unfortunate adult beguiled into parenthood by the purest accident of evolution, whereby people are born at the peak of their appeal and then have nowhere to go but down, instead of the other way around. It is only fair for these five ages to be given equal time or even a little affirmative action!

TOPIC 6

"NAZI" ATROCITIES AND "JAPANESE" WAR CRIMES

———◆———

ATROCITIES AND WAR CRIMES COMMITTED by Germans during World War II have tended subsequently to be attributed to Nazis, as demonstrated by the examples quoted below. But when committed by Japanese, they were, and still are, attributed to…well…Japanese.

This either unfairly exculpates Germans or unfairly inculpates Japanese. What are the roots of this distinction? Is it a Euro-racist phenomenon, with the implication that barbaric cruelty is somehow endemic in non-Europeans but just an exceptional aberration in people who look like us?

I don't know whether Asian publications or politicians have ever had much to say about German war crimes and atrocities, or if they have, what terminology they tend to favor for "German" and "Japanese" in this connection.

Wikipedia. "Pope Francis Visits Nazi Death Camps at Auschwitz," July 28, 2016.

The *Wikipedia* article states, "With many of their Jewish and a good number of their Christian citizens slaughtered by the *Nazi* aggressor. After the war, from 1945 to 1949, the *Nazi* regime was put on trial in two tribunals in Nuremberg, Germany by the victorious Allied powers. The first tribunal indicted 24 major *Nazi* war criminals."

Taylor, Ihsan. "No Resistance." Review of *Priscilla: The Hidden Life of an Englishwoman in Wartime France*, by Nicholas Shakespeare. *New York Times Book Review.*

According to the review, this book is "the story of a femme fatale who made painful compromises to survive the *Nazi* occupation." Wasn't it actually the *German* army?

Review of *The Short List*, by Nancy Kline. *New York Times Book Review*, March 8, 2015, p. 34.

The book uses the term "Nazi" in the following description: "now a fashionable hostess, thanks to her Nazi lover."

Donadio, Rachel. "Preserving the Ghastly Inventory of Auschwitz." *New York Times*, April 16, 2015, p. 1.

This article states, "The idea is to keep the place exactly as it was when the *Nazis* retreated before the *Soviet* army arrived." Isn't that the same army that's now called the "Russian army"? Or should it by the same token have been known at that time as the "*Communist* army"?

The article uses the term "Nazi" again, describing "the gas chamber of Birkenau...the structure that the *Nazis* blew up in their retreat" and finally on page A11 when it says, "The *Nazis* didn't want it to last."

A Russian law banning Nazi propaganda has succeeded in removing *Maus*, one of the greatest anti-*Nazi* chronicles, from its bookshelves,

Maus, the Pulitzer Prize-winning graphic novel by Art Spiegelman, has been withdrawn from Moscow bookstores. In the book, which tells Spiegelman's family's story, Jews are portrayed as mice, and—refreshing exception—*Germans* as cats. Its cover features a mouse couple huddled below a swastika bearing a Hitler/cat emblem.

TV Guide. "Nova: *Nazi* attack on America." "The Week," May 8, 2015. The description of this program states the following:

A generation after the Lusitania, *German* U-boats were attacking America again. Few Americans knew that during WW2 Hitler's navy sank more than 50 ships in the Gulf of Mexico, claiming 5,000 lives... Bob Ballard, the ocean explorer found a sunken *Nazi* sub, and helped to expose a brazen *Nazi* operation that Washington long kept hidden.

Cowles, Gregory. Review of *The Art of Memoir*, by Mary Karr. *New York Times Book Review*, October 25, 2015, p. 20.

"Oliver Sacks described in his memoir *Uncle Tungsten*—the dropping of a *Nazi* bomb on his London neighbourhood."

I doubt the post–World War II German media have ever described the bombs dropped on Dresden by the Royal Air Force as anything but *British* bombs, certainly not *constitutional monarchic* or *parliamentary democratic* bombs, regardless of whatever political regime may have held sway in Britain at the time.

A similar if not analogous case of propaganda by nomenclature was that of the morning news on WQXR, the radio station of the *New York Times* at the time of the Vietnam War.

Every morning, I would listen to the morning news before I left for work, and every morning, the first item was the report of casualties on both sides of the war.

It was always couched in these terms: "Communists dead"—usually a lot—and "Americans dead"—usually far fewer. I couldn't help hoping against hope that one morning I would turn on the radio and have the satisfaction of hearing "Today, the Pentagon announced the following casualties in the fighting: "*Vietnamese*—(a lot), *capitalists*—(a few)."

Ironically enough, the newscast was at that time always followed by this announcement: "The news was brought to you by Krakus and Atalanta Polish ham," accompanied by the boost, "delicious ham imported from Poland by Krakus and Atalanta," as advertised in the *Milwaukee Journal* at that time. Poland at that time was a member of the Communist Military Warsaw Pact.

COFFEE, ANYONE?

———◆———

THE ALMOST UNIVERSAL USE OF coffee has spawned a bewildering variety of terms connected with its consumption, which can be a veritable minefield for the unwary coffee drinker outside his or her native habitat.

It is no good assuming that if you just ask for "coffee" or the dictionary equivalent of it in the language of the country you are in, you will get what you bargained for. You will either get something you didn't expect, or, most likely, requests you probably won't understand for further specification.

In Brazil, you will probably be asked to specify *café* (some version of Nescafe) or *cafe-cafe* (the real thing).

In Chile, if you ask for what you think *cafe con leche* means in your language, or by some vague association with "café au lait," you are in for a (probably unpalatable) surprise (coffee made with milk and nothing but milk).

In Vienna, if you don't know your *verlaengete* from your *melange* (half milk and half coffee) or your *Brauner* (very little milk) from your *Einspaenner* (in a glass with cream) or your *Kapuziner* (a little milk), you had better ask for tea. As for *Schwarzer*, maybe you had better just ask for your coffee *ohne milch*, just in case there are any politically sensitive New Yorkers within earshot.

In Jamaica, however, if you do ask for "tea," you should be forewarned that it seems to be used as a generic term embracing tea, coffee, and possibly even the whole range of warm, brown, nonalcoholic beverages, including cocoa, Ovaltine chocolate (hot), and even, for all I know, Instant Postum.

In Geneva, when you are asked if you would like a *renversé*, your dictionary, which will offer you a range of possibilities from "upside down" to "knocked over," will be of absolutely no help.

If you think you have a notion about something called Turkish coffee, don't ask for it in Greece if you value your security, or in Turkey if you value your stomach lining.

If you come to the United States from another English-speaking country, comfortable in the security of speaking a common language, are you ready to cope with the notion of "regularity," which is sure to crop up in connection with your innocent request for coffee?

Conversely, if you leave the United States for another English-speaking country, you probably wouldn't think twice before asking for your coffee "regular." Well, you really should! In the case of the United Kingdom, even if you overcome the nomenclature problem and have figured out what to say when asked if you want it "white," you should brace yourself for another culture shock when the actual "coffee" comes.

In Japan, although the fact that the nearest phonetic approximation to it will sound something like *kohee* will not prove an insuperable obstacle to your consumption of that beverage and will probably not burn a hole in your stomach, the same cannot be said for your pocket; the last time I was in Tokyo, at the airport, admittedly, a cup of coffee cost seven dollars (ca. 1988).

CHRISTMAS FARE OR FOWL PLAY: TALKING TURKEY

———◆———

LANGUAGES ARE ALWAYS USING THE names and nationality adjectives of foreign countries to stigmatize undesirable phenomena. English, for example, describes as "taking French leave" the phenomenon of unauthorized absence from one's appointed place. The French return this noncompliment by describing it as *filer à l'anglaise* and give back as good as they get for "French letter" with *capote anglaise*, but I have no idea how the citizens of the Netherlands get back at English speakers for being forced to take the rap for "Dutch courage," "Dutch treat," and "double Dutch." Even the American founding forefathers are not immune. The spin imparted to the ball in various ball games by wily practitioners, causing it to deviate from the straight and true, is described by Americans as "English," or, for all I know, "english," thus tainting the word with a certain aftertaste of deviousness.

Against this background, it is hard to understand what so many language cultures have against the poor turkey—the innocent and, so they say, severely intellectually challenged victim of the annual sacrificial rites practiced every Thanksgiving in the United States and at Christmas wherever the Anglo-Saxons have imposed or bequeathed their culture. By their choice of nomenclature, most insist on ascribing it to some alien and exotic culture. The few exceptions, which do not name the turkey according to where they think it comes from, do so either according to what they think it sounds like or according to a salient feature of its appearance. Rarely has a creature been the victim of such an anarchic cacophony of conflicting nomenclature.

At some point in history, the English blamed the name on the Turks, on what, according to the consensus of the recognized etymological authorities, appear to be the flimsiest and most implausible of grounds. The *Oxford Dictionary of English Etymology* claims confusingly that the name was applied to an *African* bird, the guinea fowl, probably because it was originally brought from *New Guinea* by the *Portuguese* through *Turkish* dominions. As if that were not enough, the name was then misapplied to the *American* bird that now bears the name. This is clearly a case of mistaken identity, since the American bird bore only a superficial resemblance to the guinea fowl. If it was really the Portuguese who were responsible for bringing the bird home "through Turkish dominions," it is particularly odd that it did not end up being called "turkey"—or its equivalent—in Portuguese itself, which appears to have passed the buck to a Brazilian neighbor that calls the turkey *peru*! In Peru itself, they have been sporting enough not to retaliate and are content to use the Spanish word *pavo*, which becomes a peacock when it is "real"—that is to say, "royal," as in "real" tennis, which in no way implies that the version played at Wimbledon is somehow phony or bogus.

The Turks themselves, of course, refuse to assume sponsorship of this hapless, stateless, and hopelessly unaerodynamic fowl and have laid it at the doorstep of the Indians, calling it *hindi*, as do, mutatis mutandis, at least two of the Slavic tongues, which call it *indeyka* (Russian) and *indyk* (Polish).

Czech, however, prefers a form of the word *kroc(ts)an*, which appears with slight variations in the Scandinavian languages (*kalkun*), Dutch (*kalkoen*), Romanian (*curcan*), and Uzbek (*kulkul [tovuk]*), although the Uzbek dictionary does offer *hind (tovuk)* as an alternative. The common ancestor of this group of names seems to be Calicut, from which we also get *calico*. Thus, the attribution is still to India, albeit by the back door or specific port of call.

The French, in defiance of all considerations of linguistic or geographical affinity, line up in this onomastic free-for-all with the Poles, Russians, and Turks. But why not, after all? One must never underestimate the power of the *esprit de contradiction* of the French. Why else would they add a gratuitous *e* to the Concord and so strenuously eschew the proper name for the strip of water that until only last year insulated them from the British, and call it "The Sleeve"? (The Channel Tunnel opened in 1994.) Clearly, then, there was no way the French were going to acquiesce supinely to "turkey" or still less *pute* (as it is known in Austria), a word of "disrepute" with which the French mind by no means spontaneously associates a table companion. Uninfluenced by the

English "turkey" and the German *truthahn* flanking them on either side, the French—vive la différence—came up with *dinde* (from India), which may well, of course, have been a Talleyrandesque curtsey to the Russians for agreeing to call the English Channel *La Manche*.

The only theory I have been able to track down for the origin of *truthahn* is that the *trut* element is a German phonetic approximation of the mating call of this species of *hahn*.

The Italians too have stoutly resisted the example and influence of their nearest geographic and linguistic neighbors and have come up with the maverick *tacchino*. True to their vocation for the vocal, they have, like the Austrians, taken what linguists call the "bowwow" route; they appear to have derived it from their phonetic approximation of the sound it makes in the barnyard, *tac-cha-taccha*, which we describe as "gobbling."

It is ironic that while the French were cozying up onomastically with the Russians—with the Poles obbligato—the Greeks were pinning the rap on them in the form of *galopoula* (although appearances are deceiving, and it probably doesn't actually mean "little Gallic person"). I know far too little of the history of Franco-Hellenic relations to begin to imagine what slight or indignity the French may have inflicted on the Greeks to deserve such retribution.

Arabic pins it on either the Ethiopians, with *dik habash* ("Abyssinian cock"—pardon me—"rooster"!), or the Europeans or Westerners, with *dik roumi*. *Roumi* seems to embrace pretty much all those west of the Bosphorus.

What, you may very well not be wondering, are wattles? They are the fleshy folds that droop from the faces and necks of *Meleagris gallopavo*, or the common turkey, and it is this feature that has determined the name *shichimencho*, by which it is known in Japanese. The *kanji*, or Chinese character-based written version of the word, is made up of three characters meaning "seven," "face," and "bird," respectively. For the Japanese, a turkey is a creature they are far more likely to see alive in a zoo than frozen in a supermarket, and it is therefore not surprising that their attention has been captured by its appearance rather than its taste. Turkey watchers—for this exercise, the turkey has to be alive—will be rewarded by the spectacle of its wattles changing to several different colors in turn. As to "seven"—well, perhaps the Japanese share the Western convention that this is the number of colors in the rainbow. In this case, the relationship between the name and the thing named is the opposite of that of the chameleon and *its name*. The chameleon (from the Greek *chamai-leon* or *ground-lion*) lent its name to one of its distinctive features—namely, its propensity for changing color according to its surroundings. The *shichimencho*, on the other hand, derives its name from precisely this feature of the creature.

The Chinese, who are, like their neighbors, more observers than consumers of the turkey, name it accordingly, with two characters meaning "fire" and "chicken," or *huo-ji*, because of the red or fiery color of its jowls.

As to what on earth Anglo-Saxon celebrants of Christmas are doing eating on December 25 every year a bird that came centuries after the events in question from a land that could not be more remote from either Northern Europe or the Middle East, that is a whole other story. December 25, after all, is, if it is anything, a date commemorating an ancient Northern European pagan winter solstice, or "yule" festival, and may or may not have anything to do with the date on which Jesus was born in biblical Palestine—but in either case, where do turkeys come in?

And just for the record, turkeyophagy is by no means universal among celebrants of Christmas; Danes eat goose, Czechs carp, and Icelanders ptarmigan.

TOPIC 9

JEW-ISH

IN *BEYOND THE FRINGE*, THE revue written and performed by four recent Oxford and Cambridge graduates to great acclaim in London in the 1950s, there was a sketch performed in front of the curtain. Two members of the cast, Dudley Moore and Alan Bennett, came out and engaged in a dialogue about how decent it was of the two "middle-class" members, Peter Cook and Jonathan Miller, to perform on the same stage with them—members of the working class. As they left the stage, one of them remarked, "Well, at least we're not Jews!" At this, Jonathan Miller came out from behind the curtain to say, "I'm not really a Jew; I'm just Jew-ish."

It is reported that the late Sammy Davis Jr., during a round of golf, was asked what his handicap was and replied, "I'm a one-eyed black Jew."

It has been said that if you wonder whether you are in love, you're not. However, for most intents and purposes, if you wonder or are cogitating on whether you are "Jew-ish," then you are (acknowledgments to R. Descartes).

HIDING THE FACT

What follows is predicated on the notion that "Jew-ish" or, still more, "Jew" is *not* just one more religious or even ethnic label like any other. In the headlines on September 10, 1985, is the hijacking by the PLO (Palestinian Liberation Organization). As in other similar cases, passengers whose names were thought by the hijackers to be Jewish-sounding, have been earmarked for slaughter. This raises the question of changing Jewish names for non-Jewish names—that is to say laying oneself open to the charge of "hiding what you are." This may or may not be the same as "failing to proclaim publicly" something that you are not—that is, someone who possesses attributes, mostly negative, that the majority of your fellow citizens believe are ineradicably yours. Is this "hiding what you are," or is it giving yourself a chance of being judged for what you are—and not for what others have decided to label you as? Or indeed, are you actually avoiding being taken for what you are *not*? For example, if you are not greedy and are Jewish, and people in general believe that Jews are greedy and grasping, then by accepting the identity of "Jewish," you are also accepting the identification of "greedy" or "rapacious" in the eyes of the beholder.

A complication is the fact that almost all derogatory racial or group epithets are essentially indicators of degree, with "greedy," for example, lying somewhere along the spectrum from "generous" to "avaricious" or "miserly" and on the undesirable side of the line. Thus, by acquiescing in these imposed equations—that is, to be Jewish is to be greedy—you are implicitly accepting inferior status.

There is a story that a certain Goldberg, who, tired of living among the unsympathetic English, changed his name to Jones and went to live in North Wales, where he promptly became known as "Jones the Jew." So, for example, if you change your name like the hapless subject of the anecdote, you may be not only denying or withholding your "Jewishness," whatever that may mean—and in the eyes of the beholder, it may well mean nothing but the sum of the undesirable and odious attributes that "Jews" are traditionally and popularly held to possess—but you are also denying or rejecting negative labels like greedy, pushy, ostentatious, or whatever opprobrious epithets are fashionable at a given time or place.

When I first went to school, "big" boys would corner the new ones and insist on an answer to the question, "Are you a PLP?" If you said yes, they revealed that it meant that you were "a public leaning post" and immediately treated you to a practical demonstration of the function you had conceded. If you said no, you were advised that it meant that you were not "a proper living person," and treatment appropriate to your "freely acknowledged" subhuman status was promptly administered. The rules of the game are basically the same. You are being invited to accept a label without knowing, caring, or daring to find out what your interlocutor means by it. The stick is just as cleft; in the one case, one way or another, you will either be publicly "leaned on" or beaten up, while in the other, you will either be letting "your side" down or conceding your own general undesirability.

The Goldberg story also raises the question of the "Jewishness" of Jewish names. Why is it somehow more authentically "Jewish" to go around as Goldberg, a Germanic name artificially imposed by non-Jewish oppressors or assumed under duress in a German-speaking environment, than as Jones in an English-speaking (or Welsh-speaking) environment? Or, for that matter, why is it more authentic than being known as Dayan or Eban in a Hebrew-speaking environment?

The answer is, partly, that Jews over generations, by passively accepting the names artificially assumed or imposed upon them by what was an alien and hostile linguistic/ethnic environment and by cultivating an ethos whereby it was somehow shameful or a betrayal of authenticity to adopt names appropriate to the linguistic environment in which they may have lived for generations, have continued to bear "authentically Jewish" names like Goldberg, which have encouraged non-Jews to think of them as "authentically" Jewish. Why is a Jew born, bred, and raised in Avignon somehow less authentically a Dupont than his ancestor born, bred, and raised in Munich and most probably far less "assimilated" was a Rosenbaum?

In the spring of 1997, around the time of the "furor" over the "revelation" of her Jewish descent, the *New Yorker* published a cartoon accusing Madeleine Albright (who was appointed US secretary of state in 2003) of "purporting" not to have known that her family was Jewish. At this time, parallels were being drawn between this "purporting" not to have known and the ethics of Newt Gingrich's equivocations about his misuse of funds for what he described as his "college courses."

The fact is that there is a whole range of things about yourself that you can lie about, conceal, or simply fail to announce: that you are Presbyterian/ are homosexual/are Jewish/are a convicted child molester/have been practicing medicine without a license/wear shoes with lifts in them—and worse. After all, is being of Jewish descent and being a practicing Catholic any more or less a contradiction in terms than being a child molester and a Baptist?

To put it another way, would Madeleine Albright have been just as legitimate lampoon fodder if she had been generally thought to be Jewish and had "concealed" her family's true Christian and/or gentile origins?

Concealment of Boris Yeltsin's true state of health or his criminal record has something to do with his (un)fitness for office and is thus wrong and unsavory. Now, either it is true or not that being "Jewish" (not in this case a matter of religious belief or still less affiliation but a question of "descent"—an interesting equivocation in its own right) affects one's fitness for office. To the extent that this may be held to be true in some quarters, then concealment of the fact is only a way of leveling the unequal playing field; if it is not true, then what is all the fuss about? It is not insignificant that the media in the course of this furor made free with such tell-tale words as "confess" and "admit," which are normally reserved for untoward or unsavory conduct of some kind, where guilt and shame are involved. Would this kind of vocabulary have been wheeled out in the case of some public figure—even Madeleine Albright herself—who had "purported" not to have known that she was "really" a Baptist or even of Native American descent?

TOPIC 10

GLOBAL WARMING AND THE
SEPARATION OF POWERS

———◆———

THE EXPRESSION "GLOBAL WARMING" SOON ceased to be a term coined by the scientific community for the notion that planet Earth was getting warmer, with the corollary of its potentially harmful consequences for the planet, and became fighting words, a "red rag to a bull," an article of faith—or bad faith, as the case may be—a credo, a shibboleth. What started out as a descriptive term has now become 90 percent emotive.

On April 22, 2015, rising sea levels were reported in Florida and were causing the salinization of fresh water. This was threatening the flora and fauna of this environment, among other direct and indirect harmful consequences. If observable phenomena of this kind, whether they are or not symptoms of global warming, were presented to the American public without ascribing it to, or even mentioning it in connection with, what has now become an irredeemably emotive term, people might not feel emotionally committed or conditioned to a "knee jerk" reaction to it and might be open to regarding it simply as a regrettable fact, as they are forced to do in the face of major disasters like earthquakes, landslides, tsunamis, hurricanes, and tornadoes, especially when they themselves are actual or potential victims of them.

What does it matter what name we give or deny to whatever it is that causes these disastrous events? If palpably, observably, and measurably, small island nations *are* being imperiled by rising sea levels, if glaciers *are* melting all over the planet, if deserts *are* spreading, if people *are* no longer able to skate on the river Thames, if even Britain *is* producing wine from homegrown grapes, if California and Sao Paulo *are* now in the throes of a water crisis, does it matter what we do or don't want to call the underlying cause—even if there is one?

Well, of course, it does matter, because if we know the underlying cause, experts can propose remedial action, and governments can take measures to implement it. *But* if the very name that has been given to that underlying cause has become so politically and emotionally fraught as to alienate and antagonize a sizable proportion of the American public in particular, this is clearly going to hamper, obstruct, inhibit, and even defeat the efforts of governments to deal with the problem. Governments are thus confronted with a dilemma; either name the malaise and be damned, let events take their destructive course without intervening, and let the devil take the hindmost, or simply go on dealing in turn with each individual symptom as it arises, because the name of the syndrome has become anathema and if used, it would polarize the population and paralyze remedial action.

It is worth pointing out, however, that polarization doesn't necessarily paralyze government, because not all governments are endemically prone to division. Interestingly, there are two kinds of government that, although not immune, are not constitutionally wired for division, as is the United States.

India has its sacred cows, and the United States has its Constitution—both are sacrosanct and unconditionally venerated. In their fear of the accumulation of power to the point of monopoly, the founding fathers sought a "separation of powers," possibly without much consideration of the possible downside of the arrangement.

It has been said on the highest authority, and also by no less an earthly figure than Abraham Lincoln, that "a house divided against itself cannot stand." If the founding fathers had heeded that warning, they might have foreseen that a government divided against itself cannot govern—a chicken that has most decidedly come home to roost in the Washington barnyard in recent times. Never have powers been so cruelly and damagingly separated, and government so hamstrung.

Totalitarian and authoritarian governments are free to govern by definition—for good or ill. The governments of parliamentary democracies, while not entirely immune to gridlock, are free to govern when they are in power, because the opposition, although it is entirely free to oppose the government as vigorously as it wishes, cannot actively *obstruct* it or veto its legislation. The checks and balances, however, are there, but they take on a subtler form than those of *division* of powers—namely, that of the *alternation* of power. The effect of this is that the government in power at a given time is inhibited from straying too far from the center in pursuing the direction it might like to go, for fear that doing so might alienate the "floating voters" in the electorate, who are often decisive in voting out a sitting government from office and replacing it with what had been the opposition.

So don't ask people if they "believe in" global warming. If you feel impelled to ask that question, don't! Ask instead whether your interlocutor believes that tidal waves, hurricanes, and floods happen; that glaciers everywhere are melting; that sea levels are rising; that coastal areas are being eroded; that rivers like the Thames used to be frozen in winter and skated on; that wine is now being produced in Britain from homegrown grapes; that California and Sao Paulo in Brazil have become drought ridden. Then ask if they think action should be taken by governments to remedy these problems. If the answer is yes, ask whether they should try to find out what the causes are. If the answer is once again yes, then ask whom governments should ask about the causes. Should it be experts in the field? If so, should the general population be invited to vote on the findings of the experts (something they are, happily, not invited to do in the case of other disasters and scourges regardless of whether or not they are the effects of global warming, such as Ebola, forest fires, mining disasters, landslides, industrial pollution of the environment, mad cow disease, and avian flu)?

The best of luck, however, if you should happen to find yourself tangling with an opponent of "big" government or a global warming denier, who may eventually figure out where you're coming from and that you are trying to strip him or her of a cherished belief, a gut conviction, or a cherished disbelief.

THE POWER OF NOMENCLATURE AND ITS ABUSE: "LIE DETECTORS"

THE VERY NAME FOR THIS device, which has become universally accepted, unfairly influences the results of its use, and for this reason alone, the term "lie detector" should never be permitted in court or in other proceedings in which its results are represented as evidence of lying—or not lying! By the same token, the use of the term should be banned in media reports of any such proceedings.

Polygraphs, as they are formally and less insidiously known, should be presented only as devices for taking certain biochemical and physiological readings, which, if "significantly" higher than "normal," may at best be held to indicate an unusual degree of agitation or nervousness, something that, like all other similarly derived medical readings, is itself open to conflicting interpretations. Calling polygraphs "lie detectors" is like calling metal detectors "gun" detectors—that is, incorporating one possible interpretation of a positive reading into the very name of the device and thus loading the "reading" in favor of the desired interpretation.

What is worrying about this is that it seems more than likely that the most gifted liars, including chronic exaggerators, braggarts, and con artists, owe their gift precisely to a lack of accompanying embarrassment, agitation, and other such symptoms when they are lying. This casts doubt on the usefulness of negative readings. As for positive readings, I have the strong feeling that if I were under serious suspicion of having committed a crime, my nervousness about the reliability of the machine itself would generate positive readings betraying the very agitation that, according to the experts, is evidence of lying.

In any case, how can experimental data possibly be gathered for testing the usefulness and reliability of this device for its proclaimed purpose? How, for example, can you run a lab test on a thousand subjects by arranging for some to "lie" and others not to "lie"? For it is precisely in artificial, experimental conditions that "lies" are purged of the tension and anxiety that register on a polygraph. If, however, you try to gather data in "field" conditions, you are faced with the contradictory task of determining whether people have lied by (a) asking them if they did and (b) believing them when they say yes—or no!

"RANK INFLATION" AND TITLE DEPRECIATION IN AMERICA

———◆———

WHEN I ARRIVED IN THIS country many years ago from London, it was something of a surprise to learn that in fact I was from a place called "Europe." It was also something of an eye-opener to realize that I had spent all my life eating "London" broil and "English" muffins without knowing it. No doubt visitors from Copenhagen and St. Petersburg have the same minor readjustment problems when it comes to "Danish" pastries and "Russian" salad dressing.

One culture shock I have never quite absorbed is the freedom with which titles such as "veteran," "professor," and "doctor" are awarded—or claimed—in this country, titles that are so much harder won in "Europe." A related phenomenon is the drive for euphemism, which generates such a rapid (unplanned) obsolescence or turnover in these titles.

A fresh-faced youth in his early twenties can be a "veteran"; the podiatrist who removes your corns and softens your calluses will take it amiss if you do not address him as "doctor"; and the penniless graduate student who needs to work off some of his or her own tuition fees by teaching freshman composition is suddenly a "professor."

The US government itself boasts but a single vice president, but businesses and bureaucracies of every kind are positively teeming with them. In banks, practically everyone above the rank of bank clerk or teller is a "vice president," a term that must have started life with the strong implication that (a) you were the only one of your kind and (b) you were second in command to the president and would replace him in his absence.

In US post offices, employees who man—or should I say "person"—the counters have now been elevated to the more sonorous title of "associate." Those who, up to now, have borne this title with pride are no doubt scurrying for cover, shedding this now-tarnished title as they run, but they are sure to emerge with a new and improved one.

"Doctor" was not too long ago a title proudly borne by MDs, but it is now giving way to "physician," partly under pressure from dentists, chiropractors, or even foot doctors—pardon me—podiatrists. There seems to have been a parallel evolution in the case of lawyers, who now tend to refer to themselves as "attorneys" and to each other as "counselor."

Not too long ago, the Furtwanglers and the Toscaninis had no difficulty in sustaining even their immense dignity with the title of "conductor," but now, even the humblest community orchestra performs under the baton of no less a personage than its "music director."

Managing director, chairman of the board, president of the company—pardon me—corporation, all molder in the vast lumber room of discarded titles, elbowed out by the newly, but how ephemerally, grandiloquent CEO, who receives nothing so commonplace as "pay," "salary," or even "emoluments." No, nothing less than "compensation," or better still, "compensation package," does justice to his or her exalted status. Not too long ago, "compensation" was what ordinary mortals got to make up for some damage that had been done to them.

Over the years, I have put in sporadic appearances in TV studios, and I am no longer astonished to see the kind young ladies and gentlemen who have brought me coffee and water and shown me the way to the men's room billed in the credit titles as "associate producers."

This undemanding and indulgent approach to the attainment of at least the trappings of achievement is well illustrated by the pomp, circumstance (it is not for nothing—and not without a certain irony—that the music of Edward Elgar at its most heart-swellingly imperial is de rigueur on these occasions), and accoutrements that attend high school graduation. In my day back in "Europe," high school was something that one "left." It was indeed something that one could not help leaving once one had served out one's time. It would have seemed grotesque for this nonevent to have been marked by solemn rites and ceremonials from which, as if from the field of academic triumph, even the dimmest-witted dunces, arrayed in rented academic garb once designed to grace the noble brows and stooped shoulders of scholars, were borne in exultation by their jubilant kith and kin to the huzzahs of the multitude—only to show up the next semester in a thousand "freshman composition" classes conducted by the hapless academic drudges mentioned above.

It has taken me some time to come to terms with a country teeming with campuses and campuses teeming with "professors," but I now realize two things that I did not at first. One is that in this country, apart from conferring an unseemly and premature venerability on the absurdly young and largely undeserving, part of the function of the title "professor" is to indicate what the bearer does for a living rather than how exalted he or she is of his or her profession. The other is that the exalted title is clearly meant to compensate for, or help numb the pain of, earning so much less than his or her titular inferiors, such as the defensive backfield coach, the groundskeeper, the campus policeman, and the janitor.

To its credit, it must be said that the title of "professor" has stood its ground much more staunchly than most of the others, and there seems to be little danger of any imminent supersession by some grander-sounding upstart. Its horizontal proliferation is, however, another story. Has anyone calculated how many "professors" there are per capita in the United States, and would that figure tell us any more or less about the state of American education (about which none complain more bitterly than do American politicians and educators themselves) than the number of doctors tells us about the state of American health and the number of lawyers about the state of American justice?

TOPIC 13

BLACK AND WHITE IN AMERICA

—————◆—————

DR. WATSON: "BUT SURELY, HOLMES, seeing is believing?"

Sherlock Holmes: "Up to a point, Watson, up to a point."

Wesley Lowery is a journalist who in November 2016 published a book titled *They Can't Kill Us All*, a chronicle of the black men who have been killed by the police over the previous year or so. In it, he also refers to his personal feelings about covering the deaths of "people who look like [him]."

What he actually looks like is a man who could conceivably "pass for white" in current society but who wouldn't have a hope of "passing for black" in the "bizarro world" that would have resulted from the hypothetical, historically inverted circumstances I describe below. This is a hypothesis that seeks to explain how such a person has allowed himself to be placed in, or has perhaps simply been painted by circumstances into, the uncomfortable corner he now occupies—namely, a corner in which he finds himself spontaneously and sincerely misdescribing "the dead black men" in question as looking like himself—*they don't!*

An idea that seems to be unreflectingly shared on both sides of the color divide is that whoever is not "wholly white" is ipso facto "black" and is properly described as such. This makes no more or less sense than its mirror image that whoever is not "wholly black" is "white."

Unfortunately, this implicit acceptance, even by blacks, of "whiteness" as a norm, from which any dilution is a deviation, is to swallow a distortion or a fallacy that paints "blacks" into corners in which they would not have to be if only white to black were properly seen and understood as a spectrum with differences of degree instead of a binary, yes/no choice.

This is going to be like one of those optical illusion tests. You see a picture or a drawing of a goblet or pitcher. Then you are invited to focus unblinkingly on it for long enough to see it turn into a drawing of two faces in outline. Or the drawing could be a cubic figure shaded so that it starts off looking like the inside of a box but after a time resolves itself into the outside of a box.

Usually, after making the effort to focus, you eventually succeed in seeing the image change before your eyes. The trouble is that once you relax your gaze or turn away from the image, it always reverts to the one you first saw—or to put it more accurately, the image you first *interpreted* it to be—since it is by now clear that the drawing can be seen, or interpreted, in two quite different ways.

With such optical illusions, most people eventually succeed, first in seeing the same picture as a totally different image from the one they saw at first, and second in realizing that the "seeing" that they are doing is really "interpreting" the lines and shades on the page in a way that comes most readily to their minds.

In these cases, the images people "see" are uninfluenced by either emotion or conditioning. To most people, whether they see a pitcher or two faces on the page is a matter of total emotional, moral, or political indifference or neutrality. But what would be the result if such "seeing" were to be complicated by emotions or conditioning of merely an aesthetic nature, and the picture could equally well be "seen" or "interpreted" as a rose or a pile of steaming turds? Now let even stronger and deeper emotions enter the picture and the "seeing" of it. Even the classic example of the pot filled to 50 percent of its capacity will divide its viewers into those who see it as half full and those who see it as half empty.

Now imagine two line drawings: The first is the outline of a shaded geometric figure, like a rectangle or a circle. If a cross section of Americans were asked whether they would describe it as white or black, x percent would say it was white, and y percent would say it was black. But if the second drawing were the outline of a human figure still shaded, can there be any doubt that the y percent who saw it as black would be greater than the value of y in the first case?

So it is with the perception of "white" and "black" people, in the sense in which these words are used in America—but not only in America. As in our experiment, to begin with, you can't even imagine seeing what you are looking at in a different way or seeing it as something else. And this is because you are not so much seeing as *interpreting*. But even when you have realized you have been interpreting, it is still hard not to credit the fact that the image you saw or interpreted first is the "real" one, and the second one is an illusion.

I first arrived in this country in the early 1960s, and the first impressions of a newcomer to a country tend to remain strong and vivid. I was then able to see things with the detachment of an outsider. Such impressions tend to fade over time, with growing familiarity. The same phenomenon occurs with the new couch in your living room and that new picture on your wall. How quickly they become "part of the furniture" or "part of the wallpaper" and cease to be noticed, although sometimes they can be brought back into sharper focus when a new visitor points them out.

For a number of reasons—historical, geographical, and demographic—I found race relations in the United States as relations between "black" and "white" have come to be known: highly distinctive, if not unique, in comparison with other countries, whether in the United Kingdom, South Africa at the time of apartheid, Latin America and the Caribbean, and other places with a sizable population of African origin.

The epiphany occurred on the day when I saw a "white" woman sitting with a "black" child at a table in a coffee shop. I would now rephrase that more accurately as "I caught myself reacting unthinkingly and spontaneously to what I had just seen"; I would have left the scene secure in that conviction, but for some reason, it occurred to me to wonder what I would have "seen" if it had been the child's "black" father sitting with the child instead of his or her "white" mother. Undoubtedly, I wouldn't have batted an eyelid, turned a hair, raised an eyebrow, or given it a second thought, since there is absolutely nothing eye-catching about the sight of a "black" child with a "black" father. I then found myself wondering why a child equidistant in pigment from both his "white" mother and his "black" father should automatically be seen as belonging to a different "race" from the mother and to the same "race" as the father. Just to reinforce the point, imagine the standard eyebrow-raising reaction of someone, white or black, to the sight of a "white" father sitting with his "black" child, compared with that same observer's lack of reaction to seeing the child's "black" mother sitting with the selfsame "black" child.

Now let's imagine a reversal of the historic roles—*but not of the pigmentation*—of the white and black inhabitants of the United States, such that the first alien settlers to arrive on this continent in their counterpart of the Mayflower were from Africa and not Europe. Those early settlers later expanded the territory they had initially occupied in the face of the resistance of its indigenous inhabitants, known as Indians—resistance they eventually overcame. Those Indians who survived the struggle were ultimately confined to "reservations."

Then came slavery, but in this scenario, the slaves were captured in Europe by slave traders and shipped to America to toil in the plantations of their African masters. There followed a civil war between the Unionist North and the Southern Confederacy, leading to emancipation and the outlawing of slavery. This in turn ushered in a Jim Crow regime and the rise of the Ku Klux Klan, whose members would clad themselves in black sheets and hoods as they terrorized the newly emancipated white European slaves, many of whom found their way to the cities of the victorious North and settled in what became known as white ghettos.

After a long and bitter struggle for civil rights and against the various forms of discrimination through which they were suffering, they achieved at least de jure equality with their former masters in the South and their neighbors in the North. They discarded successive opprobrious epithets, such as "blancos"—or even more opprobrious, in the defeated South, "blancahs"—and eventually became known, according to current political correctness, as European Americans; since over the centuries of their forced immigration to the United States, the traces of their links to their locations of origin had been obliterated, although in any case the Europe of that time had not been tidily divided into what have only relatively recently, in historical terms, come to be known as countries. These came later to Europe, when it was carved up, divided neatly, and clearly demarcated as such by African colonial masters.

This ongoing process of gradual progress toward de facto equality has by 2016 reached the point where the first "white" man was elected to the presidency of the United States—and at the time of writing is nearing the end of his second term of office. His name is Barack Obama, and he is the same man of exactly the same pigmentation as the Barack Obama who happens to be known in real life as the first "black" president.

Amid the welter of talk and commentary inspired in the 1990s by speculation about General Colin Powell's political intentions, there are two things that are held to be self-evident and unarguable: one is that the intensity of public interest in his intentions is, to say the least, heightened by the fact that he is "black," or African American, and the second is that he *is* "black." Well, he is "black," but only if you believe, as Americans both black and white seem to have been thoroughly conditioned to do for generations, that anyone who is not "wholly white" is "black." This credo is so deeply entrenched that it would be hard to persuade believers that it is something they "believe" rather than something they actually see with their own eyes.

In the same way—with the historical roles reversed, but with exactly the same pigmentation—Colin Powell would have been hailed as the first *white* chairman of the Joint Chiefs of Staff, and later the first serious *white* potential presidential contender.

However, as things are, on August 26, 1995, *The Times Magazine* (London) published an article titled "Left Right Left Right" on Colin Powell's presidential prospects, which said, "with a better chance of becoming the first black man in the White House...Sam Donaldson asked him if he would like to be the first black on a national ticket."

Note that he did not ask him simply whether he would like to run "on a national ticket" but instead imposed on him a premise he might not wish to accept—or to respond to. What if he *would* like to run for national office, but would not care to run "as the first black," but simply on his own merits.

The article continued, "He went on to become, in 1989, the first black chairman of the Joint Chiefs of Staff...Powell's race is crucial to his appeal. A black man who defies racial stereotypes..."

How about "a *predominantly white* man who *conforms very well* to the racial stereotype"? Or "*a Caribbean American who falls outside American racial stereotypes*"? As the article says, "His racial philosophy is less African-American than West Indian."

Colin Powell is, in fact, of mixed race. If the historical roles had been reversed, the same man, in the same circumstances, would be seen as a "white" making a historic breakthrough in "black"-dominated society. For example, Colin Powell has been on the cover of *Ebony* magazine. If the roles had been reversed, he would have been on the cover of *Ivory* magazine—as a "white" hero or role model!

By the same token, Muhammad Ali would have become an iconic hero of the oppressed "white" community—in fact, a great white hope, and the pigmentation of Adam Clayton Powell, that other iconic black leader, wouldn't have permitted him even a hope of passing for black.

What, among many other things, would have happened under this scenario is that the color demarcation line would have been drawn, not between 100 percent white citizens and all the rest, regardless of even their predominantly white heritage and "blood," but between those citizens of undiluted black heritage and "blood" and all the rest, even if *their* heritage and "blood" were predominantly black.

White and black Americans have both been conditioned to see blackness and whiteness of pigmentation in terms of a strictly binary and clearly demarcated frontier between the two "colors" without any no-man's-land or "gray" area between them, and not, for instance, as in Caribbean countries, as a continuum of infinitesimal gradations between two extremes. These and other countries, such as India, have been usefully—although dys-etymologically—described as "pigmentocracies," where lighter skin tones trump darker ones. Even apartheid-era South Africa found it relevant and meaningful for its purposes to draw a distinction between what it termed "black" and "colored" members of its nonwhite population. It also saw its East Indian population as a separate segment, although not primarily distinguished by skin pigmentation. It was a group that was classified at times as part of the "nonwhite" population and at other times as "Indian," and, as such, its members were permitted under the Group Areas Act to live only in designated areas.

Significantly, in the United Kingdom, East Indians, sometimes categorized as "Asian," at times have self-identified as "black" for political purposes, thus aligning themselves with the Caribbean immigrant population.

The truth is that many "black" Americans are of mixed race, and in other societies they would identify themselves and be identified as such. What is revealing is that the term "colored" and its synonyms have fallen into disuse in the United States, although for some purposes, the more genteel expression "people of color" is in polite use.

For historical reasons, "colored" (mixed race) and black people have been forced into the solidarity of victims of the same oppression, and for the same reason—"nonwhiteness." As a product of this solidarity or common victimization, they begin to respond to the outside perception of themselves by also perceiving themselves as "black" (i.e., nonwhite) first and foremost, and only secondarily, if at all, as possessing different degrees of blackness. This blackness, if the historical roles of "black" and "white" had been reversed, would have been perceived as different degrees of whiteness—that is, nonblackness.

Of course, 100 percent blackness—the line that would have been used to divide "black" from "nonblack"—is a distinction or category now barely perceived either by "whites" or "blacks." Terminologically, at least, the South Africans had got it right.

It is interesting that at the Wimbledon tennis championships, "predominantly white" as an on-court dress code counts as white, while for demographic purposes in America, it can count as black!

Examples abound of the way Americans "see" all fellow citizens who are not 100 percent white as black, even if they are somewhat white or even *predominantly* white.

CNN. *Sonia Live*, interview of a "black" filmmaker lately returned from visiting the Gullah people in Africa, September 2, 1989, 1:40 p.m.

Sonia: "Apart from the fact that your *skin is the same color as theirs...*"

In actual fact, his skin color was about equidistant between that of Sonia and the Gullah, but as always, this (mis)perception is fed to and swallowed whole by all concerned.

Review of *Sour Sweet*, by Timothy Mo. *New York Times Book Review*.

"The author is of mixed Chinese-English parentage." Contrast this characterization with the nonexistence of the description "mixed European African" in the United States, where only whites regard offspring or descendants of such unions as alien, other, or nonwhite, while those of "pure" African descent *and* those of mixed race regard them as black and not nonblack.

South African blacks, however, unlike US "blacks," had the same automatic perception of "coloreds" as alien as do whites both in the United States and in South Africa—but from the other end of the "color" spectrum.

New York Times. Article on "coloreds" in South Africa.

"As a group they are consciously aligning themselves with the Nationalist [White, predominantly Afrikaaner], Party because they feel their interests are threatened by 'black' rule."

In the United States, by contrast, there is no way that mixed-race or lighter-skinned "blacks" could conceivably or self-consciously align themselves as a distinct interest group with "whites" against their brother "blacks." Significantly, at the time of writing during the current (2016) presidential election campaign, from a psephological standpoint, there is constant reference to the "black" vote, period—as a single, undifferentiated block with an overriding common cause.

CNN. Conference of urban mayors to meet Clinton, November 10, 1992.

Sharon Pratt Kelly, formerly Sharon Pratt Dixon and now known as Sharon Pratt, was the third mayor of the District of Columbia, from 1991 to 1995. Pratt was the first *African American* woman to serve as mayor of a major American city (Wikipedia).

Andrew Young, mayor of Atlanta (1982–1990)

David Dinkins, mayor of New York City (1992)

 Coleman Young, mayor of Atlanta (1992)

These mayors of Atlanta, Detroit, New York City, and Washington DC were all in fact "colored," or of "mixed race." And that is how they would have been perceived, and would have perceived themselves, in South Africa by both blacks and whites alike, and, as such, they would not have been integrated into a "black" political movement, let alone be its leaders.

Delaney, Paul. "The Myth of the M" (on Jesse Jackson's run for the US presidency). *New York Times*, Sunday, April 29, 1984.

"Ever since light-skinned and free blacks held themselves different from those with dark skin and those still in slavery, blacks have disagreed on how to fight slavery."

In spite of this albeit dismissive reference to the notion that all "blacks" might not be "black," the author is locked tight within the blanco-centric perceptual and terminological straightjacket and writes *"light-skinned blacks"* where he might just as reasonably have written *"dark-skinned whites."*

Shipp, E. R. Review of *Black Robes, White Justice* ("black" New York State Supreme Court justice), by Bruce Wright. *New York Times Book Review*.

"In this slim volume, which Justice Wright describes as 'reflections and musings…on a view of America based on an entire life spent as *a black male in a white world.*'"

 Or, mutatis mutandis, one could also say *"a white male* (however sunburned) *in a black world."*

Again, the same old interpretation or perception masquerades as objective fact.

British "blacks" in London speak with the same authentic cockney accent as other Londoners, and Chinese urban poverty in the 1970s was much more severe on a per capita financial basis than the poverty of "black" ghettos in American cities;

yet it was not accompanied by certain untoward behavior patterns that were at the time unanimously attributed to poverty by American commentators.

What do these examples tell us about the validity of certain ingrained American assumptions, attitudes, and shibboleths about "race"—as "blackness" and "whiteness" have come to be known in America?

A. That "blacks" *do not* have to or "naturally" speak in a distinctive and identifiable "black" way in order to distinguish and dissociate themselves from their white oppressors—a straightjacket from which upwardly mobile American "blacks" have struggled, not always without mixed feelings, to emancipate themselves.

B. That the culture of the inner city ghetto is *not* primarily or even necessarily born of poverty.

First, the "huddled masses" in, say (at the time of writing in 1979), Shanghai are much poorer than those in Harlem, and second, they do not pose or suffer from the same social problems; in particular, their poverty has not destroyed or undermined their family structure or values. So if poverty is not the reason why certain behavior is undesirable, reducing or eliminating it (poverty) is not going to cure the culture or behavior.

Review of the film *Do the Right Thing*, directed by Spike Lee. *New York Times*.

"On one side of the picture are the more serious, darker-skinned blacks on the campus, who enthusiastically embrace their blackness...On the other side are the 'wannabees,' the lighter-skinned students who, according to the film, *ape white attitudes at the cost of their own heritage*."

If these students could see themselves and be seen as darker-skinned *whites* (as they would be if the historical roles had been reversed), they would no longer have to be burdened by charges and the consequent complexes and guilt about "aping" whites, although, of course, they might then be seen as baited by their lighter-skinned fellow "white" students for "aping"—or perhaps even *escaping*—the dominant culture of their "black" fellow students.

Staples, Brent. "She Was Hard to Impress." Review of *Give Us Each Day: The Diary of Alice Dunbar-Nelson*, by Gloria T. Hull. *New York Times Book Review*.

"By 1920, Mrs. Hull tells us, Dunbar-Nelson had become the first *black* woman to sit on the State Republican Committee of Delaware...Dunbar-Nelson was born in New Orleans in 1875. *Extremely fair of skin...*"

Alice Moore Dunbar-Nelson (1875–1935)

Poet, essayist, diarist, and activist Alice Moore Dunbar-Nelson was born in New Orleans, Louisiana, to mixed-race parents. Her African American, Anglo, Native American, and Creole heritage contributed to her complex understanding of gender, race, and ethnicity.

Again, mutatis mutandis, she would have been classified as "white" and have become the first "*white*" woman to sit on the State Republican Committee of Delaware.

Whether she would have been any better off and any freer of the toils, obstacles, and complexities of her tangled racial background under a racist "black" regime is unlikely.

How "white" were/are the leaders of the Black Power movement and other "black" human rights movements? Is there a correlation between their "whiteness" and militancy? If so, is it because of a connection between an uneasy or obscure consciousness of "whiteness" on the part of certain "black" leaders and the frustration born of the fact that the path to "fulfilling" that "whiteness" is blocked? The frustrated energy then takes the only other channel open to it, which is that of denial, repression, and even obliteration of that "whiteness" by a violent overreaction in favor of "blackness." Hence, "black is beautiful"—black English, "Back to Africa," black Muslims, Black Panthers, Malcolm X, Adam Clayton Powell, Leroi Jones, Andrew Young, Jesse Jackson, and Al Sharpton, all in their own different ways.

Martin Luther King Jr., by contrast, did not seem to be struggling with the demon "whiteness." Is it just a coincidence that he uniquely (or almost) championed both nonviolence and integration into the mainstream?

Is there within the black community any disparaging labeling of light-skinned "blacks" consistent and powerful enough to cause complexes from the "black" side as well as the "white"? Compare this with the analogy of males who react by assuming or cultivating macho characteristics when they have either been the victims of taunts impugning their masculinity or are troubled by obscure, uneasy feelings of masculine inadequacy. Richard Nixon, who never made it past third string guard for the team of Whittier, a small college in California, leaps to mind. Among other things, he loved to be on back-slapping terms with NFL coaches and appeared to be flattered by being seen in their company.

What is the effect on attitudes and feelings about race on the part of "black" and "white" athletes who play for professional sports teams, where the stakes and the emotions are so high that a unique situation is created where solidarity and esprit de corps with a fellow team member of whatever color are likely to prevail over solidarity or fellow feeling with a player of your own "race" on the other team?

There is probably no other experience in the United States, except perhaps for show business, in certain respects, that can match the professional team context for forging bonds of "interracial" solidarity, which, for all that they are rooted in expediency, are probably more than skin deep—at least at the time. It would be worth trying to find out.

New York Times. Report on the O. J. Simpson trial, February 3, 1995.

"The switch (of a juror) leaves the jury with eight members, of whom four are black, two white, one Hispanic, and one of mixed origin."

An incidental curiosity or aberration is the use of Hispanic as a racial category. The use of the term "race" in the United States has narrowed down its meaning to skin color and effectively to the black/white spectrum.

Evidence of this is that if a headline reads "Race Riot" or "Race" anything, it is, as it is meant to be, immediately construed as a black/white matter. Since Hispanics run the whole gamut from black to white—although not necessarily in the same proportions—and are certainly not distinct from black/white in terms of pigmentation in the way that, for example, Chinese are, what exactly is the term doing in the race category at all? Either it is subsumed by the black/white spectrum or it is not a racial category at all but rather an "origin" category. But if it is, why does it not take its place as just one of the many "origin" categories that exist in this country? And if that is the case, why would, say, Balkan or Slavic membership of the jury not be just as much a part of the breakdown?

But to get back to "mixed" race and origin, this is a rare but interesting and largely unremarked distinction in this country. Someone whose parents are *both* "black" is ipso facto "black." Someone else who has one "white" and one "black" parent (presumably what is meant in this case) is of "mixed" race, even though he or she might be blacker or whiter—or the same shade—as the other. In other words, the distinction hinges on *when* or in what generation the mixing occurred. What about the children of a "mixed-race" person? If that person marries a "white," the child is "mixed" but not "white"; if he or she marries a "black," the child is "black" but no longer "mixed."

The New Yorker. Article on Cornel West, Professor of Afro-American Studies at Princeton, January 17, 1994.

Asante [Molefi Asante, director of African American Studies, Temple University] belittles West's "unnecessary eclecticism"...his fundamentally "assimilationist" orientation. "We Afro-centrists claim that there is nothing more correct for African-American people than our experiences if we learn from them...Our solutions are within ourselves, not outside of us..." West finds his intellectual center in white tradition. He has been educated away from himself.

West responds, "I begin with radical cultural hybridity." In other words, "we blacks" are not just, or 100 percent, African heritage.

New York Magazine. January 23, 1984.

New York's "Friendly Sons of St. Patrick" is considering a membership application from Manhattan Democratic boss Denny Farrell...Farrell has made his way in politics by being black: "Both grandmothers were black but I have a grandfather whose parents were from Ireland and a grandfather who was Scottish. The bottom line is that black is a state of mind and black is what I am." Officials of the "Sons" said the black leader's Irish roots ensure his acceptance.

In other words, "black" is basic here. However perversely, just as two wrongs do not make a right, two white grandfathers do not apparently make a "white." Two black grandmothers do, however, make a "black"!

New York Times.

"The nickname 'Emerald Isle of the Caribbean' is due not so much to a faded colonial past but to distinctive Irish flavor that still pervades Montserrat. Many residents, most of whom are *black*, boast of their *Irish* ancestry."

Once again, the "default" is "white." Why not reverse "*Irish*" and "*black*" in this sentence? And why would people think you were being perverse or facetious if you did? What is significant here is the use of "boast" in the original version!

THE CASE OF ANATOLE BROYARD

Gates, Henry Louis Jr. "White Like Me." *The New Yorker*, June 17, 1996.

"In New Orleans...light-skinned blacks often intermarried with other light-skinned blacks."

In a 1950 commentary article titled "Portrait of the Inauthentic Negro," Broyard wrote that the Negro's embarrassment over blackness should be banished by the realization that "thousands of Negroes with 'typical' features are accepted as whites merely because of light complexion.

Anne Bernays knew that Broyard was black through a mutual friend... Milton Klonsky."

Significantly, both Anne Bernays and the author seem to find it unremarkable that "blackness" is something you don't *see* with the naked eye so much as something you *find out about*!

"Charlie Parker [a 'black'] spied Broyard in Washington Square Park one day and said, 'He's one of us, but he doesn't want *to admit* he's one of us.'"

Broyard sounds like someone who, maybe without articulating or formulating the logic of the issue, instinctively claimed his rightful "white" heritage and acted on it. The only way open to him to do this, of course, was by "dissembling" rather than "coming out" as "black" and basing his claim on the true logic of the facts, a course that, paradoxically, would have drastically undermined his ability in practice to do so. Even if he had achieved a clear-eyed vision of the logic, others, both "black" and "white," would have confined him to the ghetto of their own conditioned but skewed perspective.

Ellen Schwamm, a novelist, was impressed by a paradox: "The man wanted to be appreciated not for being black but for being a writer, even though his 'pretending' [my quotes—S. P.] not to be black was stopping him from writing."

He was *not* "pretending not to be black." It was the "Ellen Schwamms" who were inhibiting him from being *who he was* and insisting *that he wasn't* and thereby pinning him down. He was defending himself against the inevitable consequences—that is, penalties—of "admitting" he was a little bit black, against the unholy consensus of contumely from blacks who would not forgive him for trying to "wriggle out of" being "black." Perhaps there may be a little grain of truth in the cynical saying "the hardest thing for someone to forgive is the good fortune of his friend." He would, of course, be courting the inevitable putdowns from whites who would despise him for aspiring to rise above his station and pretend to be equal with them just because of his accomplishments. It is about as impossible for a "black" to claim mitigation for this kind of "offense" on the grounds that he is only a little bit black as it was for the unfortunate girl in the story who told her outraged parents, "Yes, but I'm only a little bit pregnant."

What a bitter irony it is that in the end it was Broyard's "blackness" that made his story interesting or worthwhile enough to be the subject of an extended "memorial" article in *The New Yorker*, that his "blackness" was the peg on which the article was hung, and indeed that, ultimately, his "blackness" was treated as if that was what he was all about.

Thus, for the thousands of readers who had never given him a second thought—or a first thought, for that matter—Broyard's claim to recognition will forever be that he was "a black writer" and that if he failed as a writer because he was black, as Henry Louis Gates Jr. contends, the hard-won image for which he made this sacrifice was stripped so ruthlessly and publicly from him, and by "one of his own"! The malevolent practice of "outing" did not begin with gays.

Geiger, H. Jack. *The Color of Water: A Black Man's Tribute to His White Mother*, by James McBride. *New York Times Book Review*.

"A white man's tribute to his *black* mother" would, of course, mutatis mutandis, be a nonstarter, an oxymoron, a contradiction in terms, according to American perceptions, since anyone with a "black" parent is black, ipso facto and by definition.

Whether the author is himself in thrall to this misconception or whether he is consciously deriding is not clear from the title alone.

The problem is how to change the deeply conditioned perception that someone is obviously and unequivocally "black" when it is nothing but a matter of perspective. A useful analogy is that of north/south—that is, the hard and fast notion that for all cartographic and visual purposes, north is up, and south is down. The analogy is all the closer for the fact that "south" has acquired derogatory connotations, as in "his business is heading south," and is irretrievably linked with the notion of "below." Similarly, the word "black" is irretrievably linked with a host of derogatory expressions, such as "black-hearted," "black book," "blackball," and "blackmail." How hard would it be for an Englishman—or a Scotsman, for that matter—to start seeing or thinking of Glasgow as being *below* London when that could equally well have become the standard, universal, or default perception, if depicting and looking at the world in a way that could just as well be described as "upside down" had not hardened into a universal tradition for certain historical reasons as "the right way up," a tradition so powerful as to have imposed itself on the world's minds as a virtual law of nature.

"Inmate Population Rises to More Than a Million." *New York Times*, October 28, 1994.

"The report also gave racial breakdowns of the prison population. At the end of last year 1,432 blacks out of every 100,000 blacks in the country were in prison—more than seven times the 203 white inmates for every 100,000 whites in the country."

A statistic like this both creates and results in a misperception! If—and why not?—everyone who is non-"black" were counted as "white" instead of the reverse, then this huge statistical imbalance between the percentage of "black" and "white" inmates would be considerably reduced, provided we take into account the fact that, mutatis mutandis, what would then have become the oppressed "white" underclass would have been demoted to the lowest social and economic strata of the American population and would thereby be committing the same "crimes" (mostly drug related), arrested and convicted for them in disproportionate numbers, and punished more severely for them, with long prison terms.

In the same way that both bigots and liberals exploit or were taken in by the false logic of the race and IQ statistics following the publication in 1994 of *The Bell Curve: Intelligence and Class Structure in American Life*, by Richard J. Herrnstein and Charles Murray, so both "blacks" and "whites" swallow the fallacious statistics (based on a totally arbitrary premise arising from an accident of history) and the exaggerated conclusions they appear to yield about "black" versus "white" criminality.

"Trial of Four White Police Officers Charged with Torturing Abner Louima, a Haitian Immigrant." *New York Times*, May 5, 1999.

"One of the white officers, Thomas Wiese, has a fiancée of 8 years, Karen Wiese, who is 'black' and [or should I say '*but*'] their son is 'African American.'"

Why is the term "European American" and perhaps "German American" or another term describing whatever other ethnic source his "black" mother may also trace her descent from automatically excluded from this "origins" background? Once you are "tarred by this brush"—a notion that is technically a thing of the pre–politically correct past—you are "black," nothing but "black," and wholly "black," so help you God.

A friend once asked me a good question: whether "Afro-Irish" is part of the national/ethnic origin of the hyphenated American.

"African American" is the latest in the longish line of attempts by American "blacks" to give themselves a name that is free of stigma and adverse implications and that also conveys equality and commands respect. The idea is, no doubt, that it gives them an equal footing in identity with other hyphenated Americans, such as Irish- and Italian- but not, interestingly enough, English-American. Scottish-American has been claimed as a title, but I have never heard "Welsh-American." I believe Israeli-American is now a possibility.

The analogy fails, however, on a number of counts because Africa is not a "country" like other "countries" and the connection of African Americans with Africa is different from that of, say, Hungarian Americans with the "homeland" or "old country" (e.g., having no meaningful or even traceable link of memory or record with any specific part or kinship group). Furthermore, many American "blacks" already have an identifiable and truly analogous "old country" such as Trinidad, Jamaica, Puerto Rico, or maybe even Brazil and Cuba, and it would be interesting to know what hyphenated label they would sport spontaneously. I don't even want to think about the complexities of considering the case of a "white" Jamaican immigrant to the United States. But one of the usual determinants in the normal hyphenated American's sense of "national" identity or origin, and also the view of that person's "national" identity by others, is the family name. Thus, for all practical purposes, if you are called "Cuomo," you are an Italian American to yourself and others. This subject itself warrants separate treatment, since the family name obscures and even obliterates other ethnic/national connections. For example, Mr. Cuomo might have only two or even one great-grandparent out of eight who was Italian even though he, the great-grandson, bears that one's name and inherits his "ethnicity."

The earlier the ancestors or forbears of a Czech American settled in America, the less likely it is that the Czech family name he or she now bears correctly or usefully identifies his or her national or ethnic origin. By contrast, most "African Americans" bear Anglo-Saxon or Celtic family names, but no one thinks for a moment that these names determine their ethnic or national identities. What is more, these names do not even slightly detract from or "mitigate" the "blackness" or "Africanness" of their identity. To put it another way, the name Campbell will not generate the slightest sense of common heritage or identity in the mind of either the "black" or the "white" Campbell with his namesake of the "opposite color" despite the fact that the "black" and the "white" Campbell are objectively just as likely to have just as much common "blood" or ethnic heritage as two "white" Campbells. For both the "black" and the "white" Jones, what separates them not only outweighs but totally obliterates their common ethnicity or "nationality." However, two Polish Americans bearing Polish family names (a) would probably never discover how much non-Polish stock there was in their backgrounds and (b) would still share a sense of common identity and solidarity toward each other and against whomever their traditional ethnic/"national" enemies might happen to be (e.g., Serbs against Croats), in spite of the fact that as much as seven-eighths of their "blood" might not be Polish.

WHATEVER HAPPENED TO "BLACK IS BEAUTIFUL"—AND BACK TO AFRICA—AND THE HAIR PROBLEM?

The "Black Is Beautiful" movement started in the 1960s as a fight for equal rights and a positive perception of the African American body.

In the early 1960s, when I was watching my diminutive black and white TV screen, it was suddenly filled with the watermelon-shaped visage of Godfrey Cambridge, who must have been hosting some show or other. His humor had an edge to it but was delivered with great bonhomie, and it left me wanting more; so when he ended his act with the words "if you don't run out and buy my album, I'm gonna move in next door," I did just that, and it has become one of my prized possessions. It was the era of the Civil Rights Movement, with its blockbusting and lunch-counter sit-ins. It was from this material he drew most of his humor, and he was not loath to skewer black targets in front of the live "black" audience he was entertaining.

Among his well-aimed shots was the line, "My wife was on a 'back to Africa' kick and had our bedroom wall painted brown. When she came out of the bathroom after her shower one night, it took me twenty minutes to find her."

Another was, "I arranged with my wife to meet me in the lobby of the Waldorf Astoria one night to attend an upscale reception, and she turned up wearing nothing except a strand of pearls. When I asked her what did she think she was doing, she replied, '*Vogue* magazine says you can never go wrong with basic black and pearls.'"

Godfrey Cambridge said that when he was in college during the blockbusting, lunch-counter, integrating sixties, white liberal folks were always inviting him to parties so that they could talk to him—and be seen talking to him—about "the problem," while he wanted to talk about his golf handicap and his Miles Davis records.

Another manifestation of the mood of the time was the Afro, on which I can offer the following, perhaps ironical, reflection.

In 1973, I was sent by the United Nations to interpret at a conference called "Peace through Law" in Abidjan, Ivory Coast, as it was then known. When I got to JFK Airport to board the plane, I hadn't realized that it was a charter flight, and I grew ever more puzzled when I saw that most of the other passengers filing on board were young black Americans (I don't believe that the expression

"African American" had yet come into fashion at that time). It turned out that they were all young members of a Washington DC black lawyers association—and were all wearing Afros—truly a "back to Africa" event. I have retained a vivid memory of the difficulty of seeing anything in front of me through row upon row of Afros blocking my view.

Strolling through the Abidjan marketplace during the week of the conference, I noticed more and more of those young lawyers sitting patiently through what looked to be the painstaking—and painful-looking—process of having their Afros converted into cornrows.

On the return journey, it was something of a relief to be able to see over the heads of the newly shorn, cornrowed heads in front of me to the other end of the cabin. I wonder whether what must have been a chastening experience for my young "*back from* Africa" fellow travelers helped to hasten the demise of the "*back to* Africa" culture somewhere around the end of the 1970s. It did not, however, put an end to what seemed to an outsider a never-ending quest for a solution to the "black hair" problem.

Is it a "problem"? Well, a few minutes on the Internet will leave you in no doubt. It's full of advice about "solutions" to it.

How would one define this problem? Briefly, it's the conflict between the urge to conform with the norms powerfully and constantly suggested by the dominant and surrounding "white" culture, and, as regards hair in particular, simply letting nature take its course, except that in this case, you can't just let it all hang out, because if you allow nature to take its course, it won't just hang out; it will twist into its preordained shapes—known as "natural" hair. Both courses have different, widely divergent downsides. Resisting nature can, as the testimony available on the Internet makes clear, be enormously time-consuming, laborious, and costly. It also runs counter to what was a few decades ago a popular rallying cry or mantra, "black is beautiful," and would at that time have earned you condemnation for "letting the side down" from other members of the black community. That rallying cry now seems to have been retired, perhaps simply because "black is beautiful" has simply lost its appeal as a rallying cry, or perhaps it just lost traction because of the sheer numbers of "black" women who have embraced the need or desirability of wearing their hair "white," something that is no longer seen as a shameful capitulation to whitehood.

Basically, hair does seem to be a problem to be solved. There seems to be almost no approach that is purely *laissez-faire*, spontaneous, and unpondered. But once again, if history had been reversed, and the United States were now populated by a majority of descendants of African colonizers and a minority of their former white slaves, it would be the latter who would be in the unfortunate situation of having a "hair problem" to solve, and there would be a lucrative minor tonsorial industry at work crinkling and curling instead of straightening their hair.

To write about "race" in the prevailing climate in the United States is to tread an exceedingly narrow path and to court misunderstanding, especially if you don't happen to be "black." This was notoriously illustrated by the furor that greeted the publication in 1994 of Herrnstein and Murray's *The Bell Curve*. The barricades were manned by partisans on both sides of the divide with an alacrity that belied any acquaintance with the actual contents of what was essentially a dry and academic 845-page tome.

With that caveat, I will venture to suggest that this problem is not just the black woman's problem, as has been clearly demonstrated by the sequence of "solutions" tried—and eventually discarded—over the past few decades, but before turning to the response to the problem of American "black" men, I will recount a personal episode relating to the "hair problem." There was a young "black" woman who was a student in a class I was teaching at the time, and after the class, we would both head to the same subway station on our way home. After a few weeks of chatting as we walked, I was emboldened to introduce her to the topic of this article, introduced, of course, by my hypothesis, as an outside observer of the US "race" scene, of the "historical reversal of roles" and its consequences.

After one of these conversations, she said she would like me to meet her mother, who was a professor of black studies at a college in the CUNY system.

This was not the first time I had attempted to broach the subject with a "black" American I knew fairly well, so even at this point, I began to wonder whether I had succeeded in getting my essential point across, and I began to realize that what my interlocutors were essentially listening for was "where I was coming from" or "whose side I was on." I imagine that it wasn't unnatural to suppose that my take on the subject came from a sympathizer, but the problem was that *that* was not what it was about. This suspicion was confirmed when I eventually did meet her mother. On the appointed day, she called me in my office, and I arranged to meet her in the lobby of the building. Before hanging up, she told me that I could recognize her easily, because, not unexpectedly in the light of the subject she taught, she had "natural" hair. This encounter took place in the early 1990s, when New York's first "black" mayor was in office.

Happily, I managed to suppress the jocular riposte that sprang to my lips— "So have I!"—which would have been embarrassingly inappropriate. I didn't attempt to turn the situation around with my "historical reversal of roles" and point out that, mutatis mutandis, I would have been the one to call her in her office and explain that *she* could easily recognize *me* by my "natural hair," and she would have been the one to refrain from tactlessly and inappropriately remarking, "Me too!"

Equally inappropriate, it turned out, would have been any attempt to introduce my "thesis" in the hope of eliciting a reaction to it. She had come armed with her own thesis, which essentially boiled down to saying that the status of black people was just as bad as ever and had shown no improvement. Although I was essentially a sympathetic listener, I couldn't go all the way with her and lamely argued that there must have been *some* progress if there were by then at least four "black" mayors of major American cities, and Clarence Thomas had become the second black justice of the Supreme Court—if that counts as "progress!"—and pointed out other noteworthy black success stories in other walks of American life. She must have left with the feeling that her daughter had misled her and dismissed me as just another wishy-washy "white liberal."

One last bastion of "natural selection" or spontaneous segregation in the United States is the barber's shop or hairdressing salon. "Black" customers are rarely to be found in white establishments—their needs are different and probably cannot be serviced by barbers and hairdressers trained on white scalps. But there are probably no "black" barbers or hairdressers, either, in establishments catering to "white" hair, presumably for the same reasons, in reverse. Similarly, "white" customers are rarely to be found in "black" establishments.

In recent decades, "black" men's solutions to the "hair problem" have run the gamut. Slicked-down, parted hair, glossy with brilliantine, were favored by Adam Clayton Powell Jr. and black entertainers and musicians such as Duke Ellington, Count Basie, and Nat King Cole. Then came cornrows and braids. There were the Rastafarian-inspired dreadlocks stuffed into tall, woolen, brightly colored headgear. Later, the bald or shaven head became popular, which either solved or disposed of the problem by getting rid of the hair itself. This fashion has been much favored in recent time by "black" men in the public eye, including athletes, more among basketball players than baseball and football players, possibly because in basketball, the head (and the hair on it) is fully exposed. This list would, of course, not be complete without the diverse variations on the theme of "natural" hair.

Probably the hair that got far more than its fair share of airtime on TV, at least in the tri-state area, were the glossy, flowing tresses of Al Sharpton, but the style never seemed to attract a following. Now (in 2016), no doubt in keeping with his transition from stormy petrel to elder statesman, those locks have been shorn and have become scalp-locked.

Perhaps significantly, it is the current (2016) first couple who perfectly embody the final—or simply current—solution. The first "black" president, Obama (he who would, mutatis mutandis, have become the first "white" president), has essentially solved the hair problem simply by minimizing it, never letting it grow more than a millimeter or two from the scalp. The First Lady (black or white)—take your choice—has uninhibitedly embraced, and no doubt reinforced, the widespread fashion of wearing the flowing locks lately renounced by Al Sharpton.

The White House serves not only as a bully pulpit, but along with the enshrinement of the title and status of the First Lady, also as a fashion pulpit.

TEACHING OR PREACHING

THE *NEW YORK TIMES* CORRESPONDENT Somini Sengupta, reporting on the recent (May 14, 2002) Children's Summit at the United Nations, referred to the Bush administration's policy of teaching: "abstinence as the best way of protecting teenage health."

Well, there is teaching, and there is teaching. There is the kind one associates with schools, where we are *taught* subjects, and the kind where we are *taught* what our elders and betters regard as appropriate behavior—which is more accurately defined as *preaching*.

When we are taught algebra, we are shown how to do something that we would not be able to do if left to ourselves. When we are taught abstinence (from sex in particular), we are being told, or *exhorted* and *admonished*, not to do something that, left to ourselves, we have a powerful, not to say overpowering, inclination to do.

If teaching abstinence meant demonstrating to children *how* to do it, like algebra, it might, accompanied by a methodology, possibly qualify as a school subject with the corresponding periodic tests and final exam to determine how well individual students have learned to do it. The injunction "just say no!" is no more a way of teaching children *how to* abstain from drugs and not get addicted to them than the Bush administration's description of abstinence as "the best way" of not having sex—and winding up with AIDS. The logic of this is akin to telling drivers that "the best way" of avoiding traffic accidents is "to abstain" from driving. It's also close to the well-meaning but equally ineffectual recipe delivered from time to time by popes for the elimination of warfare—namely, to "just say no to war!"—or, as a pope once put it at the United Nations in an appeal for disarmament, "Let the arms fall from your hands!" as if just saying no to guns were a way of teaching people *how to* prevent deaths and injuries from firearms, rather than exhorting them to say no. The reductio ad absurdum of this reasoning is the sheer tautology that "the best way of not doing something undesirable is not to do it."

No doubt the Bush administration knows best when, and indeed *how*, to abstain from abstinence.

POOR OLD ROSSI

———————◆———————

WHAT DO ROEBUCK, ROSSI, AND Royce have in common—other than their initial letter? It's the fact that they have all been dwarfed or obliterated, upstaged or outstaged, by once-equal partners who have gone on to become household names while their own have dwindled into oblivion. One can imagine the restless ghosts of Rossi and Royce doomed to haunt endless cocktail parties and parking lots to eternity until they come upon the very first guest ordering a "Rossi, very dry" after sending his chauffeur to park the Royce.

The two Byzantine brothers Saints Cyril and Methodius are another prime example of this genre. The alphabet they invented, used by Russian and a handful of other Slavic languages, and known as the Cyrillic alphabet, gives top and exclusive billing to the eponymous Cyril. I don't know whether self-esteem is too close to the sin of pride to be attributable to a saint, but if Methodius had any, it must have been sorely dented after the centuries of oblivion to which he has been consigned.

In this and other cases, one is tempted to put this down to a mere accident of alphabetical order (or at least our alphabetical order), except that this fails to account for the puzzling case of Roebuck, whose catalog no one sends for, even though he precedes Sears, whose catalog everyone sends for, in the alphabet.

Perhaps the whole thing is governed by a law of euphony that prescribes that names, or indeed nouns in general, with fewer syllables shall precede those with more. It is surely no accident that "gold and silver," "milk and honey," "Abbott and Costello," "law and order," and "salt and pepper" come in the order they do, but then why do Abercrombie and Fitch, and Gabbitas and Thring, sound so right? Is it just that we are used to them? It is intriguing to speculate about how Stan got his Laurel in ahead of Oliver's Hardy, or who first got the idea of putting Romeo before Juliet, but at least with couples who achieve celebrity for what they do rather than for what they make, like Sacco and Vanzetti, Hero and Leander, and Tom and Jerry, there is little danger that only one of them will end up eponymizing the thing or object they have jointly produced.

Fortnum seems to have just about thrown Mason out of the ring, but Wesson is holding his own very nicely with Smith. Obviously, the equal and opposite forces of the alphabetic primacy of Smith are nicely balanced by those of the rarity and identifiability of Wesson.

So the next time you're thinking of trading in your old Royce for a Benz as you swirl your olive in your martini, please spare a thought for poor old Rossi!

Americana

"A Duke's Exalted Station"

On November 30, 1995, the *New York Times* published a letter from a fourteen-year-old boy that read, "He [President Clinton] has no right to send troops to Bosnia, he never served in the armed forces. I learned that he was the only president never to have served in the armed forces."

It should be pointed out that a decision *not* to send them is equally an exercise of the president's prerogative as commander in chief!

The boy's grandfather researched the matter and found that of the forty previous presidents, twenty had served, and twenty had not served.

Ultimately, this raises the horrible specter with which the Fairy Queen threatened the House of Lords in Gilbert and Sullivan's *Iolanthe*: "And a duke's exalted station shall be attainable by competitive examination."

What would be the pros and cons of this method—competitive examination—of appointing US presidents?

Oh no, I hear you cry, that would prevent the people from getting the president they want! This is an objection that rests and falls on the most rickety of assumptions, first and foremost that the "people" are, and have always been, getting the president they want. And it would only be a valid objection, at best, if the current system did produce the president they want.

Apart from anything else, up to now, in most presidential elections, close to half—and in one recent case *more* than half—of the voting population got a president they didn't want, a situation that recurred even more recently in 2016. This, of course, does not account for the sizable percentage of people who didn't vote for anyone at all, either because they didn't care one way or the other or because they didn't feel that their vote would affect the outcome one way or the other, or even because someone they would have voted for did not happen to be one of the candidates on the ballot.

Since 1920, the percentage of qualified voters who actually voted in each presidential election has fluctuated between 50 percent and 60 percent, rising slightly above 60 percent on only two occasions.

So much for the people getting the president they want under the current system.

Presumably, objecting to entrusting the role of commander in chief to presidents without any record of military service is based on the idea either that a record of military service means that a candidate with such a record is braver than a candidate without such a record, or that any function or rank in the armed forces confers the corresponding expertise, however noncombatant the role, and however little command the function entailed—not to mention such a flimsy veneer of service of presidents such as Reagan, whose "service" in an army film unit meant little more than his dressing up in a soldier's uniform, and Nixon, who served in the navy in what appears to have been a noncombatant role, which seemed to have given him enough spare time to amass a nest egg from his poker winnings.

Would a potential President Quayle have gotten away with taking cover in the National Guard, and did actual President G. W. Bush get away with his sporadic appearances in that body—when he wasn't actually AWOL? In fact, chances are that it would be more of a shock to the system of grassroots America to learn that John "Duke" Wayne had never served in the armed forces—he didn't!

If we pursue this logic—the idea that candidates for the US presidency should possess firsthand knowledge and experience in all those areas and walks of life for which they will be expected to take the lead in policy and decision making—there would never be anyone qualified to occupy the presidency.

People might just as well object that non-college-educated candidates should be debarred because they would not be qualified to legislate—pardon me—or make executive decisions on education, those without a law or medical qualification should be debarred from nominating Supreme Court justices or surgeons and attorneys general, those who had never been postal workers would not be qualified to appoint postmasters general, and so on and so forth down to the reductio ad absurdum of barring from the presidency anyone who has not milked a cow or plowed a furrow, because he or she is thus not qualified to appoint a secretary of agriculture.

Ultimately, what is more important to nearly all electors is not how rich, smart, brave, honest, good-looking, monogamous, or educated—or, in these emancipated times, even how black or white, or male or female—a candidate may be, but rather whether *he or she is on, or perceived to be on, his or her side of the political fence.*

THE "GUNS DON'T KILL PEOPLE; PEOPLE DO" MANTRA: A REBUTTAL

———

UNFORTUNATELY, REASONING CAN NEVER MATCH the short and snappy gut appeal of slogans, mantras, war cries, and bumper stickers—except perhaps at the shouting match or school-yard level of "yes, they do, dummy!" But perhaps, in an attempt to remove its plausible glossy veneer, an analysis of it is worth a try.

There are two sliding scales involved. One is one's threshold of squeamishness (ST) about personally inflicting physical violence on others and, a fortiori, killing them, and the other is one's level of motivation (ML) for doing so at the specific time of committing that violence.

In order to kill someone with one's bare hands, one would have to have an extremely low squeamishness threshold and an extremely high level of motivation—or be a psychopath. One would also have to maintain both the ST and the ML for the relatively long time it would take to, say, overpower and strangle someone. Another factor that would stand in the way of killing someone with one's bare hands regardless of one's low ST and high ML would be the need for sufficient physical strength to overpower one's victim. So although people do kill people, there are at least these three powerful factors that inhibit, restrain, or prevent people from doing so with their bare hands.

In order to bludgeon someone with a blunt instrument, especially to the point of death, one could probably afford to be a little less squeamish because (a) the use of any weapon begins to distance a murderer from his victim; (b) it would take a little less time so that the high ML would not have to be sustained for so long; and (c) a weapon begins to equalize (not for nothing has a gun been dubbed an "equalizer") a physically weaker assailant with a physically superior victim or even give the assailant the advantage.

At the other end of the scale, there stands the old moral conundrum. If you could press a button in New York and safely, anonymously, and with total impunity "eliminate" a total stranger in, say, Outer Mongolia in return for a million dollars, would you do it?

Whether you would do it or not, it is safe to say that more people would accept that deal than the alternative deal of receiving the same reward for strangling that same person up front and personally, with their bare hands.

On all these scales, pulling a trigger is much closer to pressing a button than bare-handed strangling. With the same ML, be it fear, rage, jealousy, or greed, a gun allows someone who would otherwise be too squeamish, cowardly, or physically inferior to kill another person with his or her bare hands, or even with a blunt instrument or a knife, to do so with that weapon. A gun allows killers to kill without having to maintain their high ML for more than a moment. With a gun, how much easier is it to plead (and even mean it), "Your Honor, I didn't know what I was doing—it just went off"? It allows people to kill intimidating and physically stronger people or even superior numbers of people whom they would otherwise be afraid to attack; it allows them to kill at a distance without even showing or exposing themselves.

In hot blood, grabbing a gun is much more liable to be immediately and—please don't forget—*multi*-ply lethal and—don't forget either—more crippling—than bare hands, blunt instruments, and even knives, because in these cases, (a) death takes longer, even much longer, to inflict, and this alone gives tempers and passions time to cool down, and (b) victims have a greater chance of self-defense and survival.

How many "cold-blooded" professional assassins would have taken up that occupation if they were paid only for hacking their victims to death with an ax rather than for their marksmanship?

Ask Vietnam veterans whether it was easier to kill people on the ground in hand-to-hand combat with bayonets than to train their bomb sights on impersonal and remote targets from a height of several thousand feet and press the button.

Asserting triumphantly that it's *people* who kill people somehow suggests that those who favor gun control don't know that, don't believe it, or aren't smart or observant enough to see it. Actually, it is precisely because of their awareness of the fact that it *is* people who kill people that they don't want to make it so easy for them to do so, or so likely that they will.

Next week, we can talk about all those other countries where, although guns *are* banned, bare hands, blunt instruments, and knives *are not*, or even licensed, and where the people who kill people still go on doing so—but for some strange reason, *far less frequently*!

Yes, everyone knows and agrees that "people kill people," but what *is* in doubt is whether everyone agrees that *too many* people kill *too many* people, or whether some people feel that that is simply not true, or that it may be true, but that it is just an unfortunate consequence of a higher value—namely, "the right to bear arms" or the rights of "sportsmen."*

So if we can clear away a nonquestion that everyone agrees on, maybe the real questions can get equal time.

Do guns make it *easier* for people to kill people and in greater numbers as well as *more likely* that they will do so? And if so, is there a good reason not to make it less easy and less likely?

And if there *are* good reasons, is the argument against somewhat restricting the fun of shooting animals one of them?

Postscript

From the *New York Times*, October 17, 2015.

"A 12-year-old girl on Long Island was critically injured on Friday when a bullet fired from the street outside her home struck her in the head while she was indoors."

One cannot help wondering how many other innocent bystanders are injured, maimed, or killed by "people" with the help of "stray bullets," compared, of course, with the number who are killed, maimed, or injured—*unintentionally*—by "people" armed with clubs, knives, or bare hands.

---

* In the aftermath of one major school massacre, when Congress had drafted a bill banning the *import* of high-caliber, rapid-fire automatic weapons, President Bush the elder announced that he would veto it because it was "unfair to *sportsmen*"!

THE BELL CURVES...BUT FOR WHOM?

———◆———

THE BELL CURVE IS A 1994 book by American psychologist Richard J. Herrnstein and American political scientist Charles Murray.

The authors suggested that there was some correlation between "race" and "intelligence."

The book was heavily publicized and highly controversial when it was released, just after the death of Herrnstein. In the first several months of its release, four hundred thousand copies of the book were sold around the world. Hundreds of reviews and commentaries were written about the book soon after its publication.

If there is anything on earth that abhors a vacuum more than nature itself, it is the media. So with the untimely demise of the baseball season (as a result of a players' strike, the Major League Baseball season ended prematurely on August 11, 1994), we saw the opening of a new "race and IQ" season to engage the idling passions of the American public.

On the right, the bigots were manning their familiar barricades, and on the left, the liberals were scuttling to their familiar bolt-holes. Enormous amounts of ammunition were being expended in attempts to prove or resist the notion that different population groups, particularly ethnically or racially defined groups, score consistently higher or lower than others on IQ tests, and that this "finding" is proof of group inferiority and thus would have explosive consequences.

Let us suppose, first, that there is a more meaningful way of determining who is "black" and who is "white" in this country than the traditional and unquestioned premise that everyone who is nonwhite is "black"—after all, one could just as well proceed from the opposite, but equally valid and equally dubious, premise that everyone who is nonblack is "white"!

Suppose further that it has been established that there *is* a fifteen-point average spread in IQ between the groups the scientists have chosen to describe as "black" and "white." The truth is that the logical consequences of such findings are neither what the bigots hope they are nor what the liberals fear they are. If, for example, one of the purposes was to recruit students on the basis of IQ, all that it would mean would be that, proportionately, there would be a few more "whites" than "blacks" in the higher-IQ classes or schools and a few more "blacks" than "whites" in the lower. It would in no way follow, as the bigots hope and the liberals fear, that all "blacks" should be educated separately from all "whites." Whether high-IQ students should be segregated from low-IQ students is a completely separate issue.

The mere mention of the word "race" immediately begins to kindle passions, but in less controversial areas such as height, I doubt that it would occur to anyone that, if it were scientifically proven that, say, men over six feet tall consistently scored lower on IQ tests than their shorter brothers, they would therefore be sent to separate schools and those other "grisly" consequences feared by the *New York Times* in an editorial would come to pass.

Liberals do themselves and their cause a disservice by allowing themselves to be bullied by the bigots into accepting the premise that "proof" of collective "intellectual inferiority" makes the case for educational segregation or any other dire or—to use the language of the same *New York Times* editorial—"grisly social or political consequences." In this way, they end up taking refuge in that very obscurantism they profess to abhor, by resisting scientific inquiry in areas that they—mistakenly—fear may yield unpalatable results.

Nothing that may be even "scientifically proven" about groups collectively can detract from the principle that individual members of all and any groups should be treated on their merits. Even in the case of basketball, where it is empirically demonstrable that tall players tend to be more effective than short ones, there is no suggestion that short players as such should not be treated on their individual merits and allowed to play in the NBA if they can make the grade. By the same token, no woman is excluded from joining the New York City Fire Department as a firefighter because she is a female if she can climb a ladder and rescue a 165-pound person from a burning building.

THE NO-FAULT SOCIETY

———◆———

Exculpatory, my dear Watson!
Erewhon redux, or "Erewhemos"

IN HIS UTOPIAN NOVEL, *EREWHON*, the Victorian British writer Samuel Butler imagined a country where the sick were treated as criminals and the criminals were treated as patients.

There is a sense in which the United States today is rapidly becoming a no-fault society, where wrongdoers exculpate themselves and are exculpated by others as having exercised poor judgment, having made "mistakes," or having acted stupidly, thereby transmuting unethical, immoral, and even criminal actions into intellectual failings. In this variation on Samuel Butler's theme, those who cheat, defraud, and deceive are labeled by themselves, their lawyers, their friends, and their families as merely dumb, and those who commit "blue-collar crime" are labeled criminals and pay heavily for their poor judgment, mistakes, and stupidity.

This displacement from the moral to the intellectual also manifests itself in casual encounters in the street or on the road. Drivers or pedestrians who act inconsiderately or purely selfishly are most often excoriated by their victims with the words "stupid" or "dummy."

Among other examples of the "free pass" given, or indulgence shown, for bad behavior in this no-fault society, there was the impunity enjoyed by the young McEnroe when his temper tantrums on the tennis court, mostly provoked by adverse line calls, were attributed by commentators to his "perfectionism." This perfectionism was somehow never exhibited when line calls were in his favor.

Schoolboys, who in other climes and times misbehaved and were appropriately disciplined, are now excused on medical grounds, diagnosed with such "disorders" as attention deficit hyperactivity disorder, and treated with drugs such as Ritalin.

For those charged with—and even convicted of—white-collar crimes, especially public figures and high-office holders, the nearest thing in American public life today to confession, remorse, repentance, or acknowledgment of guilt seems to be the invoking of something known as "error of judgment," "misjudgment," or some equivalent term that removes the issue from the moral framework of right and wrong and places it squarely in the realm of brain power or IQ, as if the only failings ever at issue were intellectual ones, to the exclusion of moral issues of blame and guilt. How are we meant to understand the fault of "misjudgment" that is conceded, and then only grudgingly, after the usually prominent and highly placed wrongdoer has been caught, exposed, and convicted? Is the lapse of "judgment" then simply about the fact of having done the deed in question but misjudged the chances of exposure? And is the regret, however grudgingly—or even lavishly—expressed on such occasions, a regret at having been caught, or is it simply an acknowledgment of having miscalculated the chances of being caught?

The related concept of responsibility in public life seems similarly to have been drained of its content so that the mere mantric recitation of the phrase "I accept responsibility" or its equivalent by public officials has become what is known in linguistic and philosophical circles as a "performative utterance." What makes performative utterances interesting and special is that there is no possible evidence in the real world outside the utterance itself that can prove it true or false. If someone says, "I hit a home run in the game today," you can check whether he or she did or not by reference to the facts of the matter, which are out there to be investigated. But if someone says, "I congratulate you," the only way to check whether he or she did or not is to find out whether or not he or she uttered those words.

When President Reagan finally and grudgingly "accepted responsibility" for the Iran-Contra scandal, his "acceptance of responsibility" never amounted to anything more than his utterance of the words, "I accept responsibility." In courts where "blue-collar" defendants "accept responsibility" for their wrongdoing, they do so by pleading guilty and "suffering the consequences" of so doing.

In other times and climes, the test of whether an office holder accepted responsibility for something was whether he actually did something like compensate someone for loss or damage or resign from his post, if some major malfeasance or act of negligence occurred on the office holder's watch, thus entailing his ultimate responsibility.

If I say "I accept responsibility" for breaking a valuable vase in a friend's house, is that the end of the matter, or does it entail consequences, such as (a) cleaning up the mess and (b) offering material compensation for the damage?

Examples of the various kinds of self-serving, exculpatory language are legion. Here are a few, accompanied here and there by my own interpolations in italics.

In one example, at the time of writing (May 2, 2016), Governor Christie of New Jersey has not said that he "accepts responsibility" for the havoc-wreaking closure of traffic lanes on the George Washington Bridge, no doubt because in this case there would be unpleasant consequences and a price to pay.

In another example, Wendy Bell, an anchorwoman at Pittsburgh TV station WTAE, speculated about the identities of two men who fatally shot five black people in a poor Pittsburgh suburb. There were social media protests that her remarks had been racist. She was fired by the station, which apologized, saying that Bell's remarks showed "an egregious lack of judgment."

New York Times, November 6, 2015.

"Mr. Cherkasky had apologized for drinking too much and having a lapse in judgment, but not for injuring the woman, Kirsten Schuk."

Writing about Reagan administration's Attorney General Edwin Meese, the *New York Times*'s Steven V. Roberts reported on February 7, 1990, that "Washington is wondering how long he can keep on surmounting accusations of impropriety and misjudgment in the Med Tech scandal."

This kind of language is a prime example of the practice of transposing the conduct of public figures, in particular, from the realm of morality to the morally neutral realm of "miscalculation." How deeply rooted this transposition has become can be judged by the fact that in this example it is not even Edwin Meese himself who is using "misjudgment" as an excuse for misconduct. Rather it is the reporter who is describing as "misjudgment" some wrongdoing Meese has been accused of! In the Reagan administration, the frontiers of the language of exculpation were rolled back even further, and a special word was coined or rescued from oblivion by the president's handlers for "damage control" over the effects of his special mix of what Benjamin D'Israeli might have been moved to call "lies, damn(ed) lies, and misstatements"—namely, "the president misspoke"—that is, uttered untruths that he didn't mean, didn't mean to utter, or was unwilling actually to retract.

I believe that it was during President Reagan's term of office that his aides enriched the language with the term "deniability" in order to deflect criticism of him.

Televangelists, when finally confronted with the incontrovertible, sometimes concede that they have "sinned." This locution is designed to take the matter beyond the range of moral and even legal retribution but in a rather different direction, and the announcement is not usually long in coming that by private arrangement in bilateral and privileged communication with the "Lord," they have been forgiven. As the cases of Jim and Tammy Bakker and others show, they do not, however, seem disposed to extend the same morality—and legality—transcending privileges to those who have trespassed against them!

At a certain point in the Irangate drama, Reagan announced that he "took responsibility." This assertion, of course, remained a purely performative utterance, and he showed no sign of taking responsibility for suffering any of the consequences of "taking responsibility."

Janet Reno (attorney general) "took responsibility for" the assault by the organs under her jurisdiction (the Bureau of Tobacco and Firearms) on the Waco headquarters of the Branch Davidians.

Again, if this does not entail accepting the consequences of taking responsibility, what is there left for it to mean? When various terrorist organizations announce that they "claim responsibility" for bombings, assassinations, and the like, they are accepting the consequences and expect to be charged, convicted, and punished, or if Donald Trump has anything to do with it, "have the sh+t bombed out of them" if they are caught.

Stern, Laurence, and Haynes Johnson. "3 Top Nixon Aides, Kleindienst Out." *Washington Post*, Staff Writers, Tuesday, May 1, 1973, p. A01.

"President Nixon, after accepting the resignations of four of his closest aides, told the American people last night that he accepted *full responsibility* for the actions of his subordinates in the Watergate scandal."

New York Magazine, letter from Jimmy Roe.

"The police commissioner is caught entertaining a female guest on city property, and the mayor sidesteps the issue, calling it a '*lapse in judgment.*'"

CNN. "Sonia in LA" (regarding the indictment of Bess Myerson for bribery, etc.), October 8, 1987, 1:45 p.m.

Sonia quotes the director of the Miss America Pageant as saying "a woman in love will do stupid things." Sonia comments, "Is it only a woman? What about men? Is it true that being in love lowers a person's IQ?"

Once again, this places the issue squarely inside the realm of intelligence and outside that of "right and wrong" or even criminality!

New York Times. Letter titled "Mrs. Zaccaro's Loyalty," dated January 8, 1985, from Louis Auchinloss.

"When she described her husband, John Zaccaro's gross misrepresentation of his assets in a loan application as a *judgmental error*, I was reminded that Richard Nixon had used the same argument to explain his conduct at Watergate."

New York Times.

"Mrs. Ferraro, in a statement, linked her husband's troubles to what she termed her 'historic candidacy.' She said he had committed a *judgmental error* in trying to help a client."

"The District Attorney said that the scheme had been designed to net large commissions for Mr. Zaccaro."

Thus, a patent attempt to cheat, defraud, and evade the law motivated by greed and for the purpose of gain is described as an intellectual shortcoming motivated by compassion.

Martz, Larry, and Robert Parry. "The Ollie North Case." *Newsweek*, April 24, 1989.

"Keker made North tell how he had obtained backdated bills from the contractor and then prepared phony replies, typing them on typewriters at a local dept. store to avoid being seen by co-workers. 'It has to be one of the dumber things I'd done all my life,' he said contritely! 'If I'd been thinking clearly, I wouldn't have done this at all to begin with.'"

Ibid. Attorney General Edwin Meese, already under investigation for actions he may have taken on behalf of the Wedtech Corporation, may soon have some explaining to do for another potential conflict of interest. Senator Howard M. Metzenbaum accused Meese of a "gross error of judgment and an insensitivity to appearances of impropriety" regarding Mr. Meese's holdings in several regional telephone companies. Lieutenant Colonel North conceded that he was guilty of "an error of judgment."

New York Times, September 26, 1992.

"The head of the Texas Railroad Commission, Lena Guerrero, a protégé of Gov. Ann Richards, resigned today, apologizing for the false claims she made that she was a graduate of the University of Texas. 'I made mistakes, deeply serious mistakes,' said Ms. Guerrero."

Newt Gingrich, January 1997.

There was a lot of talk in the media about Newt and his "ethics violations." Leaving aside his semantic slithering—"inadvertent," "inaccurate," "incomplete," "erroneous," "failure to take legal advice," and so forth—what about the public relations effect or perceptions of the American public of the recurrent use of the opaque words "ethics" and "ethics violations"? If one could poll readers of the Daily News and ask them to rate "ethics violations," "dishonesty," and "lying and cheating" (for personal gain) in order of moral turpitude or disqualification for high public office, would they treat "all those imposters just the same" (phrase borrowed from Rudyard Kipling's poem "IF")? Or would they give different responses to the following three questions: (1) How much do ethics violations by politicians matter? (2) How much does honesty matter? and (3) How much do lying and cheating matter?

New York Times, December 1997.

"'While Mr. Cisneros has admitted that he made *mistakes* in his personal life,' Mr. Namorato said, 'he has attempted to put these mistakes behind him.'"

It is worth considering this interesting verb, which is often used by transgressors and their apologists in connection with their "mistakes." Does it mean "I am going to forget them, act as if they never happened, and hope that the media and the public do too"? Or does it mean "I did whatever it was, but I have been punished or have made up for it, or have made amends in some way and am therefore quits"? Or does it mean "I am going to turn over a new leaf and never do that kind of thing again"? Or does it mean "I wish I had never been caught or exposed, but if I (and the media) keep quiet about it for long enough, perhaps everyone else will too"? One thing this kind of language clearly does not mean is any assumption of guilt or expression of repentance, remorse, or intention to make amends (to the victim[s]) or to reform.

"Ex-Judge Pleads Guilty to Fleeing from Justice." New York Times, December 3, 1997.

"A former judge convicted of sexually assaulting five women in his court-house...The defendant, David Lanier, told the Federal District Court here [Memphis] that he had made a '*a bad judgment call*' in August when he fled. He was captured two months later in Mexico living under an assumed name."

Isn't that what baseball umpires sometimes do in August?

"Mets Manager Steve Phillips Accused of Sexual Harassment." New York Times, October, 1998.

"'Although Phillips did not tell the Mets initially about the matter,' Howard said, 'Steve was very forthcoming to explain to us the facts of the relationship.' Phillips said, 'I apologized for making some incredibly bad judgments.'" Asked why Phillips was not being fired, the Mets general manager said he was "receiving extensive personal counseling."

So not only is your wrongdoing OK, since it is attributable only to the intellectual failing of bad judgment, but counseling has now also become an appropriate alternative to punishment or retribution, and it has joined the lexicon of exculpation or retribution. Humbler wrongdoers, however, usually get their counseling, if any, in the course of—and not instead of—serving their prison sentences.

The words "appropriate" and "inappropriate" are coming into vogue as convenient expressions for public figures to use in confessing their sins and crimes when they are cornered, in an attempt to neutralize, mitigate, or "de-culpate" themselves and transmute wrongdoing into what might appear to be relatively innocuous differences of taste. One might, for example, be inappropriately dressed for golf.

For example, CNN and NBC on February 10, 1993, settled with the Ford Motor Co. over a report by NBC showing a Ford truck set ablaze after a staged collision with another vehicle. NBC, after admitting (a) that the colliding car was in fact going considerably faster than viewers had been told and (b) that incendiary devices had been planted on the truck, conceded that their report had been inappropriate!

Whatever happened to lying, cheating, and deceit—and, in this case, reckless endangerment?

There is an old saying: "There is one law for the poor and one law for the rich." Has that now been superseded by a "postmodern" paradox whereby white-collar criminals may now excuse themselves on the grounds of a temporary lapse of "judgment" or cerebral "brownout," which causes them to act more "dumbly" than usual, while street criminals, who may be assumed to be operating at a chronically lower intellectual level, never get to plead low IQ in mitigation of their offenses?

Hauser, Christine. "Officer Admits He Helped Thwart a Brothel's Rivals." *New York Times.*

The defense counsel offered an exculpatory passage richly larded with this contemporary "no-fault language."

"Mr. Kim's lawyer, Maurice H. Sercarz, said his client 'is not a case of a police officer who used his badge to enrich himself. He wanted to do the right thing, but ended up crossing the line and had been a capable and aggressive police officer and now wanted to put the ordeal behind him.'"

This sentiment was undoubtedly shared by each and every inmate in the nation's jails, but they were not able to share it with us (a) because they had no lawyer to act as a public advocate and (b) because neither they nor their crimes were deemed sufficiently "newsworthy" by the media to bring their cases to national attention.

What precisely is it that we are supposed to understand that stopped him from doing that "right thing" that "he wanted to do" while at the same time "using his badge to enrich himself"—which he didn't want to do?

Mr. Kim's lawyer continued, "There is a bargain police officers enter into with informants. That's what this case is about. He obtained the information and used it as a police officer is supposed to do, but in so doing he came to recognize that he may have been assisting the informant in a way that might be inappropriate."

Although Americans are so often first into the field in so many areas of life, the British usually get around eventually to climbing onto the bandwagon. So it is not that much of a surprise to come across the following headline in the Times on July 19: "My Silly Mistakes Sank Barings, Leeson Confesses."

"Mr. Leeson...who was accused...of losing 208 million pounds while representing that he was making profits admitted that he had made *some very silly mistakes*."

Leeson is in jail in Frankfurt on twelve charges, including forgery and cheating. The wording of the headline, perhaps unwittingly, condones what has by now become an almost standard self-commutation of crimes deliberately committed in the pursuit of gain and motivated by greed into some kind of intellectual shortcoming. Leeson is precisely not confessing but rather mitigating and transmuting, by the currently permissible verbal alchemy, the sow's ear of criminality into the silk purse of "silliness."

Well, who wouldn't rather be stigmatized for a simpleton than hanged for a villain, if it could be managed?

London Times, April 5, 1998.

"James Hewitt's former fiancée was arrested yesterday over the alleged theft of intimate letters written to him by Diana. Ms. Ferretti was quoted as saying: 'I now see how *stupid* I have been, but I am also relieved that they are now back with their rightful owners.'"

Politics and show business are by no means the only walks of celebrity life where wrongdoers are privileged to "weasel out" of blame and guilt through the use of such special exculpatory language.

ABC TV. Football, Syracuse versus Boston College, November 27, 2004.

The referee awarded Syracuse a fifteen-yard penalty for a face mask violation by Boston College. *The violation was gross, wanton, and flagrant; the offender threw his victim to the ground while grasping the face mask with one hand when the ball was already way downfield. The sportscaster called this a "foolish error"—that is, an intellectual failing rather than a clear attempt to gain advantage for his side by breaking the rules.*

TALKING "TOUGH": THE ALL-AMERICAN WORD

————◆————

IT WAS WHEN I FIRST began to travel on New York commuter trains that I got my first whiff of the Wild West.

When I traveled by train in Britain, I was known as a "passenger"—an effete and supine role compared with that of a "rider." This robust, rugged term of choice on American trains was so suggestive of rodeos, leather saddles, spurs, chaps, and bucking broncos that I half expected to see the commuters exiting Grand Central Station wearing ten-gallon hats and walking bowlegged—which brings me to the topic of "talking tough."

What's the difference between a "tough guy" and a "tough kid"? Most adjectives are supposed to mean more or less the same thing regardless of the noun to which they are applied, but a "tough guy" is essentially someone prone to threatening or dealing out violence, while a "tough kid" is like the kind of quarterback whom sportscasters are prone to admire, someone who can "take" violence rather than dish it out.

Over the years, I have collected a sample of the uses to which the word has been put. Large as it is, this sample only skims the surface of the tip of the iceberg of its use. In each case I have tried to deduce from context the tremendous variety of the normal descriptive words that would have been used in its place by normal speakers of English who are trying to express themselves rather than project an image. The word is a real favorite with politicians and publicists in general and is the ultimate populist linguistic sop to "grassroots America." Its use often goes hand in hand with the dropping of the final *g* (H. W. Bush, passim) in present participles, a reluctance to use the "correct," rounded version of the final "-ow" in "fellow," "yellow," and "tomorrow" (Lyndon Johnson, passim), and the substitution of "good" for "well"—an anathema to sportscasters—and "like" for "as if."

There is an undoubted link between this kind of verbal muscularity and the tradition of presidential athleticism as well as the horseshoes, jogging, fishing, wood-chopping (pardon me, joggin', fishin,' 'n' choppin'), and other rough-hewn folk activities that American political grandees are so anxious to be shown engaging in.

"Tough", with its evocation of robustness, ruggedness, and hardiness, may well be the quintessential American word and has become a kind of all-terrain vehicle of American, especially male, self-expression—good for all seasons, circumstances, and purposes. As such, it has been gradually drained of most of its descriptive meaning and has become largely emotive. It is to be found frequently on the lips of public figures. Its use seems somehow to invest its users with an aura of "toughness" itself—a "real man's" word, whose use verges on what is known as a performative utterance. Although it is not technically an expletive, it belongs in the same category as all-purpose words like "like" and the *F* word, all of which save the speaker the trouble of knowing or thinking of the words that would pinpoint the desired meaning. With the use of this word, the speaker is somehow projecting an image of being tough by association, or of someone who "doesn't mince words" or is a "man of few words"—a man, of course, who may very well be one who doesn't have many words to mince.

I had rarely, if ever, heard this expression used in this way by a woman before TV coverage of (American) football started to include women in the commentary team (rarely, so far, in the booth itself, but mostly down on the field to conduct pointlessly tautological halftime interviews with the coach whose team is ahead telling her, in so many words, that his guys played "good," and the coach whose team is trailing telling her, in so many words, that they didn't). These women all have to be young, in the same spirit in which, in the days before they became "flight attendants," "air hostesses" all had to be young. They also tend to be assigned to what seems to be considered the appropriate female task of reporting on the status of the injuries of the players who have been detained in the locker rooms after halftime.

Each example of the use of "tough" is accompanied in brackets by the "untough" equivalents it is doing duty for. The results should reveal the tremendous variety of semantic bases its users are attempting to touch with this talismanic, "macho" word.

Of course, the word "tough" itself by no means exhausts the vocabulary of toughness. On October 10, 1992, CNN described Clinton as "hitting" the books in preparation for the first candidates' debate on November 10, 1992; he was doing nothing, of course, so effete or wimpish as "reading" them, so the report managed to strike a robust, muscular note in even this bespectacled, sedentary, nerdy, and indoor context.

One of the most iconic uses of the word as a political war cry is on the subject of crime—for example, being "tough" on crime. For the most part, it's brandished by Republicans. It almost always translates as "tough" on *punishment*. Democrats should perhaps fight back by appropriating "toughness" for crime *prevention* a much "tougher" proposition by far, although not as it's represented in the following example (from the Dao, James. "NY's Top Democrat Takes *Tougher* Stand on Juvenile Crime." *New York Times*, December 10, 1996), where "top Democrat" Silver appears to be stealing some Republican thunder by advocating "tougher" sentences.

On November 2, 1992, "I haven't been afraid to take on the tough [unpopular, controversial] issues," Senator Al D'Amato said.

On October 29, 1992, the *New York Times* reported, "Like Mr. Perot...Mr. Chung is campaigning on a platform that the country's current leadership has run the economy into the ground, though it is a tough [weak] argument in South Korea, where economic growth this year is running at more then 7%."

On October 29, 1992, CNN reported that Acting Secretary of State L. Eagleburger said the problems facing the Commonwealth of Independent States were "a tough [difficult] row to hoe."

On November 5, 1992, the *New York Times* reported, "John Glenn... defeated Lieutenant Governor Michael de Wine in the toughest [closest] race of his career." "Democrats running for Congress in the face of tough [stiff, strong] Republican challenges."

On November 21, 1992, on *Monday Night Football*, John Madden said, "The closer you get to the line, the tougher [harder] it is (to score!)."

The *New York Times* reported on November 1, 1992, that the director Ridley Scott said, "We had a fairly heated discussion about our presentation of the Spanish Inquisition as being rather...tough [cruel, ruthless, harsh]."

The *New York Times* reported on November 12, 1992, that "Mr. Clinton…reassured…the armed services that he would be as tough [aggressive] with national security affairs as any of the Republicans who had questioned his mettle in the campaign."

Are these his own words or a reporter's paraphrase? If the latter, then Clinton's own words might reveal his meaning. As it stands, the word "tough" is a lot more emotive than it is descriptive. The chances are that, as his audience would no doubt feel that their own instinctive preferences on issues affecting national security would be *tough*, talk of toughness would strike a responsive chord. When it comes to "endowing the notion with concrete content," as the Russians like to say, it would no doubt mean opting for "Desert Storm" instead of giving sanctions a chance, or it could mean going into Panama to get Noriega out. In other words, it would mean to give preference to *military—or other violent—means* to solve "national security problems." Some, however, might construe it (including Clinton himself, privately) as meaning having the moral courage to resist the facile and popularity-enhancing option of "sending in the marines."

In November 1992, Frank Gifford said on *Monday Night Football* that it was a "tough [unsuccessful, frustrating, disappointing] night for the Bears."

On November 3, 1992, Bill Beutel said on ABC TV, "That had to be a very tough speech for him [Bush] to make tonight." Only the construction of the sentence prevents the misinterpretation of "tough" here as "pugnacious," "hostile," "angry," and the like. Here it means "difficult," in the sense of having to overcome his own reluctance.

On November 18, 1992, the *New York Times* reported, "As the criticism against the mayor [Dinkins] has continued, his defense has grown tougher [vigorous, vehement, defiant]."

On November 30, 1992, the *New York Times* printed, "Tougher [more effective, stricter, stringent, more unpopular] measures to fight tuberculosis urged by New York panel."

"Angry [Security] Council takes a tougher stand [firmer, stronger, more punitive, more positive]—imposing trade and other restrictions on the Khmer Rouge."

CNN's Jeannie Moos reported that in Bosnia, there were "tough [fierce, brave, fearless] Serb fighters and tough [rough/difficult to move on] terrain."

A TV commercial declared that "Alka Seltzer Plus is tough [strong, effective] medicine."

On December 27, 1992, the Seattle Seahawks played the Chicago Bears. Gelbaugh (Seattle quarterback) intercepted with three and half minutes to go and Seattle behind by 2, driving down their own forty-yard line. John Madden's partner said it was a "tough [unfortunate, regrettable] play for Gelbaugh."

On December 23, 1992, Fox TV channel 5 used the slogan, "The Fox 5 news team—for twenty-five years tough enough for New York." At this level of usage, the emotive content has squeezed out practically all the semantic, leaving little more "meaning" than the Coca-Cola commercial that tells you that you should consume their product because it is IT! Is there perhaps a suggestion that unlike the faint-hearted, lily-livered, and squeamish competition of the newscasters at rival TV networks, Fox reporters and cameramen are, of course, *unflinching and remorseless* when it comes to seeking out and covering the corruption, mayhem, and murder that goes with this beat?

Other examples:

CNN: "Tavis-D relieves tough [severe, bad] congestion."

New York Times, April 17, 1997: "Mr. Packwood denied the accusations [of sexual harassment] near the end of a tough [embarrassing, revealing, damaging] session."

"Every reason to hang as tough [uncompromising] as Mr. Bush in rejecting partial deals [with Saddam Hussein]."

New York Times, April 28, 2001: "Journalists from the second state-dominated network, ORT, were noted in 1998 for their tough [critical] coverage of events in Belarus, a close Russia ally."

Pam Shriver, commenting in the course of a tennis match that was trespassing on the time allotted to rain-delayed car racing: "It's been a tough [bad, with adverse weather and surface conditions] day up in Bristol [Tennessee]."

ABC TV, December 28, 1996, Ford truck commercial: "What tough [resistant, stands up to rough treatment] is, what tough does." This immediately followed an Advil commercial that said, "Advil, tough on [effective in relieving] pain." Since the commercial was broadcast during a football game, it was clearly targeting the aggression/violence nerve of its audience. The screen depicted San Francisco 49ers quarterback Steve Young being "hit"! Interestingly enough, the ad was doing its best to avoid the opposite, unflattering implication that people who "are afraid of a little pain" and rush to buy pain medicine are the "weak sisters," the real un-tough!

Australian Open Tennis Tournament, January 19, 1997: T. Muster versus J. Courier at one set all, 4–4 in the third, advantage Muster: "That's just a tough [at a particularly critical juncture] double fault there by Muster." Is the commentator being sorry for Muster in his misfortune, or is he criticizing him for his failure of nerve—or, if neither of those, what?

New York Times, March 13, 2000, Calvin Sims: "Fusae Oto, the first woman governor of Osaka, Japan's second largest prefecture, a tough [grim/harsh/heavily industrialized, or whatever it is that the media mean by "hardscrabble"] commercial region 250 miles SW of Tokyo..."

One of the few products that I have not seen—yet!—boosted by the use of the attributive adjective "tough" is toilet paper, but believe it or not, a once well-known brand sold in Britain was called "Bronco," perhaps more of a tribute to that nation's reputation for eccentricity.

However, toilet paper has now been seen on display in the aisles of your friendly neighborhood supermarket proudly bearing the nation's currently highest accolade: "as seen on TV"!

THE COMPASSIONATE CONSERVATIVE: OXY-MORON-IN-CHIEF

———————

You Iraqis will thank me for it when you're older—if you live that long!
—*Washington Post*, "Bush Marks Fifth
Anniversary of Iraq Invasion"

FIVE YEARS AFTER LAUNCHING THE US invasion of Iraq, President George Bush marked the anniversary with a speech at the Pentagon.

I'm pleased to be back here with the men and women of the Defense Department. On this day in 2003, the United States began Operation Iraqi Freedom. As the campaign unfolded, tens of thousands of our troops poured across the Iraqi border, *to liberate the Iraqi people and remove a regime that threatened free nations.* Five years into this battle, there is an understandable debate over whether the war was worth fighting, whether the fight is worth winning, and whether we can win it. The answers are clear to me. *Removing Saddam Hussein from power was the right decision*, and this is a fight America can and must win. Bush's stated war aim, the removal of Saddam Hussein from power, had been achieved five years before this speech was delivered. What then could possibly be the meaning of "a fight that America can and must win"? What was America still fighting for in 2008 as Bush was speaking? The men and women who crossed into Iraq five years ago *removed a tyrant, liberated a country, and rescued millions from unspeakable horrors.* [emphasis mine]

So five years after launching his invasion of Iraq, President Bush felt unable to offer any reason for doing so, other than the purely altruistic one of rescuing the Iraqi people from a brutal dictator—significantly enough, not even Saddam Hussein's "weapons of mass destruction" were invoked.

The following letter, published on March 31, 2015, in the Scottish newspaper, the *Herald Scotland*, well illustrates the fact that this myth is still being swallowed—and regurgitated—in places and times far removed from the time and place of the invasion, even after so much time has elapsed as to make unmistakably clear its continuing and disastrous consequences, and disastrous above all to the Iraqi people themselves, whose welfare Bush had so much at heart.

The letter was headed: "It was right to remove tyrant Saddam."

"31 March 2015.
Your correspondents David Stubley (Letters, March 25) and Ian Johnstone (Letters, March 30) should move from continual attacks on George W. Bush and Tony Blair over the second Iraq war.

They should remember it was Margaret Thatcher who first took the UK into war with Iraq, *but it was President Bush and Mr Blair who finally removed a monster from the world. Saddam Hussein was killing many thousands of his own people.*"[emphasis mine]

The problem is that it suggests that since the *effect* of the US intervention was to "remove an evil tyrant," it was also somehow its *motive*, and that, in spite of its "misplaced emphasis" and clumsy, bad-faith manipulations of public opinion, it somehow still "meant well."

1. The United States is not and never has been in the business of removing tyrants as part of its foreign policy.

The list of "tyrants" that the United States has not and is not removing is endless. The incomplete list of those it was actively supporting and has actively supported includes Saddam Hussein *himself*, Manuel Noriega, Nikolai Ceasescu, plus a host of Latin American military juntas—and indeed, including those the United States actually had a hand in creating (the Pinochet regime in Chile, for one). This list is only a little shorter than the list of those brutal dictators it has countenanced with equanimity, tolerated, or ignored: inter alia, Idi Amin, Papa Doc, Emperor Bokassa, President Mubarak, Zia Ul Haq, Chairman Mao, and even Fidel Castro, although not from want of trying to overthrow him, and even Manuel Noriega, until he had outlived his usefulness—not to mention Joseph Stalin.

2. "Tyrants," like "freedom fighters," "terrorists," and "war criminals," tend, like beauty, to lie in the eye of the beholder. That is why the whole fabric of international law, including the Charter of the United Nations, has given absolute primacy to the notion of national sovereignty. Only recently have exceptions been made for interventions strictly under the aegis and with the sanction of international and regional intergovernmental organizations like the United Nations or NATO.

Once an individual nation claims the right to remove another nation's "tyrant" by force, then it is open season on any head of state or government whom any other government decides for its own reasons as someone who is or has suddenly become a "tyrant"—provided, of course, that the tyrant-removing nation has the necessary firepower!

3. As for that flimsiest of propaganda fig leaves—that the United States, or any other nation, for that matter, is in the business of "removing tyrants" because it feels sorry for the "tyrant's" victims—consider the following:

a.   What about the victims of all the other still-unremoved "tyrants"— Mugabe?

b.   What about the victims of Saddam Hussein and Manuel Noriega during all those years when those "tyrants" were still doing some of Uncle Sam's dirty work and had not yet outlived their usefulness?

One thing that has become unmistakably clear to me from my work in the United Nations is that "victims" are chosen and their causes espoused by member states strictly in accordance with and because of the identity of the "oppressor." Two of the most vocal champions of the antiapartheid cause during the Cold War were the USSR and China, two of the most racist countries around.

Were they sorry for the "victims," or could it be that they had an interest in "getting at" their oppressors?

The Kurds are a "victim" people, without a country of their own, if there ever was one. I never heard the Kurdish question raised in the United Nations, except once, by, of all people, the representative of Mongolia, at a meeting of what was then the "Afro-Asian caucus group," where the chairman immediately gaveled the proceedings into adjournment. There's no cigar for guessing which nations at that time were the most vociferous champions of "self-determination"—except, of course, when it came to places like the Falklands population, and, of course, the Kurds.

By contrast, while the "inalienable rights of the Palestinian people" were a cause that had for years a whole standing committee devoted to it, served by a full-time secretariat, the plight of the people of East Timor was never mentionable in polite company. Was it because no one was "sorry" for them, or was it because no one had any political mileage to gain from pillorying their Indonesian "oppressors"?

"Only in America": "America No. 1"

———◆———

In *At the Drop of Another Hat*, the two-man musical revue by Flanders and Swann, Michael Flanders remarked about the English, "We don't go round telling people how wonderful we are—everybody knows that!"

When I first arrived in the United States, with my eyes, ears, and pores wide open, there was a multitude of first impressions competing for my attention. One of these first impressions, which has become a lasting one, is the frequency with which politicians and other public figures feel impelled, at the drop of a hat, to proclaim the worldwide primacy of the United States in whatever area of life catches their fancy, ranging from the sublime to the ridiculous.

Well before my arrival, I had read a newspaper article that reported that a visiting Texan bishop had declared that "the people of Texas are the guntoting-est and churchgoingest people in the USA." I put this down at the time to the fact that he was from Texas, and I didn't realize until later that it was in fact a pan-American conditioned reflex.

To prove to myself—and perhaps others—that this was not a misimpression, I started to collect examples, but the pickings were so easy that I had to give up after a while. To quote Ecclesiastes 3:1–8 (King James Version), "To everything there is a season"—and the author proceeds to enumerate them at great length but not as exhaustively as he might have thought. He reckoned without a country where claiming "number-one-hood" is never out of season.

Here are a few examples. After reading them, some may think that Shakespeare had a point when he gave Hamlet's mother the line: "the lady doth protest too much, methinks."

To put the matter in perspective, there are two hundred or so sovereign nation-states in the world. Has it ever occurred to Ms. Schreiber or any one of the authors of the preposterously and immodestly inflated and chest-thumping claims quoted below to wonder whether one or more of the other two hundred "competitors" might, for example, have a "greater" military academy—even supposing there were an internationally recognized, reliable method of assessing the relative "greatness" of military academies?

Costa Rica was, and may still be, the only country in the world that, as a matter of principle, does not have a military academy at all. Does that make it a worse or inferior country?

If anyone is inclined to defend this practice on the grounds that "others do it too," it should be pointed out that bad behavior is no less so because of that. There is also the matter of degree, and it may well be that in this particular respect, America really is number one.

Women's Tennis Association Tournament, May 2, 2016, Charleston. Pam Schreiber, in the commentator's box, while chatting with Cliff Drysdale about how great it was that the military was being honored in Charleston that day, said, "The Citadel…one of the greatest military academies in America [short pause], and *in the world*."

Well, well! American exceptionalism does pop up in the most unlikely places. The Soviet newspaper *Izvestia*, December 10, 2003: "However, the Declaration [of Human Rights] raises the bar very high, and it would be fair to say, that no nation, *not even the USA,* has always and completely acted in accordance with all its provisions."

New York Times. December 6, 2010. Page 1 photo. Afghan poppy field. Caption: "The Afghan opium trade is just one source of money for extremist groups that has been hard to staunch, leaked cables say." The chances are very good that America is the biggest market for heroin. If so, that makes America number one in financing terrorists through this trade.

Where else could there be a program like the one advertised to be shown on NBC on Saturday, July 7, 1990, called "Is America still the greatest country in the world—is the US still #1?" Where else would it be offensive to question this assertion, as if suggesting that it may not be number one is to say that there is something wrong with it?

This need to "superlativize" manifests itself everywhere in American life; after all, it took America to contribute the superlative's superlative to the language: "the mostest."

New York Times. "Mistakes Will Be Made," by Bob Herbert, December 10, 2001: "Overzealous public officials might pose a threat to the principles of justice and fairness that have made this nation the jewel of the planet."

A Chorus Line closed on April 28, 1990, after six-thousand-plus performances. It was, according to TV news, "the longest-running show in the world."

Does anyone ever bother to research these claims? The last I heard was that, *The Mouse Trap* had been running in London for thirty-six years. At six performances per week for fifty-two weeks, that makes some eleven thousand-plus shows!

President Bush, addressing the National Association of Broadcasters, said, "The voice of freedom will never be stilled as long as there is an America to tell the truth."

CNN. February 1988. Al Haig, on withdrawing from the race for the Republican nomination for president, said, "Only in America could a nonpolitician have done as much as I have…and now a word about that unique American phenomenon, the media…"

This, of course, is one way of putting it. Another way, among a thousand others, would be, "Only in America could a former secretary of state/foreign minister have failed so abjectly to be nominated by his party for the presidency."

CNN. March 6, 1990, 9:35 a.m. Announcing the rise in first-class postage from twenty-five cents to thirty cents, the head of the Postal Workers Union said, "The US Postal Service is the best in the world."

ABC News. December 10, 1995, 11:25 p.m. Bill Beutel said, "Even with the fears about the US blood supply (because of HIV infection, which has affected thousands of samples), it is still the safest in the world."

CNN. December 22, 1988, 2:40 p.m. President-elect Bush, nominating cabinet officers, including the secretary of transportation, said, "We all know the American system of transportation is the best in the world."

CNN. May 11, 1990, 11:15 a.m. Travel program. Bella Shaw said, "Lombard Street in San Francisco is well known as the world's most winding street for traffic."

New York Times, November, 1992. Ex-president of Costa Rica on op-ed page: "Some weeks ago Pres. Bush, on the occasion of the U.S. sale of F-16 fighters to Taiwan, described them as 'flawless pieces of craftsmanship,' and a symbol of 'what only Americans can do.'"

August 20, 1989. David Brinkley: "Americans are the tax-payingest people in the world."

CNN. May 5, 1986, 12:30 p.m. Larry King, boosting his show: "See Walter Cronkite, the world's best-known anchorman."

New York Times on the right of the press not to reveal its sources: "This country depends on law more than any other on earth."

Brinkley, Alan. Review of *Pledging Allegiance: The Last Campaign of the Cold War*, by Sidney Blumenthal. *New York Times Book Review*.

"'The American presidential election,' Theodore H. White wrote in 1961 is 'the most awesome transfer of power in the world...no people has succeeded at it better or over a longer period of time than the Americans'"

Thus began "The Making of the President 1960."

Ehrlich, Thomas. Review of *How Can You Defend Those People? The Making of a Criminal Lawyer*, by James A. Kunen. *New York Times Book Review*.

"And this country provides a better balancing between the rights of society and the rights of the accused than any other."

Ambrose, Stephen E. Review of *On Bended Knee: The Press and the Reagan Presidency*, by Mark Hertsgaard. *New York Times Book Review*, November 20, 1988.

"But in 30 years of doing research on recent American history, much of it in the newspapers, I've become convinced that the American press is not only the best and freest in the world, but the most critical, thought-provoking, thorough and diverse."

How is it possible to venture a comparison on the basis of "research" on only one of the items being compared?

New York Times, December 28, 1992. Photo: Cathedral of St. John the Divine.

Caption: "Mayor Dinkins at a celebration at the world's second largest church."

Lewis, Neil A. "Schools Open with Focus on Chancellor." Report. *New York Times*, September 7, 1988.

"Dr. Richard R. Green, the city's Schools Chancellor…said, 'if…maybe very nearly at the end of this century, the greatest institution America has ever given to the world, public schools, will perhaps breathe its final breath.'"

The mindless, self-congratulatory inanity of this one is truly breathtaking.

A. When, how, and in what sense could America have "given public schools" to a world that either had them already, evolved them itself, or still doesn't have them?
B. What are these other institutions that America has given to the world?
C. In what way are they "greater" than these other unnamed institutions?
D. How can they be "great" at all, when the whole tenor of Dr. Green's speech is what bad shape they are in? As the writer of the article states, "Students began returning to NY City's public schools today in an atmosphere of intense public concern over whether the school system will improve or whether that is even possible."

Fishman, Robert. Review of *The Park and the People*, by Roy Rosenzweig and Elizabeth Blackmar. *New York Times Book Review*, October 18, 1992.

"Those mid-19th-century New Yorkers who set out to build the greatest central-city park in the world, and succeeded."

New York governor Cuomo, March 1993, after the explosion at the World Trade Center and the effect of fear.

"What we want to do in this greatest city [pause] and state and country in the world is to…"

CNN, November 25, 1992, President Bush, pre-Thanksgiving speech: "Only America has set aside a special holiday just for the purpose of giving thanks."

Since America is the only place where its inhabitants are supposed to be so grateful to have got away from other, less thanksworthy places to be, why should America also get credit for having the ingenuity or humility to go to the trouble of stuffing themselves with turkey and turkeys with stuffing? Clearly Bush is claiming higher marks than all other countries for some virtue or accomplishment. What exactly is this virtue or accomplishment? If this holiday involved fasting rather than feasting, then at least there would be some grounds for self-congratulation for the virtues of austerity or self-denial, but what grounds for self-congratulation can there possibly be for this unabashed orgy of self-indulgence—indeed, overindulgence—where by no means universal minimal and momentary lip service paid to giving thanks, as often as not without any direct or indirect object, is "swallowed up" by the gullet and belly service that is the primary purpose of the exercise?

Senator Orrin Hatch, October 9, 1991, on Senate hearings on the nomination of Clarence Thomas to the Supreme Court: "Only in America could this happen."

Just for a start, what about all the black judges in African and Caribbean countries—if this is what Hatch meant? If he didn't mean that only in America could a "black" become a top judge, what did he mean? Among others, Leopold Senghor, former president of Senegal, and Houphouet-Boigny, former president of Ivory Coast, had both held important ministerial positions in the French government.

Channel 11, WPIX, July 1, 1990. Editorial on proposal for representative "recall" law in New Jersey: "For all its faults, our democratic system works better than any other in the world; don't tinker with it!"

Madeleine Albright, Council on Foreign Relations, November 15, 2008.

"We are about to inaugurate the forty-fourth president of the US...we have turned over power peacefully that many more times, and we can consider ourselves very proud of being able to do that—the oldest democracy in the world."

Iceland's democracy had been going for about nine hundred years by this time. Oh yes, let's not forget ancient Athens, with whom the United States has had in common the fact of not allowing slaves, women, and others to vote. Was the United States a "democracy" before it gave the vote to women and blacks? So at best, democracy began in the United States only after the Voting Rights Act of 1965. Ergo, all other "democratic" countries must have become so only after 1965. Could the truth be that, in fact, the United States was one of the youngest?

Secretary of State James Baker, at a Senate Foreign Relations Committee hearing on the Gulf crisis: "America is the world's most democratic society and the best society."

CNN, December 3, 1986, 10 a.m. US Senate begins radio coverage.

"The US Senate is the world's most deliberative body."

This not too far from claiming the world's wettest rain! It would be interesting to devise a way of arranging for "deliberation" to be made an Olympic event and to work out rules that would allow the world's "deliberative bodies" to compete for medals. Most probably, it would have to consist of a number of separate events—as is the case for the running events—sprint events to determine the fastest and long-distance events to determine which body can "deliberate" the longest. And in the Winter Olympics, medals could be awarded for "deliberating" on ice. Aquatically, there could be a "synchronized" deliberating event. Ideally, the last and ultimate event, which would attract record numbers of televiewers from around the world, could be the underwater event—the last out of the pool would be awarded the gold medal. If none emerged alive, the medal could be awarded posthumously to the last man breathing.

CNN, October 23, 1986, 9:50 a.m. President Reagan, live, campaigning for Senate Republican candidates: "Our armed forces are for protecting the peace—and in that area the record of this country is second to none."

How about Nepal, Lichtenstein, Costa Rica, and Madagascar, for a start?

New York Times. On a Memorial Day (1996) trip to New Jersey, Senator Dole praised American veterans as "the best darn kids in the world."

Not to mention that they must also be either the oldest darn kids or the youngest darn veterans in the world!

"Only in America," said a woman interviewed by CNN (January 16, 1997, 11:40 a.m.) about snowfall in Flagstaff, Arizona—a rare event.

Are we to understand from this (1) that snow falls only in the United States, (2) that only in the United States does snow fall in Flagstaff, Arizona, or does she mean (3) that only in the United States does snow fall in January, (4) that only in the United States does so much snow fall, or, comprehensively, (5) that only in the United States does so much snow fall in Flagstaff, Arizona, in January?

This is, of course, true in the unexceptionable sense that anywhere that anything happens at a given time must be the only place where it is happening then and there—unless she means that this is only true in the United States, in which case...

CNN, December 24, 1995. President Clinton said that America has become the world's leading peacekeeper.

By what criteria? Number of missions? Overall size of troop contributions? Amount of fanfare? Percentage of armed forces involved? Per capita financial contribution? Does the balance sheet include the debit side—number of casualties, including "collateral damage" inflicted by US troops in unilateral as well as multilateral "peacekeeping" missions? In Panama? The Gulf? Grenada? Somalia, Vietnam, Korea, Iraq?

CNN. *Headline News*, September 15, 1998, 10:41 a.m.: "The world's best-equipped, best-trained fighting force…is facing problems."

The only indisputable element here is that of size, but even here, the US armed forces may not even be the largest. What about China?

Letter to the *New York Times* about managed care: "We have had the best medical care, training, and research opportunities in the world because we spent the requisite money on them."

How about being thirteenth in the world for infant mortality rates—to name but one statistic?

CNN. Commercial for Multi-Media Tutorial Services: "Never before and in no other country in the world has it been so easy to secure high grades in math."

New York Times, July 1, 2000. Mr. Mulholland said his party would not waste "one ad to campaign against the green candidate. Nader became famous because of the Corvair…and now he wants to be president? It's a joke; it's ridiculous. Only in America can someone completely irrelevant run for President."

What about countries where someone "irrelevant" has actually become president? Where does the US Constitution mention "relevance" as a requirement for running for office? How is "relevance" determined and measured? How would Mr. Mulholland rate the relative "presidential relevance" of a totally unknown former KGB officer, now president of Russia, against that of a well-known consumer advocate and nominee of a recognized political party? So at least one other country can match and even surpass America in the "irrelevance" quotient. However, it must be conceded that right now—in May 2016—the United States has produced a presidential candidate of an "irrelevance" rivaling that of candidate Putin. Or is it only in America that someone can run for president of America, irrelevant or otherwise? What relevant thing did Hillary or G. W. Bush or Forbes fils or Kennedy *frère* become famous for—not to mention the odd astronaut, quarterback, basketball pro, or actor—even if we grant the premise that either fame or relevance has been or is a prerequisite? If "relevance" were ever to become an Olympic event, I would back to the hilt the chances of David Edward Sutch winning the gold medal way above the chances of Ralph

Nader. He was also known as Third Earl of Harrow, or simply Screaming Lord Sutch, an English musician. He was the founder of the Official Monster Raving Loony Party and served as its leader from 1983 to 1999, during which time he stood in numerous parliamentary elections. He holds the record for losing more than forty elections.

UWSA?

UNITED WE STAND AMERICA WAS the name selected by Texas businessman H. Ross Perot for his citizen-action organization after his 1992 independent political campaign for president of the United States.

In the highly successful revue *Beyond the Fringe*, written and performed by four recent Oxford and Cambridge graduates, which came to Broadway in the sixties, there was a sketch by Jonathan Miller. In it he ponders—aloud—the possible meanings and implications of the unpunctuated inscription that was displayed in British Railways and other British institutional bathrooms of the time:

Gentlemen lift the seat.

I was sharply reminded of this by the title of Ross Perot's new postelection organization, known as "United We Stand America." Interestingly enough, on at least one occasion, the *New York Times* placed a comma between "stand" and "America," no doubt because its sensibilities could not tolerate the unpunctuated implication that it—America—must otherwise be the object of the word "stand" and that, singly, "we," whoever "we" are, could not stand it. Are we meant to supply an exclamation point and understand that "America" is somehow being invoked or addressed?

In the good old days of "family values" and the "three Rs," there used to be things called sentences, and there were a couple of things you had to do to them, known as parsing and analyzing. "United We Stand America" defies both.

Sometimes an awkward, labored, or even well-nigh senseless title is justified by the pithy, witty, punning, or high-impact acronym it yields, but UWSA? Maybe the final version of the title is simply the result of a computer's despairing attempt to assemble a sentence out of the four words fed into it, which were revealed, by assiduous subliminal research into the nation's psyche, to be those in the nation's vocabulary that evoked the most powerful emotional response—namely, "America," "stand" (see Bush on Desert Storm passim!), "United," and "We."

No doubt, Perot, who seems curiously unwilling to pronounce his name the "American way," not wishing to stand for anything that "grassroots America" won't stand for, felt he might as well stand for anything that turns it on.

Grammar, syntax, and sense are a very small price to pay.

TRUMP'S SEVEN DEADLY SIN-DROME

THIS YEAR, MY OSCAR FOR the most mindless inanity stirred up by the Trump campaign juggernaut goes to the evangelist interviewed on TV who was asked why he was voting for him. He said that it was because Trump "*shared his values*" and was a "*good Christian*." It should be pointed out that one of the extraordinary features of this (2016) campaign for the nomination of a Republican candidate for the US presidency, a feature that enjoys a remarkable degree of consensus among the punditry, is that the electorate is disillusioned with, mistrustful of, and skeptical of politicians and "government." That being the case, it's hard to imagine why the electorate (elect-irate?) wouldn't be at least equally alienated by someone who so desperately wants to join the ranks of the detestable politicians and to become part—or even all—of government itself.

The only things that his supporters know or care to know about Trump are what he says about himself. These unfailingly extravagant, self-promoting, uncorroborated, and often contradictory boasts seem to be swallowed as eagerly and unquestioningly by his fans as the reservations, questions, and criticisms of his critics and opponents are dismissed.

Let us consider how Trump rates in terms of what one would imagine evangelists of all people would regard as the paramount criteria of the character of "a good Christian" and a person who shares their values.

How does he stack up against the seven deadly sins on a scale of 1 to 10, where 1 is the lowest and 10 the highest rating? These ratings are based on public knowledge of the man, his record, and his career as well as those elements of his character that have been so extensively revealed in his campaign for the

Republican nomination, his public statements, his many appearances on interviews and talk shows, and his published "writings."

PRIDE: 10. This is better translated as "hubris."

GREED/AVARICE: 10. His hubris is so overwhelming that he cannot resist boasting about his acquisition of wealth in amounts wildly surplus to his requirements.

LUST: 10. For example, in his book *The Art of the Comeback*, Trump bragged about his sex life, writing "If I told the real stories of my experiences with women, often seemingly very happily married and important women, this book would be a guaranteed bestseller." This is what he said on Howard Stern's talk show about how irresistible he was to women: "They'll walk up, and they'll flip their top, and they'll flip their panties," he said of his alleged, unnamed fans.

It's too bad that so much was made of his unguarded remarks about "grabbing them by the pussy," which was casually batted away by his supporters as "boy talk" and "locker room talk," when published quotations that he acknowledged and indeed even prided himself on having said, could not have been so easily brushed aside.

On other occasions, even when videotaped evidence was available of other outrageous utterances, he was allowed to get away with flatly denying having made them—even to the point, on one occasion, of claiming that someone had been pretending to be him on the telephone.

ENVY: Insufficient evidence. However, anyone who goes to so much trouble over his (own?) hair must be envious of other men's hair; for all we know, he may be wearing some of it. But of course, only his hairdresser knows for sure, and I doubt whether his address appears in that French guidebook for New York that once included in the list of New York landmarks the address of Al Sharpton's hairdresser when his locks were at their most luxuriant.

GLUTTONY: His clothing seems to be as carefully tailored as his hair. He wears dark and capacious clothing, with his jacket always carefully left unbuttoned so that it does not appear to be straining against his paunch. He does not look underfed. (Only his restaurateurs know for sure.)

WRATH: 10. He is right out of the closet in this regard and has made "anger" (simulated or not) his stock in trade. He both stimulates and feeds on the "anger" of his supporters.

SLOTH. 0. Have to give the devil his due. But how SLOTH ever got into this list is a mystery. Maybe it's a mistranslation from the original, since, if anything, it is hyperactivity that has caused so much more harm, havoc, cruelty, suffering, death, and destruction throughout history.

In fact, the original Latin, *acedia*, a calque of the even more original Greek, never meant "laziness" but something that today would be akin to "depression," which I doubt any observant Catholic would confess to a priest rather than a psychotherapist.

However, the original list of original sins offered eight items, and the one that for some reason no longer appears on the current list is *vanagloria*, vainglory or boastfulness, which if anything is Trump's besetting sin, for which I have no hesitation in awarding him a top score, and so:

VAINGLORY: 10.
And how about a little homework on those Ten Commandments?

THE GREEKS HAD THE RIGHT IDEA

———◆———

NO NOOSE IS GOOD NOOSE FOR THE
RASCALS IN WASHINGTON
—"The Furlough"

SOME OF THE BEST IDEAS the Greeks ever had about effective governance have been allowed to molder unharvested, scattered randomly as they are over the pages of Herodotus. Traditionally revered as "the father of history," he was in actual fact a wonderfully uninhibited raconteur.

Herodotus reports that in a certain city-state, a legislator was only allowed to propose going to war with his head in a noose. The rope to which the noose was attached was slung over a beam or rafter, with the other end firmly in the grasp of the public executioner, who had strict instructions to begin hauling on the rope if the temerarious legislator failed to secure a majority in favor of his proposal.

Some might find this procedure a mite draconian, but short of this, couldn't the public pollster—currently the closest equivalent that now exists to the public executioner for the purpose—haul on the equivalent of his rope? The pollster could thus have the public decide which of their "servants" are and are not "furloughable" and whether they prefer to continue to be able to visit their parks, monuments, and libraries, even at the cost of sacrificing their seats at the Washington circus. Of course, the chances are that the circus artists would no doubt continue performing free of charge in any case, in their oft-proclaimed self-abnegating zeal to "serve the people."

Because of wrangling over the federal budget, the federal government was shut down at the end of 1995 and the beginning of 1996. The net immediate effect was that some eight hundred thousand federal workers were told to stay home, without pay, and the members of Congress went home, with pay! Meanwhile, millions of Americans were shut out of everything from their national parks to small-business loans.

Democrats (small *d*) tend to be very proud of the noble political ideas we have inherited from the Greeks—the ancient ones, of course—although it does not take a great deal of erudition to realize that (a) while a word may be of Greek origin, it may not have actually been used much, if at all, by the Greeks themselves, and (b) if they did, it may not have meant to them what it means to us. The Greeks themselves would have been hard put to figure out what an "economist" or a "seismographer," let alone an "orthopedist or a "taxidermist," does, and even the uses to which we put the word "democracy" itself would have boggled the Greek mind—well, at least some of the uses that some put it to. To wit: The "Democratic" People's Republic of Korea?

Apart from anything else, this one is actually a triple tautology in one, when you consider what the first three words used to mean when they were at home ("demos" = "people" in Greek, "people" = "people" in English, and "publicus" = "people's" in Latin).

Meanwhile, back in Washington, the politicians are wrangling over the budget, federal employees are being "furloughed," and their salaries, at least temporarily, are being withheld. Not enough attention seems to have been drawn to the fact that Clinton, Dole, Gingrich, et al (no, not D'Amato) are also on the federal payroll and have not been furloughed. We are told that the distinction between the "furloughable" and the "unfurloughable" hinges on the indispensability of their services. Now, the services currently being rendered by the above-mentioned gentlemen consist precisely in creating the situation for which the "dispensable" librarians and park custodians are being penalized and for which they themselves are not. Furthermore, the same gentlemen are no doubt the ones who are ultimately responsible for deciding which of our public "servants" are dispensable as well as for excluding themselves from that category.

Surely no system of good governance should countenance a situation where public servants—and no one brandishes derivatives of the word "serve" with more pride and mock humility than politicians, when it suits them——can legislate, or, as in this case, fail to legislate, to the detriment of the public they "serve" (and of which they are also members) and yet opt out with impunity of the ill effects of their legislation. It is worth recalling that a publication, the *Evergreen Review*, during the Vietnam War was disobliging enough to report that of the six hundred or so members of Congress at the time, only sixteen had sons in military service in Vietnam, of whom one was in combat. Besides, as a matter of course, all of those members themselves were exempt from conscription, although it is worth remembering that those who had voted for that war were free to volunteer to fight in it if they had chosen to..

AMERICAN FOOTBALL

—◆—

WHEN I ARRIVED IN NEW York City in 1962, I came armed with typical British scorn for what appeared to be a grotesque, spasmodic, and unfathomable travesty of rugby.

Over the years, without intending or trying to, I found myself becoming a zealous convert to what I believe to be the world's most compelling spectator sport since the Roman gladiatorial shows—especially now that you can fast-forward through the commercials. Its unique charm is that you don't have to be a fan or supporter of either team in order to find it entertaining, even gripping. There are one or two rules I would tamper with to make it even more so.

1. The "damp squib"

I propose a rule change to discourage the possibility of the game fizzling out like a damp squib when one team has a lead near the end of a game and simply sits on the ball in order to use up the time still on the clock and deny the opposing team a chance to score. One way of doing this would be to allow the end-of-regular-season "aggregate points for and against" differential to count for more in determining the ranking of teams for the playoffs, thus providing an incentive for a team with even an unassailable lead to score even more points.

Proof of the "damp squib" effect on spectators of this phenomenon—especially the fans of the losing team—is that they start to leave the stadium in droves once it is clear that the game has hit the doldrums and that no further entertainment or scoring can be expected from it.

One would gather from the occupants of the commentary booth that there is something ungentlemanly, or as they would put it, "lacking in class," for a team to pile on still more points once they have gained an unassailable lead. That's pretty ironic, if not hypocritical, in a game where both commentators and spectators seem to derive particular gratification from the most vicious and damaging "hits" on the field, a gratification which is conspicuously and theatrically shared by the assailants. In their defense, it can be said that hitting, and hitting as hard as possible, is what they are paid for and is tactically justifiable in that it can, and is meant to, have a deterrent effect on the effectiveness of the victims, quarterbacks and pass receivers in particular. Indeed, there have been times when the media have charged that some teams have offered players financial incentives or rewards for damaging hits.

2. "Overtime"

Cut out the artifices and complications of so-called overtime, designed to produce an artificial "winner" and "loser"; after all, a draw or a "tie" simply "tells it like it was"—namely, that the teams were evenly matched.

Allowing games to end in a "draw" or a "tie" in no way prevents determining which teams shall advance to postseason playoffs, and there are a number of different ways of factoring in "draws" or "ties" for this purpose. One is the method employed by the English Premier Soccer League, which awards teams 3 points for a win, 1 for a draw, and 0 for a loss.

It is noteworthy that that august body, the US Supreme Court, is composed of nine members—the same number as the starting lineup in baseball; so what could be more American? Whether or not it is also the reason, its effect is that, with all the members present and voting, there can never be a tie. Nature abhors a vacuum, and it would appear, somewhere deeply embedded in the American psyche lies an abhorrence of inconclusive competition. This credo was famously formulated by the legendary football coach Vince Lombardi when he said, "Winning isn't everything—it's the only thing." Equally significant is that the word "loser" is probably the most offensive and humiliating put-down in the American lexicon of insults. In terms of this credo, the Supreme Court is a model, and indeed in recent memory, by a vote of five to four, it even awarded the presidency to the candidate who won fewer votes in the general election than his opponent.

Since there are vastly more votes at stake in a presidential election than points in an American football game, and still more than in a soccer match, it would be highly improbable for a presidential election, if allowed to take its normal course unimpeded, to end in a tie. For the same reason, there are undoubtedly more "draws" in English Premier Soccer League soccer than there are "ties" in the NFL, because there are far fewer goals scored in the former than points in the latter.

3. "The touchdown"

Here is just one example of a recurrent problem.

On November 23, 2014, in the game between "Ole Miss" (University of Mississippi) and the "Razorbacks" (University of Arkansas), the "Hogs" scored their second "touchdown" when, on fourth down and a foot, the ball carrier leaped straight ahead and was a good five feet above the ground when he came to rest on a pile of defensive players and stretched his arms forward toward the goal line—or the upward extension thereof. After "review," he was awarded a "touchdown" on the highly notional and debatable Euclidian grounds that he had "broken the plane."

And a solution? Make the current misnomer of a "touchdown" into an actual *touchdown* on two-dimensional *terra firma*, as it still is in rugby, football's increasingly remote ancestor. This would not only make more sense but would also obviate the need for bringing into play all those high-tech devices required to make those unsatisfying hair's-breadth decisions about whether an invisible and intangible three-dimensional "plane" had been broken—with the bonus of ridding the game of what is yet another gratuitous delay of the proceedings, which is, of course, creating yet another "commercial opportunity."

Having discarded, or at least tampered with the meaning of most of the other terms used in rugby, why has American football clung to the one that is probably the least accurate and most misleading description for the purpose? This three-dimensional "touchdown" could only exist as part of what is already such a referee- and rule-ridden game that it is not and could not be played without its regiment of officials, referees, umpires, judges, "trainers," medical attendants and practitioners, timekeepers, scorekeepers, stretcher bearers, the gentlemen on the touchline who "move the sticks" (a.k.a. "the chain gang"), coaches, and assistant coaches as well as its panoply of state-of-the-art electronic equipment.

This overload of officials and minutely calibrated rules leads to too many questionable results or outcomes that depend on one or more of at least half a dozen referees—on and off the field—and their often divided opinions about rule infractions, especially when the score is close. This, once again, generates unnatural delays in the play of what is in any case a highly spasmodic sporting spectacle. It also often increases the "elapsed" time of a game, which on paper lasts for sixty minutes, to well beyond the three hours of TV coverage allotted to it and even encroaches on programs that have been scheduled to follow.

This overload also has the effect of limiting the possibilities of the game ever being played by anyone except a highly select band of professionals (NFL), pseudoprofessionals (college football), and protoprofessionals (high school football).

While it is only actually played by this tiny fraction of the population—that is to say, the male population—it is often claimed that football is the American national sport. Well, it is certainly the most telegenic and the most popular with the TV-viewing public—provided they are on the right side of the screen and can identify with this most macho of sports from the safety and comfort of their living rooms.

A good part of this top-heavy "overload" stems from the need to limit (and if possible, inhibit) what would otherwise be a spectacle of pure, unrestrained violence and counterviolence, violence that has been essentially engendered by reversing a single rule of rugby—namely, the rule that bans "blocking." This factor has been compounded by another, namely that of "specialization," which is either the cause or the effect of a further factor—that of increasing the number of players on the "squad"—which at the college and NFL level can mean that there are as many as forty-five players on each team fully equipped, in uniform (for Super Bowl 50 there were some ninety players on the roster of each team!), and ready to play, waiting on the sidelines. For some reason, it is now a matter of course that there are essentially three separate (although sometimes having overlapping personnel) eleven-man "teams" on each side, which take the field at one time or another during the game: offense, defense, and "special teams."

Now, why have I rated this game so highly as a spectator sport? That's because of its scoring structure.

The amount of scoring in American football is something of a golden mean; and football not only has the virtue of having just about the right amount of scoring (unlike basketball, which has too much, and soccer, which has too little), but it has also the added attraction of intriguing, extra possibilities of scoring apart from the standard variety (the "touchdown"). These include the field goal, the extra point, the safety, and the optional two-point conversion.

Second, the factor of meaningful possession and of maintaining it by territorial advance makes for a steady buildup of tension and expectation, and the microtouchdown of a first down provides the possibility of micro-orgasmic relief of tension for spectators at intervals short enough to prevent tension overload. This may help account for the high incidence of spectator violence in European and South American soccer—a game only minimally violent in itself—and the almost total absence of spectator violence from American football, an inherently violent game. In soccer, no amount of play can ever result in a mini-orgasm, such as a tension-relieving score, because no other scoring possibilities exist in the game except that rarity, an actual goal, short of which there is nothing to relieve the constant building of pent-up tension among the spectators.

In Britain, there is a saying that "football [soccer] is a game for gentlemen played by ruffians; rugby is a game for ruffians played by gentlemen."

It has been said that "possession is nine-tenths of the law," and possession is also a major factor in American football, in that it provides spectators with the intense gratification of dramatic reversals of fortune in the form of *changes* of possession. This can occur in three ways: the team in possession of the ball cedes possession to the opposing team by failing to advance ten yards after four downs, a pass is intercepted, or the opposing team performs a "fumble recovery." In soccer, possession is always precarious and fleeting and almost never leads to scoring, and it is this that robs it of the drama of alternating threat and hope inherent in possession in American football. Indeed, in soccer, there are long stretches of aimless and futile ricocheting during which possession is never clearly established—entirely natural when one thinks how vastly more prehensile are hands than feet. This endless titillation followed by very little consummation generates a buildup of spectator frustration, and there's nothing like frustration for generating aggression.

EXTREME SPECIALIZATION
This factor generates and brings into play the widest variety of athletic skills, something that is reflected in an equally wide variety of player physiques. In

professional soccer, by contrast, all the eleven players on a team, except the goalkeeper, must be able to keep running in repeated short bursts at top speed for ninety minutes of play. This alone means that variations in player physique are minimal; the common denominator is close to that of a human greyhound. In American football, physiques must run the gamut from the elephant to the gazelle, and the skill sets are equally varied.

A spectator with some experience of the game can make a pretty good guess at the position of a player by his silhouette alone. Even quarterbacks now tend to be much taller than they used to be because when they throw a forward pass, they are handicapped if they cannot get a clear line of sight to their receivers over the heads of the gigantic linebackers who are converging on them, bent on mayhem.

PHYSICAL VIOLENCE

This is a factor that undoubtedly lends an extra "frisson" to the attraction of the game but which commentators tend to shy away from describing as violence, preferring to use the euphemism "physical" instead to describe those players who are best at inflicting it. Happily, our athletic entertainments are a good two thousand years more civilized than the barbaric rites of the Roman gladiatorial shows, and the violence inflicted on the field in American football is only extremely rarely a matter of life and death, except, of course, in the long run, when the players who have sustained debilitating and ultimately lethal injuries on the field of play die quietly, off the field, out of sight and out of mind.

Physical violence sanctioned by the rules, although not as random as it may appear to the unfledged spectator, puts a premium on the kind of physique best equipped to inflict it. It exists essentially because of a single rule difference with its ancestor. "Blocking," which is outlawed in rugby, is allowed in American football and has become an integral part of the game. Hence, it adds to the attraction of the game because it places a premium on the nerve and physical courage of players to stand up and expose themselves to it, particularly quarterbacks and pass receivers.

THE SEXES

THOUGHTS PROMPTED BY THE
BRITISH CHESS CHAMPIONSHIPS

———◆———

SOMETIME IN THE 1980s, I had noted that in the recently concluded British Chess Championships, there were separate tournaments for men and women. It appears that this tradition has been maintained until this very day in most major championships. Why?

Can this separation be due to an unreflecting following of the tradition that it is unfair for women to compete with men in sports because of inherent differences in physique? Surely today, in 2016, when there are still separate chess championships for men and women, no one, least of all women chess players, would want to claim that an inherent inferiority in brainpower debarred competition with men on an equal footing.

The rationale might be advanced that separate tournaments were necessary to determine the standing of women chess players relative to each other, but as the examples of marathon running as well as all timed and measured Olympic events have shown, there is no need for a *separate* race or competition to determine how the women competitors, or members of different age groups for that matter, compare with each other.

Competitors emerge from chess tournaments with a certain number of points, and the woman, and the man over sixty-five, with the highest number of points would be declared the women's champion and seniors' champion, respectively.

So why must there be a women's chess championship at all? The only sense in having separate categories in competitive events is an acknowledged inherent or congenital handicap or disadvantage suffered by various categories of the population. Hence, there are separate competitions for the sexes in athletic events and special age categories in athletic and nonathletic events such as chess, not to mention wheelchair Olympics, or Paralympics. Significantly, I don't believe that there are separate championships for the physically handicapped in "mind sports" such as chess, bridge, crossword puzzle solving, or Monopoly.

Men and women competing together on an equal footing, even in athletic events and sports, would also help to create a more realistic and healthy perspective on the relative abilities of the sexes, which separate competition tends to obscure.

To understand how this unrealistic perspective arose, we have to go back to 1973 and a much-publicized media event with the preposterously inflated title of "The Battle of the Sexes" accompanied by an orgy of hoopla, ballyhoo, and hype.

In ancient times, a much more sensible, economical, and, in a way, civilized and humane way of settling an armed conflict was by single combat, with each party choosing its "champion" to be sent into the arena to fight it out with the other. One of the earliest recorded such "single combats" took place in 725 BC, when Romulus defeated and stripped the *spolia opima*, the armor and weaponry, from the body of his slain opponent, Acro, the king of the Caeninenses.

The victory of thirty-year-old Billy Jean King, then the reigning women's tennis champion, over the fifty-five-year-old Bobby Riggs, well past his prime and then reduced to the role of tennis "hustler," was sold to—and bought by—several million TV viewers as conclusive evidence of, at the very least, the equal standing of women with men as tennis players and was, largely owing to Billie Jean's militancy in the cause, ultimately responsible for men and women receiving equal prize money in major tournaments.

However, any analogy with "single combat" as waged in the ancient world is fatally flawed in that in those days, each side chose their best warrior to fight for them.

Billie Jean King was not only a boisterous and militant women's champion but also would undoubtedly have been chosen by her peer group to represent them.

However, the by then long-unranked Bobby Riggs could by no stretch of the imagination have been appointed champion by *his* peer group.

A more modest and realistic assessment of the relative tennis prowess of the two sexes was given in 1998, when another "battle of the sexes" took place.

Venus and Serena Williams had claimed that they could beat any male player ranked outside the world's top 200; so during the Australian Open, Karsten Braasch, then ranked 203rd, challenged them both. Braasch was described by one journalist as "a man whose training regime centered around a pack of cigarettes and more than a couple bottles of ice cold lager." The matches took place on court number twelve in Melbourne Park after Braasch had finished a round of golf and two beers. He first took on Serena and beat her 6–1. Venus then walked onto the court, and again Braasch was victorious, this time winning by a slimmer margin. Braasch said afterward, "500 and above, no chance." He added that he had played like someone ranked 600th in order to keep the game "fun." The Williams sisters readjusted their claim to being able to beat men outside the top 350.

In 1992, a third "battle of the sexes" match, titled "Battle of Champions," was played at Caesars Palace in Paradise, Nevada, on September 25, 1992, between Jimmy Connors and Martina Navratilova, aged forty and thirty-five, respectively. The match was played under hybrid rules to make it more competitive; Connors was allowed only one serve per point, and Navratilova was allowed to hit into the doubles court. Each player received a $650,000 guarantee, with a further $500,000 for the winner. Connors won 7–5, 6–2.

My own respect for Billie Jean King or Martina Navratilova as the world's number one women tennis players of their times would not be diminished if it turned out in the course of truly *open* competition that they ranked somewhere in the 400s–500s, although the disproportionate esteem, based on fanciful and untested assumptions, in which they are doubtlessly held by many would sink to its proper level.

All this might, of course, raise the uncomfortable question of whether there was perhaps something wrong with the idea of the world's 450th-best tennis player being paid incomparably more than, say, the world's 200th-best tennis player, for being a lot worse. But that is another story.

As for the principle of equal pay for equal work, something that women deserve and for which they have long striven, the fact remains that at all major tournaments today, women receive the same prize money as men, although their "work" is equal neither qualitatively nor quantitatively (they play only three sets; the men play five).

This state of affairs can, of course, be viewed from a different standpoint.

Professional sports can legitimately be seen as part of "show business," where considerations of equity or fairness simply don't enter into the question of how much performers should or do get paid. It's probably the most extreme example of the unbridled play of market forces, and performers are paid according to what promoters and impresarios deem to be their "drawing power"— that is, how much people are willing to pay to see them perform.

As far as tennis is concerned, both men and women compete in the same major tournaments and championships. These events attract both live spectators and TV viewers and correspondingly large sums of money. The fact that both men and women perform in these tournaments makes it impossible to calculate the relative drawing power of men's and women's matches, especially since show business and TV in particular can create or build "stars" or celebrities out of practically anyone they choose to (the current [spring 2016] superstardom of Donald Trump is an extreme example of the genre and is in direct proportion to the amount of TV coverage the networks are prepared to grant him, or—take your choice—how much he is able to command). He is in fact the reductio ad absurdum of the current TV-dominated culture, summed up succinctly in the accolade "as seen on TV," an accolade that is conferred even upon the toilet paper in your supermarket.

So it is with the stardom and celebrity status conferred on male and female tournament players alike. Once they have attained celebrity status, they can parlay that into even greater celebrity status by being hired to appear in product advertising and accumulate even more "as seen on TV" points by appearing in TV commercials. Player-celebrity tennis matches can always draw a large crowd of people who have paid large amounts for seats to watch Pavarotti, talk show hosts, and Hollywood actors in action on the court. Decide for yourself whether it's the tennis or the celebrity that is the attraction.

Interviewed after winning the 2016 Indian Wells Paribas recent tournament, Djokovic said, "I applaud them for that; I honestly do. They [the women players] fought for what they deserve, and they got it. On the other hand, I think that our men's tennis world, ATP world, should fight for more because the stats are showing *that we have much more spectators on the men's tennis matches.*" Djokovic's comments came after the tournament's CEO, Raymond Moore, said women tennis players should "get on their knees" and thank the men's players for growing tennis's popularity.

Djokovic's comment, so carefully guarded and delicately phrased, was making essentially the same point as the now former CEO Raymond Moore, who was forced to step down because of his incautious utterance.

I'll leave you to ponder your preferred implications of the following quotation from Sean Randall when he wrote on March 23, 2016, at 1:02 p.m.:

The Miami Open is selling tickets for the men's and women's final at DIFFERENT prices when the prize money for both events is equal.

The cheapest Saturday WOMEN'S FINAL ticket (which includes the men's doubles final) is listed at $69.

The cheapest Sunday MEN'S FINAL ticket (which includes the women's doubles final) is listed at $105.

TOPIC 2

"SEX, AMERICAN STYLE"; OR, "HOW TO CONFOUND THE SCROOGES WHO CUT OFF FUNDS FOR YOUR CHERISHED PROJECT AND ASTOUND THE PUBLIC INTO BUYING YOUR BOOK AT THE SAME TIME"

———————

New York Times Book Review. The Social Organization of Sexuality: Sexual Practices in the United States, by Edward O. Laumann, John H. Gagnon, Robert T. Michael, and Stuart Michaels, 1994.

"*The Social Organization of Sexuality* reports the complete results of the nation's most comprehensive representative survey of sexual practices in the general adult population of the United States. This highly detailed portrait of sex in America and its social context and implications has established a new and original scientific orientation to the study of sexual behavior."

There almost seems to be a kind of orchestrated mindlessness in the gleeful delight with which the media have with one accord seized on and purveyed what they have distilled by some kind of instant alchemy as the "message" of a "seven hundred-page tome" titled *The Social Organization of Sexuality.* The message, or "finding," as a *New York Times* editorial has it, is that "sexually speaking, this is a nation of squares." Whose "finding" is this, exactly—that of the compilers of the tome, or the editorial writer's own, based on a painstaking study of its seven hundred pages within a week of its publication? In a strangely unanimous surge, reminiscent of the start of the New York marathon, the blur-like sprint of the media from dubious premise to startling conclusion at a speed faster than thought cries out for an instant replay—in slow motion.

126

Did all the subjects contacted in the survey agree to be interviewed? If so, it would be an extraordinary coincidence, unless, of course, there was some element of pressure or inducement. If not, their places must have been taken by others who were willing to be interviewed, or only those willing to be interviewed in the first place responded. Either way, the sample must have been skewed in favor of people who were either willing, pressured, or induced to talk to an interviewer about their sex lives, a factor that makes it unrepresentative in a particularly significant respect.

What means could there be, and what attempts, if any, were made, to check the veracity of respondents? For example, were the responses of spouses or sex partners checked against each other to see if they matched? In areas such as eating and sleeping, where estimates of or claims by subjects about their own practices and habits can be objectively checked, researchers have consistently found that individuals are notoriously unreliable witnesses and observers of their own conduct.

This unreliability increases when actual or perceived established norms are involved. In no area of life more than sex is there likely to be more temptation for some to exaggerate the nature and frequency of sexual encounters in order to impress the interviewer or to minimize practices of which the interviewer might disapprove.

It is significant that in the recent (November 2016) presidential electoral campaign, most polls repeatedly, consistently, and wrongly predicted victory for the Democratic candidate, and ultimately it was her opponent who won the presidency by a clear majority in the Electoral College. And in this case, people being interviewed were asked only about their political preferences, a subject far less sensitive than their sex lives.

Indeed, according to Paul Robinson, the reviewer of *The Social Organization of Sexuality* and the author of the editorial "Sex in America" in the *New York Times Book Review*, October 30:

"The authors repeatedly confess that because homosexuality continues to be stigmatized, their findings probably understate its prevalence."

Homosexuality—in the early nineties—is by no means the only kind or aspect of sexual behavior that individuals are likely to be ashamed of or, for that matter, proud of and therefore motivated to suppress or exaggerate in the presence of an interviewer.

An editorial in the *New York Times* on October 8 states:

"There is no better way to measure one's own sex life than to compare it with the well-documented…sex lives of others."

In fact, what makes this survey peculiarly unusable for precisely this purpose is that it is unaccompanied, at least according to the available press reports, by any breakdown by age, and in practically no human activity more than sex would it be more natural to expect habits or performance to vary with age. On the basis of these "findings," couples in their twenties as well as couples in their fifties, if they are at all normal for their age groups, will be forced to conclude they are actually aberrant.

Another variable that is ignored and must surely powerfully affect the rate of sexual activity is how long the couples in question have been together; there is such a thing known as "the first fine careless rapture"—and you do not have to be a Kinsey, a Masters, or a Johnson to know it.

Why does the survey lose interest in the sexual behavior of citizens once they hit fifty-nine, which in a swiftly aging society with a spiraling number of healthy and active oversixties is a strangely low cutoff age? Even more questionable a distortion of the true and full picture painted in "Sex, American Style"— the title of the editorial itself—is the blithe disregard of what must surely be the most sexually active segment of society, its adolescents. This is, after all, precisely that segment of society that is the source of most anxiety about, and hence the principal target and beneficiary of, "appropriate warnings and advice" about "prevention of sexually transmitted diseases and unwanted pregnancies." Paradoxically, not only is this high-risk segment of the population left out of account in the survey, but the fact that it is left out of the account is itself disregarded in media commentary. The editorial actually commends the survey on providing the information on "sexual attitudes and behavior" necessary for the "prevention of sexually transmitted diseases and unwanted pregnancies."

It is with "surprising" frequency that the word "surprising" and its synonyms crop up in media commentary on the study. One might almost get the impression that part of the authors' agenda was to produce "surprising" results. The reviewer finds the authors expressing "surprise" on at least two occasions, once about the "rarity" of marital infidelity and once about the (high?) rate of anal sex. If the authors did have an agenda, other than the properly scholarly one of pursuing the truth, wherever it may lead, the reviewer provides a motive. "Perhaps still stinging from their political mauling (the withdrawal of federal funding for their project), the researchers seem eager to confound the dire expectations of their (conservative) critics."

Maybe next week's arresting paradox could be a "finding" that American society is "surprisingly" nonviolent because statistics show, as they undoubtedly would, that the number of violent crimes committed by the average American between the ages of eighteen and fifty-nine was infinitesimally lower than usual—even if the statistics were drawn from objective sources and not based on what discreditable facts individuals were prepared to reveal to interviewers.

SEXUAL HARASSMENT: A GREATER SILENCE

———◆———

TOPIC RAISED IN A LETTER by Pamela Monday in the *New York Times*, October 18, 1991.

"Sexual Harassment Flourishes in Secrecy"

Like "domestic violence," the term "sexual harassment" implies two-way traffic. In practice, however, and rightly so, domestic violence is usually taken to be synonymous with "wife beating" rather than "husband beating." Similarly, in the workplace, sexual harassment, in spite of its "gender-neutral" formulation, is taken to mean a form of mistreatment of women by men, or a built-in disadvantage suffered by women and exploited by men because of their hierarchical power over women.

The "gender neutrality" of the term allows, of course, for the remoter possibility of the sexual harassment by women of men. The further implication is that if sexual harassment were banished from the workplace, the unfair advantage enjoyed by men over women, and their exploitation of it, would disappear.

The fact is that the true counterpart exploitation of gender difference in the workplace is "sexual preferment"—namely, the way that a woman, if she chooses, can divert to her own advantage that very same male hierarchical power and the male drive to win the sexual favors of desirable female colleagues that is the basis of "sexual harassment."

The beneficiaries of "sexual preferment" have nothing to gain individually or collectively by coming forward, and the victims of it, unlike the victims of sexual harassment, are a collective, often a large number of people to whom something (getting jobs or promotions) has *failed* to happen, a failure to which they are largely oblivious. As in a cinema queue, only those who are immediately behind a queue jumper are aware that they have been victimized. In the case where too few seats are available to accommodate all the people waiting in the queue, each successful queue jumper will have made victims of the first and each successive person to have been turned away. So, paradoxically, only the people immediately behind the queue jumper will feel the resentment and indignation that properly belong to the actual victims, who remain oblivious to their victimhood.

If a woman chooses to manipulate the power given to her by the sexual interest in her shown by her male superiors, her career can advance more rapidly than that of her male peers as well as, it should not be forgotten, her female colleagues who do not happen to arouse the sexual interest of the men they work with. Of course, they may or may not prefer it that way.

A GREATER SILENCE

Pamela Monday calls for a breaking of what she appears to think of as a silence by women about the sexual harassment they have suffered. Any call for the breaking of the *greater* silence surrounding "sexual preferment," and thus for restoring the proper balance between "sexual harassment" and its true counterpart, "sexual preferment," and putting the whole matter of sexual power politics in the workplace in its true perspective is, of course, going to fail for the very same reason that the silence about sexual preferment is so much greater in the first place.

The victims of "sexual preferment" have nothing to gain individually or collectively by coming forward, for the reasons previously mentioned, but it should also be pointed out that they are also largely *unwitting* victims, and the victimhood of any one of them is only fractional, since the loss or damage sustained is divided among them. And it is on that obliviousness that "sexual preferment" thrives.

In essence, the relationship between "sexual preferment" and "sexual harassment" can be described as the means whereby the "harasser," usually male, uses power to get sex, while sexual preferment is the means whereby the "beneficiary," usually female, uses sex to get power.

The French, who make a lot less fuss about such matters than Americans, have, of course, a word for it—*promotion-canapé* (couch promotion)!

Sexual preferment, the counterpart of sexual harassment, is a truth that surfaced nowhere in the interminable talk and writing prompted by Anita Hill. In 1991, she became a national figure when she accused US Supreme Court nominee Clarence Thomas, her supervisor at the US Department of Education and the Equal Employment Opportunity Commission, of sexual harassment.

This case leaves some unasked and unanswered questions.

In what sense do asking whether her charges are true and, entirely predictably, hearing her answer "yes" and him answer "no" constitute an investigation? Did Anita Hill stay and listen to Clarence Thomas's descriptions of porno movies? If so, why? Did she attempt to stop him? If not, why not? Did she voice objections to him? If so, what effect did they have on his conduct? If none, what was his reaction? Did he indicate when or where he saw these movies?

The benefits of "sexual preferment" usually accrue in terms of promotion once the beneficiary is already on the job. But the key question that went unasked and unanswered is whether Anita Hill, no doubt unwittingly, benefited from sexual preferment at the point of *selection* for the job. Who is to say, for example, that Anita Hill, rather than being a net victim of the sexual harassment she alleged, was not a net beneficiary of sexual preferment in being chosen by Clarence Thomas in the first place as an assistant over other equally or better-qualified candidates precisely because of what she alleged was Thomas's sexual interest in her?

Krauss, Clifford. "The Case of Senator Bob Packwood of Oregon Charged with Multiple Sexual Harassment Offenses." *New York Times*, November 28, 1992.

This case illuminates further the complexities of the simplistically titled issue of "sexual harassment."

"Throughout the period, he was known as an active backer of women's issues and had one of the strongest records in Congress of hiring and promoting women."

How ironic it is that this should be offered in his *defense*, when this is precisely the "other side of the coin" or "true counterpart" of sexual harassment itself—not the opposite of it. Why else is it known in French as *promotion-canapé*, or, in Hollywood parlance, the "casting couch"? Some of those who did complain are just as likely to have done so not so much because they were sexually harassed but because they were "screwed" in the sense that they were cheated of the promised, or implicitly promised, promotion or some other favor rather than because they were simply outraged or offended by the sexual harassment itself. This may be the reason why, in some cases, charges of sexual harassment take so long to surface. Interestingly, the implication here is that Packwood's record as "an active backer of women's issues" somehow mitigates the offense rather than corroborating it. In fact, not only is this kind of record not incompatible with sexual harassment, but it is actually likely to accompany it.

A striking parallel with that even more notorious sexual predator and also a notable promoter of women in his employ—the current (November 2016) president-elect, Donald Trump.

The same fallacious reasoning is even reflected in a *New York Times* editorial on the subject: "Ten women who worked with or for Packwood charged him with unwanted sexual advances [see below], charges which, if true, are lamentable, not least because Mr. Packwood has been a leader in the fight for women's rights and *has promoted women to positions of responsibility.*"

This is by no means the paradox that the *Times* seems to believe it is.

The editorial continues: "That betrays a basic misunderstanding [on the part of Packwood] about the charge against him...it's that he used the power of his position for sexual purposes."

In fact, it is the *New York Times* that doesn't get it. Some of the women who brought the charges may well have been using the power of sex for advancement purposes and failed to secure the expected quid pro quo, while some of those who didn't bring charges had probably succeeded in securing it.

Senator Packwood, October 12, 1992: "What I did was just wrong, but no one's job or promotion was threatened. I just didn't get it; I do now." Neither he nor anyone else much seems to "get it" yet. What about the women who accepted his advances and saw their careers prosper—to the detriment of competitors, male or female, who, unknown to themselves, were thereby denied promotion?

U*NWANTED* S*EXUAL* A*DVANCES*

This seems as good a point as any at which to skewer this mindlessly repeated mantra.

What is wrong with the reasonable-sounding idea that if people want to avoid food poisoning, all they have to do is not to eat tainted food? Nothing, except that you only discover the food you have eaten was tainted when the stomach cramps start—that is to say, *after* the event.

"Sexual advances" are no more "unwanted," or tainted, by definition, than food is. The expression "unwanted sexual advances" is frequently used in connection with sexual harassment.

Is this a synthetic (as in "cows are quadrupeds") proposition, or an analytic one (as in "cows are in short supply")? Presumably, if sexual advances were "unwanted," by definition, the formula would be a sheer tautology. The only point in using it in debate would be the propagandistic one of giving the whole idea of sexual advances per se an unsavory complexion or ring. If the phrase is analytic and used meaningfully to draw a distinction between "unwanted" and "not unwanted," this undermines the whole notion of the a priori culpability of sexual advances.

For, unless the whole matter has been discussed beforehand in cold blood by the two parties concerned, and positions on the matter have been stated, sexual advances only become "unwanted" *after* they have been made, and the same goes for unwanted gifts. Neither are *inherently* "unwanted." Since all that can logically and legitimately be claimed about sexual advances per se is that they *may* be unwanted or undesirable and that reprehensible or culpable behavior can begin only after advances have been *made* and *rejected*, and then only if the man (or woman) is ungentlemanly enough to persist.

If, however, those who are attempting to stigmatize sexual advances as such by making them "unwanted" by definition were to succeed in making this definition the law of the land, they might find that the consequences were more than they had bargained for.

The Chinese are often credited with saying that the longest journey starts with the first step; it is equally inconceivable that any sexual relationship, love affair, romance, or even marriage could start without "sexual advances" of some kind. In the eyes of the proponents of this definition, are the only acceptable and legitimate relationships to be ones that start by some kind of spontaneous and, above all, *simultaneous* mutual touching maneuver? No matter how gentlemanly—or inhibited—a man may be, it is the man's traditional burden in courtship rituals to take some initiative, at the risk of rebuff. This part of the tango is at least as tough on the male psyche as is the other, much more highly publicized part, on the female psyche—namely, to be faced from time to time with "unwanted" sexual advances.

Every successful relationship, including marriage, starts, and always has started with, some kind of "advance," usually made by the *man*, and some, perhaps most, of the time, by a *gentleman* who knows when his advances are unwanted and backs off. But he would never have known if he hadn't tried.

In those (i.e., most) parts of the world where arranged, and indeed forcibly imposed, marriages are standard practice, "unwanted" sexual advances are par for the course. What *is* deemed "scandalous" in such societies is when women reject or attempt to reject them.

When Adam delved, and Eve span,

Where was then the gentleman?

I wonder who made the first move.

OTHER PIECES

"No, We Will Not Pardon your French!" or, "A Bit of Lit. Crit."

———

Toujours Provence, by Peter Mayle, with a cameo by Erich von Stroheim.

This book not only leaves me cold but actively offends me. This is largely because of a phenomenon known to me privately as the Von Stroheim syndrome.

Here, the author reports the speech of his French interlocutors in English, interspersed with little phrases and words in French. This takes me back to a less critical, more accepting, and impressionable time of my life in World War II and after, when I was exposed to what now seems like an endless series of movies where brutal U-boat captains - no doubt all played by Erich Von Stroheim, that all-purpose jackbooted and be-monocled Nazi officer whom British filmgoers of the epoch loved to hate - peered into their periscopes. U-boat captains would, in a way that the adult me now finds wildly implausible, bark out a few phrases, like "Donner und Blitzen," "Englische[r] Schweinhund," most probably "Feuer!" and above all "Achtung![,]" reverting for the rest of the dialogue to a stagey, comic opera style of German-accented English that, for some reason probably unconnected with phonetics, my generation was brought up to think of as "guttural"——and, as corollary, ipso facto, ugly, and detestable.

The villain at the periscope of his U-boat would then go on to direct his dastardly, downright unsporting, machine-gun fire at the blameless British merchant seamen clinging desperately to the wreckage of their torpedoed ship as they floundered helplessly in some two-feet deep, man-made puddle in Shepperton studios.

If we can safely assume that the author of *Toujours Provence* does not intend us to believe that the French——ahem!——*bribes de phrases* with which he is so fond of peppering his dialogues are an accurate representation of the actual speech patterns of the natives, what can possibly be the explanation for his serving it up to us in this fashion? For example, on page 31, we find a M. Gregoire saying "*Alors!* He has not been *tatoué*." On page 34, we find, "Unfortunately, he has grown to resemble a *mouton*," thus pandering to the inbred, scornful, *combien anglais* notion of the automatic "quaintness" of foreigners—a slightly amused and lofty tolerance from a vantage point of unassailable superiority akin to the fond, indulgent attitude toward children who say the "darndest things."

In the same vein, he also holds up for our disdainful amusement, the labored—and no doubt doctored—attempts of the "natives" to express themselves in English. For example, on page 80, one "native" is represented as saying "now I want to *make* another one but more *professionEl*."

The author also treats us to schoolboy renderings of French uttered by the "natives," either in order to retain the idiosyncratic charm of the original or because he is simply unable to do a better job of translation into idiomatic English. For example, page 81 contains the following: "She works well, the little one."

However inconsistently and unaccountably, the author at times leaves some of the original French of his interlocutors untranslated, thereby subtly flattering and tickling the vanity of the reader with the "of-course-ness" of the implication that the reader doesn't need a translation. Otherwise, when reporting a conversation in a foreign language, why would the author ever leave it untranslated in the first place? Could an author get away with the same approach in a book titled *A Year in Izmir/Vladivostok/Tirana?*

Perhaps the author of *A Year in Provence* feels on safe ground making fun of these particular foreigners and their particular language because he is operating within a particular context, namely that of a distinctive and special cultural relationship between the British (of a certain class) and the French. Or perhaps he feels he is speaking to an upward-striving attempt by this class to embrace and appropriate what are felt to be status-enhancing elements of French culture—elements that, of course, would not include watching French TV, reading *Paris Match*, or vacationing at resorts that are too *populaire!* This is a compliment, by the way, entirely unreturned by the French. After all, as the French say, or the returning British bourgeoisie would enjoy saying they say, *de deux choses l'une!*

Either the author expects his readers to understand the French words and phrases that he sprinkles around the text, or he doesn't. If he does, why not put the whole damned sentence in French? If he doesn't, why do it at all, since his reader will get only the "charm" or the "flavor" without the substance?

For Michael Frayn's take on how the languages spoken by our nearest neighbors and/or traditional enemies are irresistibly comical, see his *Guardian* piece on Auberon Waugh's take on how the Germans cannot possibly keep a straight face when speaking German—especially when passing an *ausfahrt*.

Turkish Reflections, by Mary Lee Settle, gives us a whiff of the same aroma.

On page 20, she mentions *beyaz sarap*, the "white wine of Turkey." Since she must be assuming that English-speaking readers wouldn't have understood the original Turkish, how should we understand the point of telling us what it is in Turkish? Surely it couldn't be just to let us know that *she* knew what it was. The same goes for *ekmek*, *beyaz peynir*, and *cicekler*. Attentive readers may have astutely deduced from *beyaz sarap* that the *beyaz* may mean white, and—if they have studied enough menus in Indian restaurants—that *peynir* may mean cheese. But it's hardly likely that the author was relying on that outside chance.

"Dolma" and *dolmus* are, however, fair game since they both represent genuinely distinctive realities that have no counterpart in British culture or the English language. This book is also marred by another flaw typical of the gushing-with-enthusiasm type of writing about strange exotic peoples. Here the Turks are said to be "born gourmets," among other things, because they like eating this, that, and other food items unknown to, or unfavored by, ourselves. Who knows, perhaps there are travel books by Turkish authors attributing exotic tastes to the English because they eat porridge for breakfast and regard overboiled cabbage as a delicacy.

You may have heard of the young man who discovered that his friends found him pretentious. Chagrined, he confronted them with, "Pretentious, *moi?*"

Further examples of the genre are the following:

Amis, Martin. "Books." "Family Romance." Review of *Experience*, by Joan Acocella. *The New Yorker*, June 19 and 26, 2000. "That two-year *saison en enfer* is unquestioningly part of the reason."

Ibid., "The Critics-Books." "The Get Ready Man"

"The civilizing power of thinking in French." E. M. Cioran would "pace the walks…in an effort to wear himself out before another *nuit blanche*." Is there any other reason for this than authorial showing off and the titillating flattery mentioned above?

"He walked the streets meeting prostitutes and clochards and intellectuals." How too terribly Parisian! How on earth did he avoid meeting any shoe salesmen, accountants, and *midinettes*?

"His [Cioran's] reputation as a pure stylist, as a master of elegant French is perhaps the highest of any writer of this century."

A typical example of the literary reviewer's knowing, sweeping, and totally unverifiable—and unverified—hyperbole. Note the nice touch with the "perhaps," suggesting either that he has just spent a sleepless night judiciously evaluating the competing claims to this lofty title of the thousands of possible candidates, or that he couldn't be bothered to do any "judicious evaluating" and is banking on the likelihood that no one else will, using the "perhaps" just to give himself wriggle room.

"Some of his aphorisms seem likely to live as long as any aphorism can: "Every thought should recall the ruin of a smile"; "There is a God at the outset, if not the end, of every joy"; and "A civilization evolves from agriculture to paradox." It would be hard to imagine utterances so devoid of pith, moment, wit, sense, or humor, perhaps, except that doing the uttering at a Parisian salon in French invested it with (ahem!) a certain *je ne sais quoi*.

We now welcome the inevitable appearance of other "celebrities" to validate the importance of the chosen and hitherto totally obscure subject and—incidentally—to enhance the "insider" status of the reviewer himself.

"It was said that they, Sam [Beckett] and Cioran, passed each other at twilight in the Luxembourg Gardens and inclined bowed heads in greeting, two recognized masters of lowered eyes and expectations."

Meanwhile, we poor mortals, in our hopeless conventionality of unlowered eyes and no expectation of having our oh-so-profound originality immortalized by some "pretentious, *moi*?" literary reviewer, can think of nothing less banal than to greet acquaintances and even—God forbid!—actually engage them in conversation in whatever obscure and glamorless park we may happen to take our evening walk.

"Cioran left Romania before the worst...and it is possible—in Paris it is almost compulsory . . .."

(Visitors to Paris may possibly have missed the signs, usually obscured amid the multitude of NO PARKING signs, giving the date of the (ahem!) *loi* in question and the penalties for violations.)

". . .to read his fifty years of wit and sleeplessness as an act of expiation... and his choice of France, French and the classical style as a rueful renunciation of the Romantic, hysterical style that led him so close to the Iron Guard."

Again, the reviewer is boosting himself as the insider with privileged access to arcane or hitherto and justifiably obscure information to which the profane but quite possibly culturally snobbish reader can now have secondhand, privileged access via the reviewer.

"Taking the poison in small doses [reading Cioran]...and telling yourself that it is medicine.

(But then homeopathic medicine is the favourite of Paris pharmacies)."

This is more insider posturing!

"He [Cioran] was heavily influenced by Nietzsche and was obsessed, like *most of his generation*" (i.e., by that microscopically minute fragment of it that *counts*, of course!) "by the ridiculous 'mediocrity' [emphasis mine] and confusion of Romania."

"He himself seems to have felt that he was transformed...by the great Parisian trilogy, the three 'F's more powerful than Wilson's four."

(I don't, of course, need to tell you, my dear, sophisticated, insider, cognoscenti readers, what they are!)

"Fornication, food and French."

(Well, where else could you get the first two? And in any case, without the French to go with them, where is the charm, the authenticity, the significance?)

Asking The Impossible

—————

In 1970, the Conservative Party, led by Edward Heath, won the British general election, defeating the Labour Party, led by Harold Wilson, and Heath became prime minister. Amid widespread industrial turbulence, Heath called a snap election in the hope of achieving a larger majority with a stronger mandate for governing during this crisis.

I was moved to send him the following letter:

Dear Mr. Heath,

Last week I heard a broadcast here in New York which referred to an electoral campaign speech in which you were reported to have called upon the British electorate to make "a clear choice" in the forthcoming general election.

As a member, albeit disenfranchised since I work for the U.N. in New York, of the electorate to which this exhortation was addressed and as a connoisseur in a modest way of political utterances, I would like to ask the following question. Although I am denied the right to a postal vote, I hope my disenfranchisement is not so absolute as to preclude heckling by correspondence.

A few years ago, Michael Frayn in his Observer column confessed to some perplexity about an appeal by the then Prime Minister, Harold Wilson, to the country to work harder to help Britain out of its current economic plight, and wondered how, say, a satirical columnist might be expected to respond to such an appeal. By making his columns longer, shorter, funnier or perhaps by writing them faster?

I wonder if you could tell me how any *individual* voter, however strongly moved by your appeal and with the very best of intentions, could actually set about complying with it once inside the polling booth, since there is no way that a voter could do anything but cast one vote for your party or the rival party. No matter how clear his choice, that voter has no way of knowing whether or not, by so doing, he has actually helped, as requested, to return [Heath's] party to power with an increased majority. Yours faithfully...

On reviewing this letter, I became uneasily aware that it is liberally sprinkled with what is now a politically incorrect, if not "sexist," pronoun. On the other hand, if I had amended the text to make it acceptable to the politically correct of 2016, I would have committed an anachronism, because that's the way it was in those benighted days.

The French proudly assert that their language is "more logical" than English, but they do so in defiance of the biblical injunction "And why beholdest thou *the mote* that is in *thy neighbour's eye*, but considerest not the beam that is in thine own *eye*?" Not only do they call a machine that spends half its time going *down* an *ascenseur* (no more logical than the British, with their "lift," aided and abetted by their American cousins with their "elevator"), but their notices advertising concerts and other gatherings of all kinds invite the public to *venir nombreux*. Again, with the best will in the world, how can any single individual do that—any more than the lone British voter can comply with Mr. Heath's exhortation?

ATHEISM VERSUS THE REST

CHRISTOPHER HITCHENS, ONE OF THE world's most outspoken and best-known atheists, died this year (2012). He believed there is no afterlife. Either he now knows he was wrong and will be spending eternity mortified (if that is the right word) by that knowledge, or he doesn't know and will never enjoy the satisfaction of knowing that he was right.

Pope John Paul II, can, if anyone can, be assumed to have believed in an afterlife. If he was right, he knows, and has the satisfaction of knowing that he was right. If he was wrong, he remains ignorant, blissfully or otherwise, of the fact that he was wrong.

If this were a betting game, there is no doubt about which horse to put your money on. If you are an atheist, you are doomed either to an eternity of kicking yourself—or worse, having others do it for you!—or to an eternity of oblivion. If you are a believer, you are in a win-win situation; you are destined for either an eternity of triumphant vindication of your belief or an eternity of obliviousness to the fact that you lost your bet.

It would clearly be a truly humanitarian act to do everything possible to raise your children in the unshakable belief in an afterlife—if it were not for the fact that this belief is so often indissolubly linked with some other, far less humanitarian, credos.

"CADS"

JOSEPH A. "JOEY" BUTTAFUOCO WAS an auto body shop owner from Long Island. He is best known for having had an affair with seventeen-year-old Amy Fisher, who in 1992 subsequently shot his wife, Mary Jo Buttafuoco, in the face. Buttafuoco later pleaded guilty to one count of statutory rape and served four months in jail. He appeared quite frequently in court, both civil and criminal; disappeared somewhat less frequently to jail; and became a minor TV celebrity—further corroboration of an American adage, "There is no such thing as bad publicity." On March 5, 2009, he sued a woman who had attempted to pay for $4,700 in repairs to her Corvette in sexual favors rather than money.

Such adverse criticism as there was included allegations that he was a "cad." Could he have been?

The notion of the cad was in its day essentially that of someone who had let the side down. In order to let the side down, you had to belong to it in the first place. Among other things, it also meant, in the most literal sense, wearing the uniform of the side. To do this, you had, of course, to be able to afford it—or rather them, since a gentleman's wardrobe had to be compendious enough to encompass the kaleidoscopic sartorial diversity dictated by the ever-changing times of day, seasons of year, and vagaries of climate, location, and activity. Expense has always and everywhere been one of the means used by elites to keep outsiders in their proper place—outside—although it is never a sufficient condition, only a necessary one.

A cad in a boiler suit or overalls is a contradiction in terms. The boiler-suited classes could only be "yobs" or "oiks," a status that precluded caddery, since in order to be a cad, you had to "know better" to start with. Only a presumptive "gentleman" could be a cad, and he could only be that by acting in an "ungentlemanly" fashion. If you are not already on the side, you cannot join it, since, by impeccably calculated definition, refined centuries before anyone had ever heard of *Catch-22*, anyone who has to learn how to be a gentleman obviously cannot be one. In the same way, anyone who has to ask the prices in a restaurant obviously cannot afford to be there.

Nothing aroused the scorn of a gentleman so much as the spectacle of his inferiors attempting to ape him. When the occasion arose for taking punitive action against a cad, there were appropriate hierarchical niceties to be observed. It had to be administered out of the sight and earshot of ladies—usually somewhere beyond the French windows at stage rear and with nothing so coarse as a blunt instrument. The implement of choice was naturally something that only the equestrian classes were likely to have at hand—the riding crop or the horse whip. The errant cad, unless he were an unmitigated "oik," would not, of course, bleat, yelp, whimper, or blubber, and his tweedily complacent assailants were expected to saunter serenely back into the drawing room, most probably through the French windows, without a hair out of place.

The truth may lie a fingernail deeper. Can any American be a cad—that is to say, a lapsed gentleman? One or two have tried to qualify by becoming gentlemen first (Henry James and T. S. Eliot leap to mind), but they had to leave home to do it. The trouble was that, in however discreet and genteel a fashion, there was no getting round the "oiky" fact that they worked for a living.

Caveat Lector! Castro Did Ante Up!

Pope John Paul II visits Cuba (January 21–25, 1998)

In a *New York Times* article titled "Pope Captivates His Marxist Host" ("The Pope in Cuba," International Section, page A9, January 26), Celestine Bohlen wrote: "He [Castro] went on to praise the Pope for his efforts to admit and correct the errors of the *church's past—candor that Mr. Castro has not so far reciprocated about the errors of his own rule.*"

This slippery and tendentious use of *reciprocate* may have sold unwary readers the notion that the pope's admission that *previous l*eaders of the Catholic church had made errors somehow morally and logically required Castro to confess that he, the *current* leader of a Marxist regime, had made errors, if he was to be equal in candor. The lingering impression remains that of the distasteful figure of the poker player who has failed to "ante up."

Reciprocity, properly understood, would either have required both the pope and Castro to admit to errors during their own tenure or for both to have admitted errors committed by their predecessors. The fact is that neither the pope nor Castro admitted errors during their own tenure and both admitted errors committed by predecessors.

Specifically, in a speech delivered on January 21, Castro stated, "I have sometimes wondered whether the conditions were right for building socialism in Poland, and perhaps this was a historical error of the revolutionary movement."

Castro added, "This pope is Polish and lived through a very special experience in a very special country, where unquestionably many errors were committed."

Castro went on to mention a number of other errors committed by the Soviet Union and the East European socialist camp. One such error, according to him, was the fate of the Polish officers who were captured when Soviet troops entered Poland. Another was the war launched by the Soviet Union against Finland.

LANGUAGE CRIMES

——◆——

SOME YEARS AGO, I WAS introduced to the ambassador of the Netherlands at a dip-
lomatic reception and thought it a good opportunity to air a proposal that had
long been on my mind, since the seat of the International Court of Justice, along
with other worthy international institutions, was in The Hague.

After outlining the current disturbing situation in which so many crimes
against language have been going unpunished, and hence undeterred, I asked
him if he would consider asking his government to offer to host an International
Conference against Language Crimes, with a view to the establishment of an
international tribunal to try such crimes. There is nothing like an international
conference for leaving the field littered with the victims of crimes against language. So this one would be a rare, if not unique, case of an international conference amply justifying the purpose for which it was convened.

Since nothing ever came of this mildly bibulous encounter, the best I can
do is to illustrate the need for such an institution by offering some examples of
the genre.

So here goes!

COMPLAINT-OID
[This item dates from the time when Ted Turner, its founder, still owned CNN.
Never having received a response, I was left a little "ann-oid."]

Dear Mr. Turner,

It has been a few years since you heard from me, but this time the dereliction by CNN which is the object of my current outrage is relatively minute and should be that much easier to fix.

My morning exercise routine is always performed to the accompaniment of CNN *Headline News* and this makes me something of a captive, if not captious, audience. For years now my sensibilities have been assaulted "every half hour on the half hour" by an item you are pleased to call a "Factoid." I had thought that if I stiffened my upper lip and gritted my teeth stoically, either the irritant or the irritation would somehow disappear. Both, however, have stood the test of time. My impression is that the powers-that-be at Headline News are under the misimpression that Factoid, means something like "a small, insignificant or trivial fact." The fact is that the "-oid," suffix means "like," or "having the same or similar shape or form." It signifies nothing about size, magnitude or significance. An "ovoid" can well be much larger than the egg it is like, and if you should ever encounter an "android" on your first visit to Mars you may only come up to his knee. If the point about the facts purveyed under the title Factoid, is their trifling and insignificant nature, then their purveyors can only be congratulated on maintaining immaculate standards, but they remain facts none the less, so why not give them a name which actually means what you intend it to mean? The possibilities are endless: "factling" "factlet" "facticulum," "facticle," "trivium," "statitisculum," or "statisticule."

Please put me out of my misery and make "fact-oid," an "av-oid"!
Yours Sincerely…

ECONOMICS 101: A "DISMAL SCIENCE" OR
"A PERPETUALLY UNRESOLVABLE DISPUTE"

———

FROM AN ONLINE ARTICLE TITLED "Is Economics a Science?" No author's name given.

"Are there some ideas about which all economists agree? Do disagreements suggest that economics is an exciting, viable academic discipline or *a perpetually unresolvable dispute?*"

THE DISMAL SCIENCE
Madrick, Jeff. *Seven Bad Ideas.* New York: Vintage, September 25, 2014.

The economics profession has not, to say the least, covered itself in glory these past six years. *Hardly any economists predicted the 2008 crisis—and the handful who did tended to be people who also predicted crises that didn't happen.* More significant, many and arguably most economists were claiming, right up to the moment of collapse, that nothing like this could even happen.

Furthermore, once crisis struck economists seemed unable to agree on a response. They'd had 75 years since the Great Depression to figure out what to do if something similar happened again, *but the profession was utterly divided when the moment of truth arrived.*

In *Seven Bad Ideas: How Mainstream Economists Have Damaged America and the World*, Jeff Madrick argues that *the professional failures since 2008 didn't come out of the blue but were rooted in decades of intellectual malfeasance.*

Paul Krugman

"How much of the problem is bad economic ideas per se as opposed to *economists who have proved all too ready to drop their own models—in effect, reject their own ideas—when their models conflict with their political leanings?*"

I believe the problem is more deeply rooted than any of the three foregoing, quite different attempts to diagnose the failure of the economics experts to predict or respond to the crisis. The rot set in the moment it was decided to misname the study of "economics" a *science*.

Read any standard economics textbook, and see how the "laws," which seem to be hung on the precarious peg of the average consumer's "*rational*" behavior in the marketplace, stack up against the realities of women's actual capricious clothes shopping practices, as often as not based upon the irresistible bargain promised by the gigantic "markdown."

Then there are the aberrations in the economics of the book trade, the chocolate-box business, and the florist industry, in which the purchaser is very often *not* the consumer, contrary to what economics textbooks seem to assume. Books, especially hardbacks, are often bought as gifts for others, gifts that are even likely to be regifted. A leading example is the fate of the celebrated best-seller *A Brief History of Time*, largely unread and thus unconsumed, unless you count its function as a coffee-table decoration as "consumption." Boxes of chocolates are rarely bought for one's own consumption, and because of the perishability of the product, even more rarely for coffee-table decor. Indeed, the end user of such a commodity is probably as hard to track down as the end user of illegal arms trafficking. The same applies to the cut-flower business, where there is at least greater pressure on the giftee to make a point of conspicuous consumption of that commodity by displaying it where it can be seen by the donor who happens to visit during its lifetime.

In the hard sciences, such as physics, chemistry, and medicine, their history is strewn with obscurantism, schisms, bad guesses, blind alleys, and violent disputes, but with the advent of modern scientific methods and the testing of hypotheses by experiments designed to test their validity and whose results are rigorously peer reviewed, hard-won consensus is eventually achieved. In this way, science, properly so called, advances more and more rapidly along a broad front.

Just imagine if the practice of modern medicine could be described, and indeed roundly condemned, as the economics profession has been by some of its own most respected and influential members in terms such as those quoted above. Who would ever have the confidence to consult a medical doctor about any ailment in the absence of any professional consensus about its correct diagnosis and treatment? So why do we put our trust, and even worse, why do our political leaders put their trust on our behalf, in those whose "expertise" is in nothing but part of a "perpetually unresolved dispute"? This is a rhetorical question, of course, but one to which there is an answer, however depressing (see below).

There is, of course, another social science, known as political science. Two professors of this "science" have in recent US presidencies been plucked out of academia to become close advisors to US presidents. In both cases, these advisors—Henry Kissinger and Condoleeza Rice—ended their political careers as secretary of state. Whether their expertise as "political scientists" influenced the avowedly purely partisan policies of their masters or the heady proximity to power seduced them into lending the weight of their academic reputations to provide a veneer of intellectual respectability to policies dictated by their masters is a moot point.

Somewhere along the way, what have come to be known as "social *sciences*," including economics, have been allowed to get away with the appropriation of the prestige-enhancing title of "sciences," and along with it, they have enjoyed all the attributes and accoutrements of that title without possessing the credentials that would justify it. Never has this "science" achieved consensus on any disputed issue, and indeed, never are these issues disputed more fiercely than at the highest level by the recognized leaders of the profession.

Franklin D. Roosevelt, Winston Churchill, Ronald Reagan, Margaret Thatcher, Joseph Stalin, and their ilk, and currently (in 2016), all the front-runners for the US presidency, however widely and wildly their economic policies (for those who have them, at least) diverge, and however economically illiterate they themselves may be, have found, or will find, a pet economics professor to validate their policies and lend them a veneer of intellectual respectability and slick and catchy titles, such as "supply side," for their gut instincts. For some reason, I have never heard of anyone championing "demand side" economics, which would appear to be the equal and opposite counterpart.

If Bernard Sanders, currently (in 2016) vying with Hillary Clinton for nomination as the Democratic candidate for the US presidency, should ever need an in-house economic guru, a ready-made, illustrious candidate for the role in the person of the Frenchman Thomas Picketty stands in the wings, and the trace of a foreign accent never proved to be a liability in Henry Kissinger's, Madeleine Albright's, or Zbigniew Brzezinski's career in the US government.

For some reason, political leaders rarely seem to need to bolster their policies by co-opting professors of other social sciences, such as statisticians, anthropologists, psychologists, sociologists, geographers, and demographers, however eminent they may be, and anointing them in-house gurus.

The seers and soothsayers favoured by such the Reagan White House and the last of the Romanovs are a whole other story.

FAMILY VALUES

ONE MORE CONVENTIONAL PIETY THAT COULD DO WITH A LITTLE SCRUTINY
THE MUCH VAUNTED—AND FLAUNTED—TERM "FAMILY values" is right up there with "motherhood," which it would be downright blasphemous to decry. With "motherhood," at least, the meaning is clear and doesn't need defining. However, "family values" (hereinafter to be known as FV) is a "feel-good" term always left undefined by its users, right up there along with "truth" and "beauty."

By using "family" as an adjective with descriptive implications that have no intrinsic connection with the meaning of the word, "pro-family" forces appropriate extrinsic, favorable connotations such as "loyalty," "law abiding," and "monogamous" for the word. "Family," in fact, has become a code word that occupies the "virtuous" end of a spectrum, at the other end of which lies the "nasty" code word "adult," as in "adult" entertainment.

It is noteworthy that, although "family values" always comes in the plural, no one ever seems to spell them out, or even name any one of them in particular.

Adjectives like "material" values and "spiritual" values at least have the merit of yielding clear contradistinctions—"material" versus "spiritual," and vice versa.

But what is the contradistinction to, or opposite of, "family" values? Could "community" or "society" on the larger hand be considered a contradistinction, or is "individual" on the smaller hand more appropriate?

FV is another one of the unarguable, self-referential assertions of political rhetoric, or more accurately, a "trigger" word or phrase designed to evoke a mood or attitude.

There seems to be a valid analogy between "family" and "nation," which can be stated as follows: "nation" is to "patriotism"—or the version of it whereby "my country, right or wrong" is considered a virtue—what "family" is to "family values." Just as one particular value, "loyalty to my family," trumps all other values, including communitywide or national values, so "patriotism" trumps all other values related to the wider community of nations. If "patriotism"—that is, "my nation, right or wrong"—is antithetical or inimical to "internationalism," what is it to which "my family, right or wrong" is correspondingly antithetical or inimical? In other words, isn't what is wrong with "nationalism" on the international plane also wrong with FV on the national level? Interestingly enough, the counterpart of FV and "patriotism" at the level of the individual is conventionally held to be a bad thing and is known as "selfishness," or more colloquially, but equally disreputably, as "looking out for number one."

Why then isn't putting your family's interests above those of society at large considered as "antisocial" and as reprehensible as putting your own personal interests above those of your family? In more concrete terms, if I cheat other people and forgive myself for it but do not recognize the right of others to cheat me, this attitude is considered to be inconsistent with civic virtue. If my country cheats another country and I approve of it but am indignant when another country cheats my own, this attitude would be considered by some to be "patriotic" and commendable but condemned by others as "nationalistic" and wrong. If members of my family cheat "outsiders" and I approve of it and even encourage it, am I to be commended for my FV or condemned for being "antisocial," for being a bad citizen, or even for immoral behavior? The fact is that the vaunters of FV, who are nearly always also vaunters of patriotic values and loyalties, are either oblivious to or are glossing over a fundamental inconsistency.

When you start to analyze them, FV are nearly always in conflict with loyalties to, and the interests of, the larger society. The politician who comes out bravely and unequivocally in favor of FV should be asked whether a mother who tries to hide her son from the law when he has committed a murder is to be commended for her FV or condemned for harboring a criminal. Or does it depend on whether the crime is "liberal" or "conservative"? Would the same politician answer the question differently if the mother is, for example, aiding and abetting her son who is a "welfare cheat"? Or would it be different if it were the son aiding and abetting the mother? The bottom line is that FV and loyalties are subversive of civic virtues and values.

Does mere membership in a family endow one with more of either the "conservative" virtues of patriotism; religious observance; "work"; and respect for authority and crime and punishment, especially capital punishment, or the "liberal" virtues of compassion; "caring"—about the right things, of course—concern for the "less fortunate"; distrust of authority, civil rights, and criminogenic considerations; and rehabilitation of criminals? In fact, membership of a family simply exposes people to a wider range of possibilities of moral depravity without making it any more likely that they will rise above it. Only a husband can commit "wife beating"; only a spouse can commit "adultery" or "cheat" on his or her spouse; only a parent (or guardian) can commit "child neglect" or "child abuse"; only a father can run off and leave his "family" to fend for itself; only a mother can connive in the abuse of her children by her boyfriend(s) or their stepfather; and only members of a family can commit incest with each other. Behind a lot of this boosting of FV is an implication or a premise that a "married man" or better still a "family man"—that is to say, a man with children—is more likely to keep to the straight and narrow and off the streets and hence less likely to commit the "blue-collar" crimes of violence. As to "white-collar "crime, I have never seen any suggestion that perpetrators are less likely to be "respectable" family men.

There is an implication that being married will somehow curb or assuage the sexual impulses that, it is felt, lead to disorder and social disruption, and that the dependency of children will keep a man's nose to the grindstone in order to provide for them. Yet it is only families that make the improvident or absentee father possible, and it is only the children of such families whose unsupervised hanging around the streets make them so unsafe for the rest of us law-abiding citizens.

It is not for nothing that the Mafia or the Cosa Nostra ape the family in their terminology and structure. They have traditionally laid great stress on "family" ties, loyalties, and, yes, "family values." Even respectable—one assumes—outsiders, like the actor Anthony Quinn during the trial of the notorious John Giotti, publicly reserved their disgust and condemnation for Giotti's former henchman who "ratted" on him, without any hint or suggestion that the "family" members who had been "disloyal" to him by "ratting" were thus doing their civic duty by assisting society in convicting a dangerous criminal who was a menace to society.

At best, one could interpret Quinn's reaction as implying that the evil represented by Giotti was by far a lesser evil than that represented by his "betrayal" by his former partners in crime.

All "values" are about relativity or priorities and are meaningless without reference thereto. When a friend asked the philosopher, "How's your wife?" he replied, "Compared with what?"

On September 24, 1992, the elder president Bush vetoed a "family leave" bill because it would cost employers too much. If you had asked him in the abstract if he was pro-family, he would undoubtedly have replied "yes." If you had asked him, also in the abstract, if he was pro-employer, how could a good Republican reply anything but "yes"? This is an excellent example of how a commitment, especially a verbal commitment, to a value is meaningless in the abstract and only begins to acquire meaning when compared with another value. Unqualified assertions of commitment to "values" are "valueless"! Someone has to be there to ask, "Compared with what?"

Everyone, including—or perhaps especially—the pope, values peace, but everyone, except for a few fringe conscientious objectors who are prepared to suffer for their convictions, is prepared to go to, or preferably to send others on their behalf to war to defend certain other "values." Sometime around 1960, Michael Frayn wrote a column in which he wondered whether the pope was so committed to peace that he would allow Congolese soldiers to continue "peacefully" raping Belgian nuns.

It was reported (in *Newsweek*, May 23, 1999) in an article titled "Rape and Aftermath," by Rod Nordland, that "although the Vatican ordinarily opposes artificial contraception, an exception was made for nuns in the former Belgian Congo during the upheavals of the 1960s." Clearly the pope's commitment to peace was so ironclad that his response was to permit them to take contraceptive pills to avoid pregnancy.

Recent US vice president Dick Cheney, a ferocious armchair warrior, famously declared that the reason why he didn't serve in the military during the Vietnam War was that he had "other priorities at the time," yet no one has been more vociferous in advocating waging war on his country's enemies. More recently still, Donald Trump, a candidate for the Republican nomination for the US presidency, in answer to a question about what he would do to defeat ISIS, fervently declared, "I would bomb the hell out of them" (well, that is, he would appoint a general to do that for him, and then that general would appoint a colonel...and so on down the line).

Such is the rush today, especially at election-tide, to occupy the high moral ground of FV that, if he were alive, Dr. Johnson might well be impelled to replace "patriotism" in his oft-quoted aphorism, "patriotism is the last refuge of a scoundrel" with "family values."

Note the frequent invocation of "protecting one's family" as the catchall excuse for a multitude of sins, crimes, and misdemeanors. The "householder," which is one of the many benign terms for what in other contexts might have been described as the "accused," the "perpetrator," or even the "alleged killer," who in May 1993 in Baton Rouge, Louisiana, shot and killed a Japanese exchange student on his Halloween rounds, was deemed guiltless by a sympathetic jury because he was "acting to protect his family." What if he had shot the student in exactly the same circumstances but happened to be single or, God forbid, gay? Why mention "single"? Because politicians, almost without exception, only ever claim to advocate or justify programs or proposals because they will help or protect American "families." Whatever happened to "people"? This is particularly ironic at a time when, according to the Census Bureau in its *America's Families and Living Arrangements* report, the percentage of one-person households has grown over the last forty years, from 17 percent of total households in 1970 to 27 percent in 2012. By the same token, gun enthusiasts always invoke the need to protect their "families," never themselves, even conceivably in cases where a given gun-toter has no family to protect.

Ancient Sparta and the Kibbutz movement are two examples of a community that implicitly recognized that for their purposes, FV were, if not inimical to, at least not entirely consistent with, the community or civic values they wanted to inculcate. Military and religious organizations have also in their different ways found it desirable to separate recruits from their families. Plato in the *Republic* and *Laws* advocates the holding of wives and children in common and the removal of budding "guardians," to be raised away from their families in order to instill higher values.

In *The New Italians* (page 126), Charles Richards writes:

This almost third-world reliance on the family is not only the source of the strength of Italian society but also its weakness. Italy is a country where the sense of civic responsibility remains very low. The family has reinforced the tendency of Italians not to contribute to the building and maintenance of civil society.

He also says (page 140):

Time and again when sons sin, in their mothers' eyes they can do no wrong…When a television program showed the story of a girl gang-raped by seven young men as she left a discotheque in Lamezia Terme, the switchboard was jammed with mothers calling up to defend the boys' action and accusing the girl of being a provocative harpy.

New York Times: "Prosecutors led Mr. Cosby [Bill] step by step through his career and what he called his emphasis on 'the moral values' and 'the family values' in his…work." He was the defendant in a paternity suit brought by his ex-mistress, Ms. Thompson, on behalf of her daughter.

As stated earlier, values quailified by distinctive adjectives are easier to define (e.g., "spiritual" or "material") because it is clear what other values they are being distinguished from. But the expression "family values" leaves unanswered the question "as distinct from what *other* values?" Is it in contradistinction to "the community" or "society" on the larger hand or "the individual" on the smaller?

Public speakers who brandish the term almost never specify or single out any one particular example of what they are talking about.

Almost the only one that is ever clearly implied is marital fidelity—that is, anyone who espouses FV and is known to have committed adultery is held to be "inconsistent" or hypocritical. The same, however, does not appear to apply to divorce or poor parent-children relations. The nearest that its advocates ever seem to come to a definition is negatively, indirectly, and by contradistinction from phenomena that are held to be inimical to FV, such homosexual marriage or homosexuals teaching in schools—not to mention homosexual couples who want to "espouse" *family* values by raising a family.

Christopher Wren's son had inscribed on a wall of St. Paul's Cathedral the words *Si Monumentum Requiris, circumspice*. ("If you're looking for a memorial, look around you.") If you are looking for corroboration of this deconstruction of "family values," it's all around you; you need look no further than your daily newspaper or your TV.

To wit:

New York Times, May 5, 2015.

"Families Back G.I.'s Held in Japan." *New York Times*, November 6, 1995: "For 3 young Americans, joining the military was a way out of their small-town lives. Now that they face charges in a rape case in Japan [Okinawa], their *families* insist that they must be innocent."

CNN, July 29, 1997: "And give American families their first tax cut in several years."

The word "families" now seems to be replacing "Americans," "citizens," "people," and so forth, thus enabling politicians to squeeze an extra drop of politically correct "feel good" out of the rhetoric tube.

New York Times. "Dean Skelos, Albany Senate Leader, Aided Son at All Costs, US Says," by William K. Rashbaum and Thomas Kaplan, April 2015.

Over the last five years or so, it seemed there was little that Dean G. Skelos, the majority leader of the New York Senate, would not do for his son. He pressed a powerful real estate executive to provide commissions to his son, a 32-year-old title insurance salesman, according to a federal criminal complaint. He helped get him a job at an environmental company and employed his influence to help the company get government work. He used his office to push natural gas drilling regulations that would have increased his son's commissions. He even tried to direct part of a $5.4 billion state budget windfall to fund government contracts that the company was seeking. And when the company was close to securing a storm-water contract from Nassau County, the senator, through an intermediary, pressured the company to pay his son more—or risk having the senator subvert the bid.

"Feisty"

Can George Herbert Walker Bush—or Any Tall, Patrician Wasp—Be
"Feisty"?

Oxford English Dictionary: "Feisty" = "aggressive, excitable, touchy, plucky,
spirited."

Merriam-Webster: "not afraid to fight or argue"; "very lively and aggressive."

The closest these definitions get to the root of the matter is the use of
the words "spunky" and "plucky," which somehow suggest that its use is only
appropriate when applied to members of an "underdog" class who are unusually
courageous in standing up to some "overdog" or other.

What is interesting about the use of this word is that it seems to be confined
to describing persons of less-than-average stature or physique—nearly always
men. Harry Truman was "feisty," and so were George Wallace and New York
mayor La Guardia.

Mayor Koch, who was every bit as pugnacious and combative, was precluded, presumably by his height, from ever being described as "feisty." It is
interesting to speculate whether Mayor John Lindsay could have qualified, even
if he had been six inches shorter and pugnacious, or whether the disabling combination of being both a WASP and patrician ruled him out. George Wallace
was, at least technically, a WASP—of the rubicervical variety—but with no
touch of the patrician about him. Given equal height, are members of different
ethnic groups more, or less likely to qualify for this accolade?

Also, does the bestower of the epithet himself have to be disqualified from
"feistiness" in order to dub another thus? For example, can a five-foot, seven-
inch sportscaster describe a five-foot-nine running back as "little" with the same

spontaneous and unselfconscious ease as Frank Gifford (six feet plus) on *Monday Night Football*?

It is noteworthy that when people (men only?) who are standing up or know each other well enough to have taken each other's physical measure are exchanging abuse, some of the opprobrious epithets likely to be hurled— "lummox," "rat," "half-pint," "shrimp," "shorty," "runt"—have stature implications. Women rarely resort to stature-impugning insults among themselves. Apart from anything else, being undersized, far from being an unfeminine attribute, often qualifies for the accolade "petite."

Motorists, however, have to be content with size-neutral insults, since they tend to come into "contact" with each other in the seated position. Indeed, the whole question of "clutch courage," which transforms the average muted, inoffensive, and circumspect pedestrian once he is behind the wheel of a car into a hermetically sealed and encapsulated thug and licenses him to hurl unheard abuse at his fellow citizens, is a fascinating one in its own right. [This was written ca. 1992. Since then, a new term, "road rage," has evolved; may I propose a compromise amalgam—"clutch cou-rage"?]

New York Times Book Review. Advertisement for the book *Contrary to Popular Opinion*, by Alan M. Dershowitz, described him as "engaging, *feisty...*" October 18, 1992.

Is it, strictly speaking, possible to describe views or opinions in the abstract as "feisty" without reference to their author and his stature, sex, ethnicity, or other qualifications for "underdoghood"? Would the *opinions* referred to here as "feisty" still be describable as such if they were known to belong to someone of the stature and ethnicity of Bill Bradley? Or would they have to be called something like "controversial" instead? Dershowitz's size is not, of course, public knowledge, in the same way as the fact that he is Jewish, but does his ethnicity alone supply the necessary element of "underdoghood"?

New York Times Book Review, October 18, 1992. Marilyn Stasio writes, "The female sleuths are smart, *feisty* and independent."

Being female in itself, especially in the private-eye milieu, clearly constitutes sufficient "underdoghood" to warrant the epithet.

Guardian Angel, by Sara Paretsky. *Sunday Times Book Review*, London, November 8, 1992. "V.I. Warshavsky...has a *feisty* courage..."

Quindlen, Anna. "The (New) Hillary Problem." Op-ed, *New York Times*, August 11, 1992. "When you read Hillary Clinton's clippings, the word 'hard-edged' appears more frequently than any other except 'headbands.' It's an interesting word, not only because it's code, but because you rarely hear it applied to men. It's like *feisty*, a word used only for women and short guys, and other spirited underdogs."

New York Times, November 28, 1992. "A *feisty* 74-year-old woman...thwarted an 'attempted' carjacking by ramming the car of her two assailants..."

A regular dog has four legs; this underdog might match this accomplishment and achieve super-underdog status of full quadrupedicity if she happened to use crutches.

New York Times, September 5, 1993. "Compliance Data Center...a firm that's made a business of compiling the dirt on investors who stiff their brokers. (Ms.) McKay White, its *feisty*, 62 year old senior vice president reigns over a four-person team..."

Clearly, sheer old age in itself qualifies as a constituent element in "underdoghood."

New York Times, October 28, 1995. An ad for "A *Feisty* Brand's Newest Frontier: Premium Colas" stated: "Attention, Coke and Pepsi: Arizona is stepping into your territory. You know Arizona; it's the *feisty* and fast-growing *upstart* purveyor of iced teas and fruit drinks..."

How to be Antiwar on the Cheap

ONE OF THE MORE SIMPLISTIC but pervasive pieties around is that works of art that depict or denounce the "horrors" of war are ipso facto somehow commendably and courageously "antiwar." The implication seems to be that those who make, promote, or participate in a war do so because they are unaware or insufficiently aware of its "horrors" and would desist if only they could become or be made aware.

The only authentic antiwar position is that of pacifism; all other positions concede the admissibility of fighting a war in certain circumstances. In practice, these positions tend to be taken over cocktails and in the abstract—never, for example, while lying out in no-man's-land in the mud with your legs blown off by a mine.

There are, broadly speaking, two classes of people who say yes to war. There are those who declare or authorize them (the political leaders, who proceed from the reasonable assumption that they—and their nearest and dearest—are not likely to end up in the mud with their legs blown off) and those who actually fight the war, their motives ranging from patriotic conviction to professional self-interest (the professional military) to those who simply take the line of least resistance and simply do nothing to avoid military service and let events run their course. None of these groups is unaware of the risk of ending up in the mud or of how unpleasant that would be. To remind them of the fact *before* they make their various kinds of commitments is unlikely to have any effect because the risk is either too abstract at that point or seems only likely to affect others, in any case. Reminding them *after* their commitment is too late to have any effect.

One of the most egregious examples of this cheap and facile "antiwar" posture—I am tempted to say IMposture—is the TV sitcom *M*A*S*H*, a posture all the more pernicious for being embodied in one of the most effective and durable entertainment vehicles to which the American public has ever been exposed.

M*A*S*H is supposedly antiwar, but there is never anything in it that remotely approaches a probing either of the issues surrounding the Korean War itself or the issues of war and peace in general, including pacifism; and ultimately it confines itself to an endless rehashing of the old song, albeit sung in "fifty different sharps and flats" and in various contexts by a variety of characters but by none more loudly and more often than the arch antiwarrior Hawkeye. The title of this old song is "War Is Hell."

In a way, the medical setting is a built-in cop-out, since Hawkeye and B. J. can rant and rave and ridicule the "war," the "military," and the like, without ever really having to put their money where their mouth is or stand up and be counted. If they had been anything but doctors (medical personnel), their vociferous antiwar cries and their demonstrative and spuriously defiant, risk-free refusals to carry or use weapons would hardly have been compatible with regular combat service, and they would have had to become conscientious objectors, dodge the draft, or desert, all of which actions were open to them, and none of which they chose to take. Of course, they would thereby have incurred the opprobrium and odium of public opinion, which they avoid by accepting military service "but only to save lives." Not once is Hawkeye confronted directly with the issue of whether he would have reported for military service if he had not been a doctor. Nor is he ever made responsible for a reasoned argument against the Korean War or war in general except for variations on the theme of the same old truism that war is hell, which, in its manifold forms and manifestations, passes for "antiwar" sentiment.

There are many things in life apart from war that call for sacrifice and suffering; are they all to be eschewed and held worthless on that account alone?

M*A*S*H is to making the case against war what golf is to exercise; the danger is that a round of golf is likely to create the illusion in the minds of the players that they have taken exercise. In actual fact, as *Aerobics* author Dr. Kenneth Cooper, Mark Twain, and others have pointed out, all that they have done in terms of making the case against war is to "interrupt a slow walk."

In-Flight Safety?

"In-Flight Safety Instructions"; or, "What to Do If You Are a Monoglot Albanian Shepherd Taking Your First Flight and the Aircraft Goes Down in the Water"

Why is the nice lady telling us what to do when we go down in the water? Is she serious? Has any passenger who understands the language being spoken, let alone the hapless monoglot Albanian shepherd on his maiden voyage, ever discovered where his or her nearest emergency exit actually is from the peremptory, laconic, and cursory flick of the finger in the general direction of the space between herself and the back of the cabin by the flight attendant whose turn it happens to be to deliver the mindless, ritual incantation? All this occurs in a language that may or may not be native to the speaker—and may or may not be native to the listener—and where speed of delivery prevails over all considerations of intelligibility, such as articulation, phonetic values and intonation, and oral punctuation.

It should not be rashly assumed, however, that on the rare occasions when all these conditions are met, the aircraft sound system is sure to deliver the message intact to the ears of the listeners, or shall we say, the *passengers*, who may or may not actually be listening.

As for the location of the "flotation cushion" or lifebelt "under your seat" *or* "overhead," have you ever actually tried to look for it? Well, of course not. In any case, when providing for an emergency where seconds count, how can doubt be deliberately left in passengers' minds as to the direction in which they should start looking for the device that is going to save their lives?

Surely, in any given type of aircraft, the lifesaving flotation devices, of all things, are not stored higgledy-piggledy in two different places. Or should we understand that of course they are not, but that flight attendants are left in the dark about where exactly they are?

If you are not supposed to practice actually donning the equipment that is supposed to save your life in extremis (as passengers on cruise ships have to do as a matter of course), the least that can be expected is that you won't have to wrestle in the dark with your immediate neighbors, who may be placing their bets on the overhead locker while you are groping around desperately by the side of your seat, in the exiguous space allotted to you; and, oh yes, what or where exactly *is* the "side" of the middle seat, in which you may have had the misfortune to have been squeezed?

At the same time, of course, what had only a few seconds before been your aircraft is now a rolling, pitching, and yawing, totally unaerodynamic tube of metal, where none of you may any longer be able to tell your arse from your elbow. As you hurtle waterward in flames to the accompaniment of the screams of two or three hundred tightly packed companions, you will no doubt be sparing a thought for your poor monoglot Albanian neighbor, who will not be enjoying your dubious advantage of knowing at least that somewhere within reach there is a potential lifesaving device.

The clear lack of impact and the general ineffectualness of the ritual litany can mean only one of two things. Either the airline doesn't really believe that the aircraft will ever go down in the water or—less comfortingly—the litany betrays the fact that there is nothing much you or the airline can really do about it if it does.

The exercise certainly fails in its purported objective, namely that of better equipping passengers to save their skins in an emergency. Its actual effect can only be to raise, quite gratuitously and futilely, the anxiety level of inexperienced passengers who up to that point may well not have been worrying themselves unduly about going down in the water until the nice lady started to tell them what to do when it happens. As for the experienced passengers, it is, I suppose, nothing worse than an irritating public distraction from their pre-takeoff private distractions.

The only instruction that has really lodged in my memory, which I shall be sure to carry out when the time comes, is to take off my high heels before launching myself onto that slide!

P.S. Meanwhile, that monoglot Albanian shepherd is probably immersed in his by now well-thumbed and tattered copy of the *Tirana Times*—that is, if he isn't also illiterate—blessedly oblivious to the prospect of going down into the sea, not in the least bothered about the actual whereabouts of that flotation cushion, and wondering why his fellow passengers are all anxiously swiveling their heads in the widest arc permitted by their necks in order to pin down the location of that "nearest exit."

Islamophobia

———

Mullik, Heider Ali Hussein. "Fear of Muslims Helps Only ISIS." Op-ed. *New York Times*, December 4, 2015.

Nice try, but not quite watertight.

He writes, "Against the few Muslims who join a group like the Islamic State stand millions who reject extremism…"

Well, they may be "standing," but they are not standing "up" to be counted.

I am afraid this account of the situation is not exhaustive. The range of Muslim opinion runs a whole gamut of nuances.

First, there are what is indeed the relatively few who are so powerfully motivated as to run all the risks and overcome all the difficulties of actually going to join ISIS.

Then there is a larger number who would like to but can't actually bring themselves to do so.

Next, there are those who decide to stay where they are and do the bidding of ISIS on the spot. The numbers of those of this persuasion are unknowable, partly because they have simply failed in their attempts or have been foiled by law enforcement.

There must also inevitably be an even larger segment of Muslim opinion made up of those who, while unmotivated to risk life and limb in the ISIS cause, are sympathizers.

At the other end of the spectrum, there is what is no doubt the largest group, to whom the existence of ISIS is an embarrassment and who have no inclination whatsoever to join ISIS. Even if Donald Trump had actually been looking in that particular direction at the time the Twin Towers collapsed, and his line of sight hadn't actually been clogged by the clouds of dust that had arisen, he wouldn't actually have seen crowds of Muslims in the streets of Union City, New Jersey, to cheer the spectacle—certainly not clearly enough to see the expression on individual faces, identify their different ethnicities, interpret their cries, or even hear them.

This largest segment—a mostly silent majority—is even more uncountable. Finally, we come to the group of "good" Muslims represented by the author of this article—represented, that is, in a purely conventional sense, since we have no way of knowing how "representative" or "unrepresentative" are the views expressed in it or how many or how few American Muslims share these views. Even among those who do, there must be an, again uncountable, number, who are unwilling to go public with them and brave the disapproval, hostility, and even retaliation from other members of the Muslim community and even their own families.

The bottom line is that we don't know how many "good" Muslims there are in this country or, in any case, how to tell them from the "bad" ones. Hence arises the temptation in some quarters to "tar them all with the same brush."

Perhaps it would help if the "good" ones would pour into the streets in protest the next time innocent people—including Muslims—are murdered in the name of Islam, thus bringing that name, however unjustly, into disrepute. We never knew how much or little of a majority the "silent majority" actually was when it was first invoked by Richard Nixon in 1963 (and since then by a succession of others, notably televangelists and most recently Donald Trump, because, well, it was "silent"—and still is).

This appeal to the notion of "few" is often used in defense of unpopular causes, inter alia, by the police.

The police apologia after every rare instance of police misconduct that (1) *happens to be caught on camera* and (2) *comes into the public domain* always contains a reference to "a *few* bad apples." The truth is that because only a "few" of these instances ever come to light—and even fewer before the advent of iPhones— the vast majority of cases must constitute the submerged nine-tenths, or more likely ninety-nine-hundredths, of the iceberg, of which only the very tip breaks the surface.

The same reasoning also applies, inter alia, to political misconduct, principally in the form of corruption, where only "a few" errant politicians are caught in the act, exposed, brought to trial, convicted (often with great difficulty), and then actually punished. Indeed, it is precisely the improbability of exposure, conviction, and punishment that, far from acting as a deterrent, encourages those in positions of power to succumb to its temptations.

I give all credit to Heider Ali Hussein Mullik for having the courage to "reject" ISIS publicly, but who are these "millions" who also "reject" ISIS, and how does he know—and how do we know—whether they do or not, since he is one of the few who are willing to stand up and be counted?

A silent majority can always be claimed by the champions of any cause to be supporters of it, but the members of it are by definition silent and could equally well be claimed by champions of the opposing cause without fear of contradiction, or the prospect of validation!

KHRUSHCHEVIANA: SETTING THE RECORD STRAIGHT—SHOE BANGING AT THE UNITED NATIONS

———◆———

IF I MAY ADD A little oil to troubled waters—or fuel to the fire...

I was chief of the English Interpretation Section of the United Nations in New York from 1980 to 1994, and I have previously had occasion to attempt to track down chapter and verse in connection with the Khrushchev shoe-banging episode. It was a little like trying to locate the other end of a rainbow; no one but a leprechaun ever found a crock of gold there.

Not only was Khrushchev never given the floor on that occasion, but delegations' desks were not equipped with microphones at that time. Hence, whatever Russian words he may have uttered to accompany his percussive tantrum are lost to history—although not to impressionistic second- and thirdhand reconstructions—and for the reasons given above, neither should nor could have been interpreted into English (or any of the other UN official languages, for that matter).

This point is corroborated by the response of Harold Macmillan, the UK prime minister at the time, who was noisily interrupted twice by Khrushchev on another occasion during the same 1960 session of the General Assembly. At the time of the interruption, Macmillan was speaking from the rostrum of the GA and was in possession of the floor and the only live microphone in the hall. After the second outburst, Macmillan turned toward the president of the Assembly, Ambassador Bolan of Ireland, and said, "I should like that to be translated if he wants to say anything." Clearly, it had not been.

Macmillan had been deploring the failure of the Paris summit meeting of the "Big Four," which had been aborted owing to Khrushchev's walkout in protest at the lack of an official apology from President Eisenhower for the U-2 incident. The official Soviet version of Khrushchev's first attempt at heckling, which was issued the following day, was, "Don't send your spy planes to our country! Don't send your U-2s!"

On another occasion, at the same session where Khrushchev was formally in possession of the floor and the microphone, he did indeed call the Philippine ambassador, inter alia, a "kholui" and a "stavlennik." An older colleague who had been responsible for the Russian English interpretation at that meeting told me that he had said "jerk" for "kholui" and "stooge" 'for "stavlennik." Khrushchev may or may not have also used "lakei" in the same tirade.

KUZMA'S MOTHER

The source of the apocryphal notion that it was on one of these occasions at the 1960 UN General Assembly that Khrushchev used the expression *Ya pokazhy vam kuzkinu mat* may have been his own memoirs, where he writes that he took a Philippine delegate severely to task, telling him, in an English version, "You'd better watch out, or we'll show you Kuzma's mother!" His memories of what he said and did on various occasions have not always proved entirely reliable.

For purposes of simultaneous interpretation—as distinct from literary or other kinds of translation—discretion is always the better part of valor; and it is always advisable not to put too fine a point on utterances that are liable to give offense, something that, in any case, is not always an easy thing to recognize in the heat of battle! Whatever the etymology or origin of the expression, it seems to have come to mean the verbal equivalent of shaking one's fist, and the somewhat open-ended "We'll show you!" would do the trick without overcommitting the hapless interpreter.

"WE'LL BURY YOU"

The endless medieval disputations about *my vas pokhoronim* also seem to lose sight of the fact that on the notorious occasion(s) when it was uttered, the interpreter's English version was the product of simultaneous interpretation and not of pondered translation. The implication is that the interpreter should have said something different, or "better." "We will bury you" is not at all a bad rendering of the original. The unwary interpreter who strays too far from the literal in the course of heated debate is in something of a "lose/lose badly" situation. If he or she says "bury" for *pokhoronim*, Monday morning translators may tell him or her loftily that it should have been "outlive" or "survive." If he or she says "outlive" or "survive" and another participant in the meeting then reacts to the Soviet/Russian delegate's remark, the original Russian speaker may hear through the reverse, English to Russian, interpretation that he or she is understood to have said *perezhit* (outlive) or *vyzhit* (survive) when in fact he or she said *pokhoronit*, and he or she will then, not entirely unreasonably, pillory the unfortunate interpreter for "not knowing how to translate a simple Russian word like 'pokhoronit.'" The complexities are endless.

Like politics, simultaneous interpretation is the art of the possible, often in trying and even well-nigh impossible circumstances. To the extent that translation is an art rather than a science, there is practically no translation of a word, expression, or phrase that cannot be second-guessed, even when it has been pondered in tranquility. As any practitioner of the art can tell you, a rough-hewn, lame, halting, or even deficient translation can in context sometimes be a salvaging operation and a heroic feat of simultaneous interpretation.

Learning the Other Guy's Language

———

The Final Document of the Fourth International Congress of Translators of Literature, held in Moscow, issued on September 9, 2016, claimed that translators of Russian literature, or indeed any nation's literature, into other languages were making a great contribution to world peace on the grounds that they were promoting international "understanding."

This is just one more example of the widespread and fallacious "feel-good" notion that "learning the other guy's language" will (a) make you like him better, (b) make the two of you "understand" each other better, and hence (c) prevent the two of you from fighting each other, or at least reduce the likelihood of it.

The term "endangered species" is not applicable exclusively to flora and fauna but also applies to words, and when they die out because the speakers of the language in question no longer have a use for them, let them rest in peace. But when an obsolescent word like "cant" so perfectly denotes a current media-driven phenomenon of epidemic proportions, it deserves to be revived and put back in service. The *Oxford English Dictionary* defines it as "affected and insincere phraseology; language implying piety which does not exist." *Merriam-Webster* says: "the expression or repetition of conventional or trite opinions or sentiments, especially the insincere use of pious words." The word "sanctimony" alone is not enough to combat such overwhelming opposition and desperately needs the word "cant" as an ally in the struggle against the barrage of cant and sanctimony with which the media are blanketing the American public, never more so than—but by no means only—in the current endless presidential campaign season (May 2016).

It is telling—and depressing—that even one of the more thoughtful and perspicacious politicians of his era, President Obama, should have proved himself in thrall to one particularly widespread, enduring, sanctimonious, and fallacious notion. During a state visit by President Xi of China, he announced the One Million Strong initiative to increase fivefold the number of US K–12 students studying Mandarin, from two hundred thousand to one million, by 2020. Obama said, "If our countries are going to do more together around the world, then speaking each other's language, truly understanding each other, is a good place to start. To be sure, the goal of seeing one million students study-ing Mandarin in just five years is ambitious, but it is achievable; moreover, it is crucial. In fact, I would argue, we should get there faster."

This particular feel-good piety is repeated everywhere and on all occasions, reflecting a strongly held belief that speaking the other fellow's language— or even some nationality-transcending language, like Esperanto—necessarily helps you "understand" him and that this in turn will necessarily encourage you to like him. Traveling along this track, we arrive ultimately at the notion that the learning of foreign languages promotes xenophilia and hence peace among nations.

What we have here is essentially a classical reversal of cause and effect. It is not their attempts to learn "the other fellow's language" that make xenophiles well disposed to outsiders, but rather it is their well-meaning disposition that prompts them to try to "understand" the other fellow and learn his language. Xenophobes who attack Turks in Germany, Pakistanis in Britain, Algerians in France, not to mention ISIS and its acolytes—the list is endless—are quite indifferent to the proficiency, or lack of it, of their victims in German, English, French, and Arabic, respectively.

Part of the lure of this comforting conviction lies in the slippery ambiguity of the meaning(s) of the word "understanding." It swivels subtly back and forth between the purely *intellectual notion* of comprehension of the word, a version I shall call "understanding (1)" and a version I shall call "understanding (2)." The first is used in such contexts as understanding how to do quadratic equations or understanding a Latin sentence in Caesar's *Gallic Wars*. The second is used in purely *emotive contexts* with the meaning of sympathy, allegiance, alignment, and support.

Unfortunately, Latin sentences and quadratic equations by no means auto-matically endear themselves to those students who "understand (1)" them any more than Serbs and Croats feel any greater "understanding (2)" for each other just because they understand each other's language. Indeed, since the ending of open hostilities between them, they have been hard at work trying to make the distance between their respective languages as great as possible.

Here is a tiny sample of the endless list of cases where knowing "the other fellow's language" and even sharing the *same language* have somehow failed—and indeed, spectacularly failed—to endear the parties in question to each other. As far as cause and effect are concerned, the shoe may well be on the other foot. Some of the most murderous conflicts seem to arise precisely because the parties *do* share a common language and "understand" each other only too well.

Examples include German "Aryans" and German Jews, American slave owners and their slaves, Serbs and Croats, the North and the South in the American Civil War, Sunnis and Shiites, the French Revolution, the Russian 1917 Revolution, the sectarian "troubles" in Northern Ireland, and the Argentinian and Chilean "Dirty Wars."

On the other hand, the populations of Switzerland and Belgium, for all their schismatic tendencies, have lived together for a long time without bloodshed—*and without a common language.*

Another related, prevalent example of cant and sanctimony, just as widespread and pernicious, is that sporting competition (especially the Olympic Games) promotes friendship and peace among nations.

On November 6, 1995, the General Assembly of the United Nations adopted a resolution titled "Building a Peaceful and Better World through Sport and the Olympic Spirit." It has been two thousand years since the Olympic Games last temporarily suspended armed conflict, although without ending it. Since in ancient Greece, the Olympic Games were connected with the worship of the Olympic gods (a cult that was shared by all the Greek city-states), a truce was observed throughout the Games, except once, when Sparta transgressed and was penalized with a heavy fine.

Yet again, this is a reversal of cause and effect. Even if there were a shred of evidence that individual competitors in the Games actually get to know and like each other, they are not the people who decide whether, when, or with which countries their own country will go to war. In the United States, during the Vietnam War, a large segment of the American public vigorously and

vociferously protested against it while their government was vigorously pros-
ecuting it.

However, even if there were an abundance of evidence that a large number
of athletes or other citizens had close ties and warm relations with their counterparts in other countries as a result of sports competition, that would not,
and did not on five occasions, starting with the 1956 Melbourne Games, stop
governments from boycotting the Games for political reasons and prohibiting
their athletes from taking part.

The other five occasions were Tokyo 1964, Montreal 1976, Moscow 1980,
Los Angeles 1984, and Seoul 1988.

In this connection, it is worth pointing out that when Britain declared war
against Germany in 1939, it did so in spite of the fact that there was a strong
network of close and warm relationships between citizens of the two countries,
particularly between the influential aristocracies on both sides.

Another event that was particularly telling in this regard was the World
War I Christmas truce, a series of widespread but unofficial cease-fires along
the Western Front around Christmas 1914. In the week leading up to the holiday, German and British soldiers crossed trenches to exchange seasonal greet-
ings and talk. In these areas, men from both sides ventured into no-man's-land
on Christmas Eve and Christmas Day to mingle and exchange food and sou-
venirs. There were joint burial ceremonies and prisoner swaps, while several
meetings ended in carol singing. Men played games of football with one another.

They then resumed probably the most colossal mutual slaughter in the history of warfare up to that time in proportion to the four years of the duration
of World War I.

And as for World War II!

"Unsportsmanlike Conduct?"
From the *New York Times*, June 23, 2012:

> Seventy years ago, on Aug. 9, 1942, the stadium became the site of
> one of soccer's most infamous and disputed games, the so-called Death
> Match. With Kiev under German occupation during World War II,

a group of Ukrainian players defeated a military team of Germans thought to be from artillery and perhaps Luftwaffe units.

According to legend, the Germans warned the local team beforehand or at halftime that it had better lose the match, and when the Ukrainians ignored the threat and prevailed, key members of the team were killed in retribution.

So much for all the cant and sanctimony about "building a peaceful and better world through sport and the Olympic spirit."

And a footnote: In the 1980s, as Reagan and Gorbachev warmed to each other, "Citizen Exchanges" as a means of promoting friendship and peace were advocated by Gorbachev and enthusiastically endorsed by his US counterpart, Ronald "Evil Empire" Reagan.

Once again—this is nothing more or less than a reversal of cause and effect. Here we have *governments* promoting and, at least on one side, *permitting* such exchanges precisely because relations between the two governments had already warmed, and tensions between them had relaxed. For decades beforehand, many private individuals had been visiting each other's countries and forming friendly relations *often in spite of government disapproval and discouragement*, and precisely when tensions between the two governments were at their height.

October 29, 1985. First Sister Keenan, representing the Holy, stated, "War is not the way to resolve conflict."

a. "War" is not decided on in order to resolve conflict but in order to (i) repel aggression; (ii) undo injustice; and (iii) maintain or secure economic, territorial, or strategic advantage.
b. "War" can resolve conflict. Would Sister Keenan deny that World War II resolved that conflict, that the American Civil War resolved that conflict, or that the Gulf War (Desert Storm) resolved that conflict?

In one of his columns in the *Guardian*, Michael Frayn asked a $64,000 question: Would the pope go to war to prevent Baluba tribesmen from continuing peacefully to rape Belgian nuns in the Congo in the 1960s?

If we were to take pairs of nations around the world, such as Chad and Paraguay or Cambodia and Ireland, and rate them in terms of the likelihood of their going to war with each other, I have the feeling that this likelihood would turn out to be in *inverse proportion* to their knowledge and "understanding" of each other. Maybe we could even learn something from studying these "league tables" through trying to identify what it is about their relationships that makes the "league leaders" so unlikely to go to war with each other. We could extrapolate these factors and consider how to apply them to the relationships between those voted "most likely to." If it turned out, for example, that one of the factors was that the nearer nations were to great-power status, the more likely they were to go to war, then those who are at present frittering away their energies and public money on "furthering international understanding" could at least divert them in the useful direction of encouraging their leaders to divest themselves of their "great-power" attributes. This is not, however, a task that would be likely to appeal to the "international understanding-mongers" who can now work to prevent international, armed conflict—World War III—with the approval and even encouragement of their governments and fellow citizens. If however, they diverted their energies and oratory to the uphill and vastly more unpopular task of advocating deep cuts in military spending and the reduction of armed forces, they would be seen as dangerous subversives playing into the hands of their countries' enemies. A perfect example comes to mind—that of the abrupt volte-face of the British Communist Party, which, after the German invasion of Poland, opposed the declaration of war on Germany by Chamberlain (the British prime minister), declaring it an imperialist war on orders from Stalin after his signing of the Molotov-Ribbentrop Pact with Hitler's Germany. However, almost overnight, the party hailed it as a war against fascism to be supported to the hilt, after Germany stabbed Stalin in the back by a sudden invasion of the Soviet Union.

Gorbachev's idea of "citizen exchanges" seemed to be that "private exchanges" would do the trick on the Western side, and that on the Soviet side it should be "official delegations," when in fact, both sides were mistaking effect for cause and nurturing a dangerous or at best futile illusion. One of the UN bodies that are in the front line of the struggle for peace, such as the Peace Studies Unit or the University for Peace, not to mention the innumerable bodies dedicated to the inherently undoable task of disarmament, could do a lot worse than conduct a poll in various countries. Citizens would be asked to rank the world's countries in order of the likelihood of a given country's going to war with their own country. They could also be asked to rank the world's countries in order of their knowledge and "understanding" of them. The results of such a survey could provide a useful and probably eye-opening empirical basis for a true correlation between the likelihood of warfare and "international understanding." I doubt the Serbs and the Croatians are at each other's throats because they know and "understand" each other less well than, say, the Irish and the Cambodians.

The only useful approach to peace studies is to analyze the following:

1. How and why governments start wars—a relatively easy task
2. How they are able to mobilize public opinion in favor of them—a wellnigh impossible task (The problem is that in most nation-states, the very fact that the citizens are told that their country is at war is enough to mobilize the critical mass of public opinion in its favor.)
3. How, if at all, these dynamics can be interfered with or undermined

Improving Relations

Does improving relations between peoples really make war less likely? What about civil wars and the Falklands War? Also, do nations that are remote from each other ipso facto feel hostile to each other? Or is it close neighbors that are most likely to? Can we extrapolate usefully from relations between individuals? Why do people within given communities murder each other more frequently than they do outsiders—for example, Chinatown, Harlem, Spanish Harlem, and the Mafia itself—not to mention members of the same families?

The Vietnam War provides further evidence from another angle. It was waged in spite of the fact that there was widespread opposition to the war *even within* one of the warring states to a war against a people the US population had little or no knowledge of or contact with.

Oral Gratification in the Course of Passive Entertainment (Ogicpe), with an Excursion into Cornflakes and Breakfast Via Popcorn

———————

Probably the archetype is the standard practice of moviegoers to eat, or more specifically to munch, while watching movies in the cinema and to a less observable extent while watching TV at home. However, to judge by the number of TV commercials that depict families watching TV and chomping either the fodder being advertised or even some other product, there are strong indications that this is a widespread lifestyle phenomenon—in the United States at least—that tends to reach its climax during the Super Bowl.

As in the case of other social phenomena, it's hard to know whether this is the result of successful marketing or a response by the market to a spontaneous human impulse or need for oral gratification while being passively entertained.

This habit is also widespread among spectators at major live sports events in the United States. There seems to be no evidence of tailgate barbecues at European or Latin American soccer matches, but this may have something to do with the extraordinarily high American rate of automobile ownership, use, and dependence, not to mention an equally extraordinary high ratio of the more macho vehicles with tailgates, all of which demand a commensurate proliferation of parking lots at sports venues.

By contrast, neither popcorn nor tailgate parties generally accompany "high culture" entertainment such as opera, theater, ballet, and classical music concerts. Nor are eating and drinking in evidence at upmarket sports like tennis and polo—that is to say, while the audience are in their seats spectating and not ingesting.

The key to the difference here might be thought to be due to class differ-ences, but a key practical difference in the "high culture" category is that the sight, smell, and, above all, the sound of food being handled, unwrapped, and eaten—precisely the "snap, crackle, and pop" that is held to be such a signifi-cant attraction of Rice Krispies—might not only be thought to be impolite to the performers but also might actually put them off their stroke. This is not so at your football stadium. Major eating and drinking took place at the old New York Giants stadium back in the 1960s and 1970s, when the actual play on the field seemed to be incidental to the partying in the stands, and a "same time next year" mood prevailed. The actual play itself was, in any case, well-nigh impossible to follow from the higher tiers, except for those zealots who tried their best to keep in touch with the play by listening to their crackling portable radios for the commentary.

So, which was the egg and which the chicken? Was the need created by the movie and/or popcorn industry, or did they somehow detect and sniff out the existence of this "need" and move in to exploit and satisfy it? Perhaps a clue would be offered by an answer to the egg-and-chicken riddle of why and how cornflakes—with shredded wheat and other attractively packaged, sugar-inten-sive cereals hot on their heels—came to be consecrated as the indispensable breakfast (and only breakfast) comestible, except for "outliers" like Seinfeld.

In 1878, the American bowel health fanatic and sex abstainer Harvey Kellogg invented cornflakes, thus creating a breakfast revolution. Actually, it was more like a religion in that it recruited more followers than most of the traditional ones and as if eating processed cereals for breakfast was a command-ment brought down by Moses from Mount Sinai. Its dictates are followed more scrupulously, and indeed more religiously, than any of the other ten, especially in the English-speaking world. Throughout human history, and today in most of the world, people ate—and still eat—whatever food comes to hand, regard-less of the nomenclature of the meal or the time of day. It's my guess that the millions who consume Mr. Kellogg's invention at breakfast do so less because of what he claimed were its antimasturbatory and intestinal cleansing effects than because it doesn't require any preparation or cooking and leaves a minimum of mess and dirty dishes and utensils.

To judge by the eating habits of his time and class, as recorded by Samuel Pepys, it seems that if the roast beef of old England was good enough for dinner, it was good enough for breakfast. To wit: Pepys recorded that "on September 9th, I went with Capt. Morrice at his desire into the King's Privy Kitchen to Mr. Sayres, the Master-Cooke, and there we had a good slice of beef or two to our breakfast." From the time of the Tudors, when breakfast started to be recognized as a meal, until the Kellogg era, there seems to be no evidence of any particular foodstuff being limited to breakfast, or indeed of any fish, flesh, or fowl ever being excluded from it.

A related egg-and-chicken riddle that doesn't quite go back as far as the Sphinx is the following: Did the creators of Rice Krispies discover through in-depth market research that out there among the breakfasting multitudes was an unconsummated craving not only for oral but also for aural gratification at breakfast time and then set their scientists to work to satisfy that craving?

Or did they happen to observe their Rice Krispies snapping, crackling, and popping spontaneously when they came into contact with milk and simply make a virtue out of necessity, thus creating a "need" instead of merely satisfying one?

More thorough research than I am prepared to undertake into the memoirs of the Roman slaves who cleaned up after gladiatorial shows at the Coliseum and chariot races at the Circus Maximus and into those of their Greek counterparts, who swept up after the Olympic Games at Delphi, might yield fascinating evidence in the form of discarded containers and wrappings as to what was being munched and crunched by ancient spectators. I would hope that it was not as insipid and dull as the panem that Juvenal suggested accompanied the circenses.

In the modern world, the OGICPE phenomenon appears to have started in English-speaking quarters, along with the advent of the cinema and television, and has no doubt spread to all those parts of the world that have been pervaded by those twin sources of the most passive kind of entertainment ever known.

Do psychiatrists and psychologists believe that there may be a deeper Freudian connection between passive entertainment and oral gratification?

PHILOSOPHY

NEW YORK TIMES WEEK IN Review, March 8, 1998

"Philosophers Ponder a Therapy Gold Mine," by Joe Sharkey

"They are hanging out their shingles. Springing from a movement that began in Germany in the 1980s, a small but growing number of American philosophers have opened private practices as 'philosopher practitioners,' offering a therapy based on the idea that solutions to many personal, moral and ethical problems can be found not in psychotherapy or Prozac but deep within the 2,500-year-old body of philosophical discourse."

If there is any discipline that should set an example of the need to define one's terms—if any enlightenment or clarity is to result from discourse—it should be philosophy. Yet it is the very nebulousness of the notion of "philosophy" and the vague feeling that it somehow enjoys a privileged connection with or access to "wisdom"—which is what the second element ("-sophy") in the word originally meant—that seems to lend it its particular mystique, glamor, and allure.

Socrates himself actually did not teach what would pass for philosophy on a contemporary college campus, and he would in any case not be allowed to, with his not possessing a PhD in "philosophy" or a degree or diploma in anything, for that matter, not to mention his dress code, unconventional even by the loose and would-be eccentric standards of the academy. Indeed, there seems to be no actual evidence that he could read or write. Nor is there any record whatever of his helping people with their "problems," for a fee. What he taught was rather how to win arguments in court, political debate, or just for the hell of it.

If Socrates could only have gotten hold of an appropriately docile and compliant interlocutor and were himself in a suitably agnostic frame of mind about the subject and wanted to get to the bottom of what exactly it was that people styling themselves philosophers were up to, he might have conducted a dialogue along something like the following lines.

Socrates: "What is it that medical doctors are better at than laymen?"

Docile and Compliant Interlocutor: "Why, Socrates, they are better at diagnosing and treating illness."

Soc.: "What about civil engineers?"

D and CI: "Well, Socrates, they are better at building bridges, roads, and airports."

Soc.: "What about historians?"

D and CI: "They are better at knowing what happened in the past—and maybe also why and how—as well as knowing how to find out about it."

Soc.: "And what about philosophers?"

(Here, philosophers are invited to supply an answer that does not include the word "philosophy" or any of its derivatives, an answer that would leave a layman understanding what it was that a philosopher was better at than himself.)

D and CI: "Well, I suppose they are better at thinking about things."

Soc.: "But surely doctors are better than the rest of us at thinking about illness?"

D and CI: "Certainly, Socrates."

Soc.: "And civil engineers are better at thinking about building bridges, roads, and the like?"

D and CI: "Of course, Socrates."

Soc.: "And historians about past events?"

D and CI: "Undoubtedly!"

Soc.: "So if all these experts are better at thinking about their specialties than the rest of us, what is it that philosophers are better at thinking about than us?"

D and CI: "Well, about those problems that philosophers think about…"

Soc.: "Such as?"

D and CI: "Well, for example, moral, political, and logical problems, problems about 'meaning' and so on."

Soc.: "But are they more likely to be 'right' about such moral and political subjects such as abortion, crime and punishment, how to combat ISIS, free health care, and the like than the rest of us, in the same way that doctors, gardeners, and civil engineers—the experts in *their* own fields—have demonstrated that they are and are largely accepted as being more likely to be right about treating sickness, planting flowers, and building bridges?"

Furthermore, in order for the possibility to exist that philosophers as a corps are more likely to be "right" about any of the problems they study than the rest of us—and it still has not been established how those problems can be categorized except by the circular definition of "philosophical"—they have to establish first a body of consensus among themselves about basic rules, laws, first principles, or findings governing their area of expertise.

After all, civil engineers proceed from an agreed consensus on the laws of mechanics—and that is why the bridges they build rarely fall down—and even historians are agreed about where and how to look for evidence about what happened in the past, even though they may disagree about interpretations of that evidence, but where is the evidence that philosophers have "solved"—to their collective satisfaction—any of the "problems" they study and thus that they possess better techniques for solving them than the rest of us?

An engineer, a historian, a computer hacker, or a basketball coach may all be as wise or smart at what they do as a philosopher or the holder of a PhD in philosophy—if that is the same thing—is at whatever it is that he does. But only Zeus knows what the somewhat above-average Joe who is prepared to part with one hundred dollars an hour for the privilege of sharing his problems with one, thinks *that* is. The only thing the general public really knows for sure about what PhDs in philosophy actually do is that they teach whatever it is to others.

The wisdom that PhDs in philosophy may be deemed to possess about whatever their subject is, has no necessary connection with know-how about solving or helping to solve such problems as "job-related stress," "marital infidelity," "parenting," "unemployment," "drug addiction," and all those "problems" that exist in the no-man's-land between the medical (e.g., arthritis and toothache) and the psychiatric (e.g., anxiety and depression).

Is there anything that would have equipped "philosophers" to help Hamlet with his problem of whether "to be or not to be"? Or to advise Julius Caesar whether or not to cross that Rubicon?

Is there anything that qualifies a "philosopher"—any more than an expert in history, computer technology, or basketball—to advise a client on "long-term goals" and "relationships"?

The author of the article and his interlocutors persistently avoid any mention of what it is that philosophers do, or what it is about the substance or content of their subject that equips or qualifies them "to treat refugees from psychotherapy"—even as "gatekeepers" under the "strict supervision of psychologists or psychiatrists." Professor Freedheim seems to suggest that the practice of philosophy vis-à-vis the practice of psychotherapy is somehow analogous to the role of nurse practitioners or "barefoot doctors" vis-à-vis properly qualified medical practitioners. Philosophy is no more the handmaiden of, or an apprenticeship for, psychotherapy than expertise in any other field or academic discipline. If it is, why is even the slightest suggestion of *why or how* so conspicuously missing from the article?

The nearest thing to the will-o'-the-wisp of a reason offered by a "philosopher practitioner" in the article was that "clients may find it appealing that there is no stigma attached to counseling on philosophy." Well, I suppose there's no stigma attached to confiding your problems to your pet cat, either.

The tenor of the article suggests that the whole point of such counseling by philosophers is that "philosophy" is *brought to bear on or applied to* the client's problems, rather than the fact that what these "refugees from psychotherapy" are looking for is *"counseling on philosophy."* But whatever the speaker of these words may have meant by "counseling on philosophy," there is just as little stigma attached to counseling on any of a hundred other academic disciplines, occupations, and areas of expertise by their practitioners.

It is not clear whether the author is defining a "philosopher," for the purposes of the clinical practice referred to in this article, as someone who holds a PhD in philosophy. Anyone who knows any PhDs in philosophy knows not only that they by no means necessarily possess a monopoly on "wisdom," but also that they may not even have more than their fair share of it.

Experts in any academic discipline may be assumed to be better at solving problems within that discipline than those outside the discipline. Because of the greater transparency of their fields of expertise, the public at large has a rough idea of what kinds of problem PhDs in archaeology, chemistry, and history are good at solving. So if a member of the public needs to know whether a potsherd he has found on the Acropolis is a genuine antique, whether he can make an explosive by mixing saltpeter, glycerin, and honey, or whether the Great War was triggered by the assassination of an Archduke in Sarajevo, he knows where to turn. If members of the public actually knew what kinds of problems "philosophers" actually spend their time attempting to solve—presumably more successfully than nonphilosophers—they would be quite unable to understand what these problems were and would certainly not recognize them as remotely connected with any problem that had ever troubled them. Problems that have bothered philosophers down the ages include what is truth, what is beauty, whether everything is made of water, whether we can really *know* anything, what to do when you arrive at the railway station and find a notice on the platform reading "The next train has just left," how much does a soul weigh, whether a priori synthetic propositions are possible, whether you can have a pain in my leg, and whether God is a proper name. For all I know, it may be that the question of whether a solution to a philosophical problem is possible is *itself* a philosophical problem.

It is hard to imagine what would induce someone suffering from depression or anxiety to invest a substantial sum of money in a session with this kind of expert, particularly when further inquiry would reveal that even—or perhaps especially—there never seems to exist any stable body of consensus among the experts about the solutions to these problems, or even about whether these are the right problems that philosophers should be trying to solve! Furthermore, their problems seem to change from one generation to another, from one country or continent to another, and from one school to another—and not because they have been solved!

This raises the whole question of what the titles or names of academic disciplines reveal or mask. There is the fluctuation or confusion between studying and teaching something and actually *doing* it. In some cases the very nature of the discipline precludes it from being "done"—for example, history and geography. Historians and geographers know a lot about their subjects, and they write about them and may even teach them, but they cannot be said to "do" them in the sense that mathematicians and biologists can, or to practice them in the sense that lawyers and civil engineers can. People are sometimes said to have "made" history, but they are not usually "historians." So only in some disciplines it is even possible for the teacher of it to be a "practitioner" or exponent of it. Even in disciplines where it is possible, the practical likelihood of the teacher also being a practitioner varies considerably (e.g., accountancy, law, medicine, literature, mathematics). You cannot teach mathematics, for example, without being able to do it, but you can certainly teach literature or basketball without being able to "do" it.

Could it be that one of the notions lurking behind the idea that philosophers are better qualified to advise people about their problems, is that, to the extent that the study of formal logic has traditionally formed part of the academic discipline of philosophy, philosophers are therefore likely to be more "logical" or better at exercising logic and applying it to "life problems" than the rest of us? If so, then the "Socratic" question again arises. Since the exercise of logic applies to all disciplines—a horse trainer cannot successfully train horses without bringing logic to bear—what reason is there to suppose not only that philosophers apply it more effectively to the study of philosophy than, say, computer experts do to designing programs, but also that they can apply logic more successfully to their own life problems and those of others? In practice, there is much more evidence that in disciplines ranging from computer technology to engineering, surgery, and aeronautics, logical reasoning has successfully been brought to bear. The crucial difference is that ultimately, all such disciplines are sustained, and progress, on the basis of a stable conceptual consensus among the experts, is something that is conspicuously lacking in the field of philosophy. To be fair, philosophers are not alone in this. Economics, which affects the trappings of hard science and whose doctrines, unlike those of philosophy, can have tangible, everyday, bottom-line consequences, presents a similar welter of conflicting, if not downright irreconcilable, views and doctrines. Any politician of whatever stripe can always be sure to find a pet economics professor to lend credibility and respectability to whatever visceral policies he or she may favor.

This article is very short on information about what "philosopher-practitioners" actually do with their clients. If, as must be the case, they draw on their professional expertise as philosophers and impart it to their clients, surely this is precisely what they do with students in their classrooms. So when all the dust has settled and the trendy nomenclature has been stripped away, is all this really just about philosophy lessons repackaged to attract "refugees from psychotherapy"?

We flounder in a culture where we are conditioned to believe that everything that hurts, frightens, or frustrates us in life is a "problem" and as such can be solved by the right expert—a culture where even the "self-help" books that dominate best-seller lists are written by self-appointed experts or gurus who tell us how to help ourselves—provided we follow their prescriptions!

Of course, the dialogue may take any number of different tacks, including some kind of retreat to the position that the "problems" studied by philosophers are somehow inaccessible to laymen. Of course, if that were true, surely it is as likely—or unlikely—that the problems of laymen, their potential "patients," would be equally inaccessible to philosophers.

Could it be that, like the character M. Jourdain in Moliere's play, who was so gratified to learn that he had been writing "prose" all his life without knowing it, I have just been *doing* philosophy without knowing it, or have I merely been philosoph-*iz*-ing?

PROFESSIONAL DEFORMATIONS

———◆———

VERY OFTEN, ONE LANGUAGE HAS coined a term for a phenomenon that is just as common in countries where other languages are spoken, but for which, for one reason or another, other languages have not found a convenient term.

There is a well-established French term for the way in which professions and occupations tend to leave their mark on the behavior, attitudes, and mentality of their members. The expression *déformation professionelle* suggests that the behavior in question is somehow not standard and perhaps aberrant, undesirable, reprehensible, even antisocial, and sometimes simply a little comical.

This thought was first triggered in connection with the media. Like spectators of an inherently dangerous spectacle, such as motor racing, even the casual consumer of the TV news product is nursing the subconscious hope, spiced with a trace of guilt—for what is known as a "thrill"—that is, the prospect that something may or will go wrong.

As the media interface and seamlessly merge with the entertainment business, so do their values and priorities intertwine.

When we watch a James Bond movie, a horror flick, or even a "serious" but equally harrowing war, crime, or disaster documentary, we get our kicks from the "sweet and sour" contrast between the mayhem and violence on the screen and our own womblike, cozy, cocooned, anonymous, popcorn-chomping comfort, security, and immunity in the darkened movie house. Coiled up slyly and furtively in that tiny cranny in a dark corner of the conscience of every one of us is this nasty little worm that thrives on the pain and trouble of others. How many of us who witnessed the midair disaster of the disintegration of the space shuttle *Columbia* experienced only those emotions we would have been willing to share in a live interview with the reporter from our favorite TV evening news program?

When reports of fresh disaster come in to the newsroom just in time for "breaking news" in prime time, how does this professional shot in the arm stack up against the civically correct distress and outrage that all of us, including those who earn their living in the media, are supposed to feel for the sufferings and afflictions of our fellow men? People who work in the news business cannot help but have a vested interest in news. News nearly always means bad news. Bad news nearly always involves the suffering and distress of others. If you have a vested interest—professional or other—in something, you can hardly fail to welcome it in some shape or form and in some degree. The logic is inexorable.

People in the news business are in the business of welcoming, and thus having hoped for, at some level of consciousness, the misfortunes of others. It is not, of course, always or entirely a matter of the people concerned being molded, formed, or conditioned by the job they happen to be doing. Some allowance must always be made for the fact that some occupations, particularly at the professional level, where the element of choice and inclination tends to be greater, are likely to attract people of a particular temperament, who are in any case predisposed to acquiring the "professional deformation" of their chosen occupation.

While few coal miners are likely to be instinctively drawn to coal dust or have a natural aversion to daylight, it is unlikely that many policemen have an instinctive distaste for disciplining others, that courtroom lawyers are averse to argumentation, that many priests are squeamish about preaching, or that many surgeons cannot stand the sight of blood.

There are different ways in which certain occupations tend to marginalize their practitioners in terms of mainstream civic virtue or public morality. Sometimes the conditioning factor is the actual purpose of the work itself, or a distorted perception of it, especially the kind of work that can attract the wrong people for the wrong reasons. Sometimes it is an occupation that offers an unusual degree of opportunity or temptation to transgress socially accepted norms.

Politics and show business may or may not tend to attract people with the appropriate propensities, but it is undeniable that they both provide more than their fair share of temptation and opportunity for corruption in the first and for sexual impropriety in the second.

Practitioners of occupations such as stockbroking, medicine, and teaching (an occupation that casts a very wide net, embracing sports instructors and coaches of all kinds) have professional vested interests that can—and do— conflict with those of the clients, patients, students, and players with whom they interact professionally. How rarely do tennis instructors or music teachers actively discourage even hopeless cases from continuing lessons? Stockbrokers can and do benefit from maximizing the number of transactions, which may or may not maximize the value of their clients' investments. Doctors—and not least fringe medicine practitioners like chiropractors—do better financially by maximizing visits and treatments rather than "curing" their patients. Stephen Potter, the pioneer and founder of "Gamesmanship," plays this element for laughs in the chapter "Doctormanship" in his book *Lifemanship*, where he warns of the "one-upmanship" of the clothed over the unclothed and offers advice about how to counter it. Other occupations that in some way or other place practitioners in some kind of authority over their clients also provide more than their fair share of opportunity and temptation. The list could continue.

All occupations breed some kind or degree of "professional" deformations or behavioral patterns that deviate from the norm. The word "deviate" has unfortunately taken on an exclusively pejorative connotation, when in fact people can deviate upward as well as downward. Ministers of religion, for example, are professionally bound to be "nicer" than average to other people, and they may actually become so in the exercise of their profession in spite of the countervailing temptations and·opportunities open to those of their calling. Of course, it may be easier for them to be "nicer," since the members of their congregations naturally tend to treat *them* with particular respect and consideration.

The acting branch of show business seems to provide more temptation and opportunity for sexual adventures. The very nature of the medium provides a much more erotic or titillating kind of interaction with fellow practitioners, who, in addition, tend to be above average in terms of physical attractiveness. Furthermore, it takes actors away from their normal domestic routines, habitats, and timetables so that they spend more concentrated, "round-the-clock" time than usual with each other "out of office hours"—time that does not have to be accounted for by having had to "stay late at the office."

The same syndrome of temptation and opportunity, not to mention impunity, actual or perceived, is inherent also in such occupations as policeman, soldier, priest, prison guard, as well as—in some societies more than others—public officials and politicians. To the extent that it is an "occupation," the landlord function is also one that is liable to be "bad for the character." Lawyers are, of course, a special case and have to be broken down into the many and varied functions they perform. The temptations and opportunities inherent in those practices where lawyers themselves not only set their hourly fees but also determine independently and, as far as the client is concerned, arbitrarily, their "billable hours" need no explaining.

Over and above the overriding influence of one's occupation, the different "roles" a person plays in the course of a lifetime can also leave their mark, although a far less enduring one, on personality and behavior.

Consider the example of motorists. For some, of course, such as taxi, bus, and truck drivers, driving, and its corollary of sharing the road with other users, is an occupation. For most others, it is a "role," or a function they perform for a portion of their waking lives. For those who live outside the major cities of the United States, driving consumes a particularly great part of their waking time and may therefore exert a correspondingly greater influence on their behavior and temperament. Motorists tend to come into "contact" with each other in the seated position, something that in itself is a great leveler, thus reducing the influence of relative size—and indeed age—in random encounters between human males. Hence, in this "role," the "clutch courage" that transforms the average muted, inoffensive, circumspect, and indeed timorous pedestrian, once he is seated behind the wheel of a car, into a hermetically sealed and encapsulated thug (citizen) and licenses him to hurl unheard abuse with impunity at what may very well be his much more powerful fellow citizen is fascinating in its own right. This phenomenon has lately become known as "road rage" and is a prime example of "role deformation."

It would be an arduous but fascinating task—one that probably only a benevolent and ingenious utopian dictator could perform—to work out the complex regulations that would ensure that the "deformations" and self-interest of practitioners of these various occupations are brought into line with the best interests of the clients or the members of the public they serve. Obviously, even "popularly elected" legislatures of the most advanced democracies cannot be trusted to do this work, as has been demonstrated by the recent revelations of the peculations of members of the mother of parliaments herself and the endemic corruption of the New York State legislature—only two of the latest in the long list of cases where politicians have succumbed to the heady mixture of temptation, opportunity, and perceived impunity afforded by their occupation to feather their own nests at the expense of the public they like to claim they "serve." And it should not be forgotten that even this long list of those who happen to have been exposed must be the mere tip of the iceberg of those whose peccadillos and peculations have escaped public notice.

Oh, did I mention salesmen?

Proverbs: the Double-Headed Coin— Thesis, Antithesis, but no Synthesis!

RUSSIANS REFER TO PROVERBS AS "popular wisdom" (*narodnaya mudrost*), but what's so *wise* about comforting Juliet, who hasn't heard from Romeo since he left for Venice, by telling her that "absence makes the heart grow fonder" while some old pessimist in Venice is telling Romeo, who is complaining that he hasn't heard from Juliet for a long time, to forget her: "out of sight, out of mind"? There seems to be no middle course to steer between the Scylla and Charybdis of these two antithetical and mutually canceling examples of folk "wisdom."

In this particular case, it so happens that "absence makes the heart grow fonder" yields another antithesis: "familiarity breeds contempt," or "no man is a hero to his valet."

If "too many cooks" didn't seem "to spoil the broth" in one instance, then how about conferring on the occasion the accolade of "two heads are better than one"?

The true wisdom of the proverb, or "folk wisdom," as it is known in Russian, lies in the canny hedging of its bets until the horse race is over and then placing your bet on the winner.

If one worked at it hard enough, I have no doubt one would find that for every proverb, there is an equal and opposite one, which if applied judiciously to the occasion seems to be the perfect, infallible, and telling epitaph to it. It would seem that whatever proverbs encapsulate, it is not wisdom, unless there can be wisdom without truth—and truth cannot be self-contradictory. What is it then that brings them into being, and what is their function? Like all clichés and fossilized, ready-made expressions, they obviate the rigors of independent thought and the evaluation of each case on its merits. When they are used *after* the results are in, they yield the self-satisfaction of a retrospective "I told you so."

During my time at the United Nations, proverbs were frequently the last—and first—resort of Soviet representatives as a way of triumphantly clinching an argument. (If patriotism is the last resort of the scoundrel, of whom is the proverb the last resort?) The corresponding resort of Hispanic representatives was the invoking of authoritative and illustrious *proceres* (heroes, legendary or otherwise), just as the favorite argument clincher of the Francophones was often the crushing and ungainsayable *pensée* of an illustrious and preferably deceased literary immortal.

Is the "wisdom" of folk wisdom, then, deeper than mere surface logic? Does each proverb contain a kernel or part of the truth in certain circumstances? Sometimes it *appears better* with hindsight—to have "looked before you leapt," and at other times it appears that you were "lost because you hesitated." But if we examine the actual use of proverbs in real life, how often will we find that such wisdom as they bring to bear is of the same "after-the-event" variety favored notoriously by sports commentators?

Is it always after the broth has been brought to the table that someone tellingly exclaims, "Too many cooks!"? Or, in this particular case, does the "wisdom" lie in the degree, or "dosage," as does wisdom in pharmacology, so that "two heads" is the optimum number of cooks for broth production but three or more are counterproductive?

In "look before you leap," however, we have no such quantitative boundary—at least, it is not spelled out. Perhaps what is implied is that one should always exercise a certain amount of caution, but not too much. The trouble is that in human endeavor, calculation has to stop at some point, and commitment has to take over before there can be certainty as to consequences. Do all proverbs, then, in the end, come down to the banal and ultimately tautological advice that we shouldn't really do anything too much or too little? If so, we only really need one all-embracing, overarching, "architechtonic" proverb and, as so often, the Greeks had a word—or a phrase—for it: *meeden agan* (nothing to excess). And what is excess? Well, if something you do doesn't work or works out badly, then clearly you went too far—or not far enough! Therein, perhaps, lies the ultimate wisdom of the "mother of all proverbs" and her teeming progeny; if you act in accordance with it, you can't go wrong—unless, of course, you did go wrong, in which case you should obviously have chosen a different proverb!

I can't help wondering if *Vogue* magazine, which has famously proclaimed to its readers, "You can never be too rich or too thin," will ever have the modesty, good faith, and of course, the wisdom to recant and come out one day with a cover proclaiming to those readers who haven't yet succumbed to anorexia, "*Too much* of anything is bad for you by definition—even *too little* food."

AMATEUR MUSICIANSHIP: QUI S'EXCUSE, S'ACCUSE

G. B. SHAW, OR AT least a character in one of his plays, once said, "Hell is full of musical amateurs."

Ah, yes, but before they get to hell, they have to serve time in the purgatory of an amateur music course/workshop/camp, where so much self-esteem is at stake that "musicianmanship" becomes as important an accomplishment as musicianship itself. Does the Yeovil School of Lifemanship have a Department of Musicianmanship? This is doubtful since, although this area of human endeavor is actually as fertile a Lifeman's terrain as golf is to a Gamesman, evidently Stephen Potter, the founder, creator, or discoverer of "Gamesmanship" was blithely oblivious to the fact that music, at least as much as games, was something that one *plays*!

What follows are a few examples picked up at random at the camps, workshops, and courses of impromptu, would-be face-saving ploys hastily produced at critical moments during play when a member of an ensemble has just screwed up.

1. "I haven't touched my flute since..." (At this point, the speaker notices the presence of x, an oboe player, and hastily adds, "I last played it with x.")
2. "I've only played this in the string version." Pianist in the Beethoven Piano and Winds Quintet.
3. "You started twice."
4. "I don't understand your 'one, two, three.'"

5. During *Mládí* (Janacek), the oboist, referring to a passage begun on the beat by the bass clarinet and after screwing up: "You didn't kind of sniff this time when you began."

6. Hindemith's *Kammermusik*, second movement, six bars after G, coach to bassoonist: "You put in an extra crotchet there!" Bassoonist: "I think I need to see what the piccolo's doing there."

7. Viola. "My A string peg's gone and dehydrated on me."

8. After a few bars into a given movement, usually, but not exclusively, a minuet, a useful ploy for slurring over a screw-up is for the guilty party to initiate the "minuet wrangle."

   Near the start of any movement, dwelling on the subject in particularly loving detail in minuets is recommended if you have just screwed up. A useful attention-distracting ploy is to start a long, drawn-out wrangle about whether to observe the repeat signs, and if so, which ones, keeping in reserve for backup the issue of whether and where to observe the da capo. Ultimately, it is important to observe the "rules of engagement," which prescribe that, after at least one participant has testily pointed out that more time has now elapsed than playing the whole damned movement "as written" would have taken, a grudging consensus is usually reached to play it as written.

   Research has revealed that this process generally takes no more than 2.7 times as long as simply playing it that way to begin with.

9. "Wincemanship"

   When playing wrong notes, learn to wince significantly in the direction of another player. Advanced—and anatomically gifted—practitioners of "wincemanship" have mastered the technique of rolling their eyes rightward to meet the eyes of a fellow winceman in the course of a leftward wince in the direction of a selected scapegoat.

10. Perfect-pitchmanship

    Both to suggest a superior—and sorely tried—sensitivity and, if necessary, to muffle, obscure, and cover up a major screw-up on your own part, with even a subtle suggestion that the affront to your sensitivity was the reason for it, stop playing and say with just a hint of gritted teeth, "maybe we'd better (re)tune."

In any case, participate with frowning intensity in the tuning-of-the-A charade at the start of the session, making a big show of minor adjustments to your instrument. You can then sanctimoniously play every other note on your instrument out of tune for the rest of the session.

11. The page-turning kerfuffle

The page turn has been known to be effective but should be seen as an opportunity rather than a nuisance. It is a ploy to be used sparingly. If you should be fortunate enough to screw up within, say, eight bars of a page turn—before or after—make a big show of clumsily mismanaging the actual page turn. In the direst of emergencies, if you have lost all hope of making a dignified recovery and reentry, with only the tiniest extra effort you can bring your stand crashing down in maximum disarray, with all the music on it flying unaerodynamically to the floor in asymmetrical heaps, and your ensemble screeching to a halt.

12. Total abstinence

This is a ploy whose effectiveness should not be underestimated in the right circumstances and one that should be used much more frequently by students of blame-and-shame evasionmanship. The greater the number of players in the ensemble, the more total is their collective and solipsistic obliviousness to what anyone else is playing and indeed to whether anyone is playing at all. It is not amor that omnia vincit, but rather a dignified silence. Ask any viola player!

13. The right note at the wrong time is no longer the right note—unless, like so many, you proceed from the premise that it is not your fault that some of the other, flashier players got through their sixteenth note/semiquaver staccato passage faster than you did.

14. Do not make the primitive mistake of assuming that the various dynamic, phrasing, and other markings with which your part is sprinkled are there to convey the composer's intentions about how the music is to be played—not at all! They are there to help you when you screw up.

When you are anything between acutely aware and dimly suspicious that you are hopelessly lost, stop the show, and with a suggestion of exasperation, scold everyone, even humbly including yourself, for failing

duly to observe some crescendo or other—or, better still, a diminu-
endo, as being slightly more of a testimony to the subtlety and sensitivity of your musicianship (not to be confused with Musicianmanship!),
or a legato (preferably a dotted one, for the same reason), somewhere
in the vicinity of the screeching halt.

15. Tempomanship

Again, do not neglect any opportunity to parlay a passing tacti-
cal advantage into a display of your superior musical sensitivity with,
of course, the payoff of the consequent discomfiture or one-downness
of your fellow players. When you have nothing more demanding than
slowish one-eighth notes, step up the tempo. If protests are entered,
counter with the confident assertion that the Berliner Ensemble or
the Amadeus Quartet always plays it at that—that is, your own, arbitrarily stepped-up—tempo. However, when confronted with acciden-
tal-strewn, sixteenth-note staccato passages marked presto - although
your own personal pain threshold is likely to be a good deal lower than
that—simply execute the same ploy in reverse.

In wind chamber music, it is often the horns who are the first to
call for the stepping up of the tempo. Here, the most effective ploy is
to lay down your instrument with great care and deliberation, walk
slowly over to where the horns are sitting, lean over, study their parts,
and then, nodding sagely, share your finding with the rest of the ensemble—something like, "Yes, just as I thought, they have nothing but
thirty-two bars of the same quarter note repeated at the beginning of
every bar." Your point will have been made. However, just one caveat:
you may have a hard time recruiting those indispensable horn-playing
colleagues—whose comparative scarcity gives them a distinctly higher
market value—for the same or another piece at a later date.

16. The last resort

It can happen to the best Musicianmen that they will run out of
diversionary ploys and devices and that the wretched incompetence
with which they have brought the proceedings to a halt will be too
painfully conspicuous for the culprits to attempt to conceal their identities. When you are the one caught with your musical pants down,

make a point of explaining in tedious detail why exactly it happened in this particular and, as you will no doubt heavily imply, exceptional instance. This implication will be reinforced if you giggle a lot—"My God, how could this happen to ME?"—at the moment of truth. If, however, you take a moment to consider your own reaction to lame— or even ingenious—excuses offered by your fellow players when they screw up, you might realize that you are only digging your grave deeper and that your squirming only adds piquancy to *their* smug gloating over *your* discomfiture as well as confirms them in their temporary collective feeling of superiority.

The trouble is that the French not only have a word for everything, but they also have a hedge for every bet. Certainly, they say, *tout comprendre, c'est tout pardonner*, but they also say, *qui s'excuse, s'accuse*. Or as Shakespeare had it, referring no doubt to the viola in one of his plays, "Methinks the lady doth protest too much!"

P.S. If you find yourself with leftover notes to play after everyone else has finished, resist the temptation to play them. Just wrap them up quietly, and take them home. You can play them there.

THE SQUELCHER

No disquisition on this subject would be complete without the last word, which can only belong to one of the rare New Yorkers ever to venture out to "Marlboro Country" to play his violin in the annual Amateur Chamber Music Workshop in Bozeman, Montana.

He came equipped with a set of printed cards, and when there was any postscrew-up attempt at self-exculpation or attenuation, he would quietly put down his instrument, extract one of the cards, pad over to the perpetrator, and deposit it on her or his stand.

It read: "Go home and practice, Schmuck!"

The Rabin Assassination (November 4, 1944): a Grim Vindication

HOW TERRIBLE, THE CRY GOES up, that a Jew has raised his hand against a fellow Jew. What I am about to say is NOT about the assassination itself, nor about the rights and wrongs of the political strife surrounding the event. The question I want to pose is whether the possibility of Jew murdering Jew is not ultimately and inevitably part of what the State of Israel is all about and, in a sense, *for*.

There are two quite distinct ways of looking at Zionism. One is that Israel is a place where Jews can go to be Jews freely, uninhibitedly, and without let or hindrance; the other is that it is a place where Jews can go and be free *not to have to be "Jews"* but just regular people, like anyone else, anywhere else—a luxury that was and is accorded only in varying degrees in their countries of origin. The point is made wryly but tellingly in the old story about a certain Goldberg who got so fed up being saddled with the burden of his Jewish identity among the unsympathetic English that he changed his name to Jones and went to live in a village in North Wales, where he promptly became known as "Jones the Jew"!*

One could probably establish a fairly precise correlation between the degree to which this luxury was or is available in a given country and the proportion of the Jewish population of that country that has chosen to go and live in Israel.

In the diaspora, there has always been a synergy at work between forces generated both from within and outside the Jewish community, which has conditioned both non-Jews and Jews alike to believe that only certain skills, values,

---

* See Dylan Thomas, *Under Milk Wood*, for relevant nomenclature background (e.g., Dai Bread, Ocky Milk, Evans the Death).

sensibilities, virtues and vices, occupations and preoccupations, vocations and avocations, and patterns of behavior were characteristic of, appropriate to, or even confined to Jews. This is why it is by no means an unmitigated compliment to Jews to be told that they are clever, musical, enterprising, or even generous, any more than it is to blacks to be told that they have "got rhythm" or are fast runners.

I was once told by an oceanographer, in a manner that suggested that he felt it was "significant," that he had never come across a Jewish oceanographer. There was somehow a suggestion of a generic lack of certain sterling qualities or the presence of certain shameful failings that accounted for this. Whatever the complex tissue of social, economic, and traditional factors that may account for this apparent reluctance on the part of nice Jewish boys to go into the ocean-ography business in the diaspora, it is quite likely that Israel has its fair share of "Jewish" oceanographers as well as practitioners of all those other robust, out-doorsy, horny-handed "Aryan" occupations, such as firefighters, lumberjacks, steeplejacks, stevedores, truck drivers, farmers, and the like, traditionally deemed, on both sides of the pale, somehow congenitally unsuitable for Jews of the diaspora. If you continue this inventory of activities for long enough, you will eventually reach murder and political assassination.

There is absolutely no reason why any even reasonably well-ordered soci-ety should not include its fair share of citizens who go in for the less reputable activities. In a largely Jewish population, the calculus of probability dictates that Jewish criminals will claim Jewish victims. What could be, however deplorably, more normal? And surely, normality in all its forms and manifestations is ulti-mately part of what Israel is all about.

What do Toilet Paper and Air Travel Have in Common?

———

OVER THE PAST FEW DECADES, the frontiers of human knowledge, ingenuity, science, and technology have been pushed back farther and faster than ever before. Two frontiers seem to have remained impervious to technological advancement. In terms of the function for which toilet paper was invented, no advance or breakthrough has been made except in qualitative terms in such areas as the paper itself and its perforations. As for air travel—for civilian passengers at least—the current speed has remained stagnant, at five hundred to six hundred miles per hour, a boundary that was reached soon after the invention of jet propulsion for military and commercial aircraft (ca. 1941).

There have been, in fact, breakthroughs in both areas, but both have so far proved to be exceptions that do not appear to have been followed up. Concorde crashed through the sound barrier in 1996 and was able to cruise at more than Mach 2, or twice the speed of sound, once reaching New York from London in just under three hours. In 2003, it was withdrawn from commercial service for a combination of economic, commercial, and environmental reasons, and the door it had opened in the sound barrier seems to have remained firmly shut— except, one assumes, for military aircraft.

Am I the only person in the world who finds toilet paper a highly unsatisfactory—and probably not particularly sanitary—means of doing whatever it is that it is supposed to do, something its name coyly refrains from indicating? And why, when everything (and everyone) is leaving the closet in droves, is it the water closet, of all things, whose mysteries have remained so obstinately sacrosanct?

Why, with all the giant strides in health and hygiene technology over the past fifty years (above all in this underarm-, body odor-, and plaque-sensitive society, where "women's products" are practically elbowing each other off the TV screen in order to be the first into our bathrooms), are we still essentially using the hit-or-miss means and method of our grandparents to rid our bodies of by far the most unsavory, malodorous, soiling, and unhygienic excremental matter of all? In all the long history of toilet paper, can it be that all we have really been longing for is a product—the comically misnamed "Charmin"— that is more fun to squeeze?

Shit is and has become the quintessence of dirt. We, the members of the world's most technologically advanced civilization, are not content to wipe minor dirt off our bodies with scraps of paper when we enjoy the unparalleled advantages of soap and water, yet we persist in wiping the filthiest dirt of all off our bodies with, yes, scraps of paper! Why?

It is the Japanese who appear to have blazed the trail in bathroom technology, but although the door they have opened has not been closed behind them, no one else much seems to have followed them through it. For them, toilet paper is now a thing of the past, and no longer of the posterior. The whole operation is now hands-free, except for the pressing of the appropriate button, and any lingering detritus is now removed by a powered water device.

Why the rest of the developed world has remained aloof from such a distinct leap forward in excremental hygiene is a mystery that cannot be explained by economic or commercial considerations, or by the unavailability of the necessary plumbing technology—the French, after all, have long since plumbed the secret of the bidet for a not entirely dissimilar purpose. In terms of hygiene and the environment, the Japanese device is a clear excremental increment.

While all around us, science and technology have been pushing ever further into the secrets of subatomic particles, seeing ever further into the outer reaches of the universe, probing ever more deeply the intricate workings of the brain and our genetic makeup, finding ways of replacing more and more body parts, and traveling ever faster on land and sea, it is toilet paper and civilian air travel that, exceptionally, have come to rest within limits that it is well within the power of modern technology to transcend. The Anglo-French with their

Concorde and the Japanese with their advance in toilet hygiene have both seen the future. In one case, it worked, but in the other, it didn't.

Before we leave the bathroom altogether, one small, related issue remains to be explored. Our plumbing carries away the obvious toxic and noxious substances excreted by our bodies, and most of us, forgivably, don't know or care where it goes and rely on the "big" government and the "intrusive," "regulating" state to ensure that this detritus does not poison us. But what must also constitute an enormous amount of waste carried away, much less obtrusively, by our plumbing is the soapy, scummy water from our showers.

What is the net polluting effect of the scum plus the chemical content of the soap waste? I believe that we all casually use an amount of soap every day far in excess of requirements.

What's Wrong with Language Classes?

IN HIS BOOK, *ANATOMY OF an Illness* (1964), Norman Cousins drew the compelling conclusion that "a hospital is no place for a sick person."

For anyone, but especially for an adult with a specific reason for wanting to learn a language, there are equally powerful reasons to conclude that "a language class is no place to learn a language." Would dentistry courses, for example, still be in business if they consistently turned out generations of students as ill equipped to practice dentistry as the typical graduate of a language class is to speak and understand a foreign language?

An article titled "Want to Learn a Language? Don't Make It a Mount Everest," by Tish Durkin, appeared in the *New York Times* on September 26, 1992. The article at least scratches the surface of one fundamental question—usually left unasked by the would-be student of himself and almost always unasked by the teacher or institution anxious to enroll the student: "Why exactly do you want to learn a language, or what exactly do you want to be able to do with it?"

In actual fact, there is a vast gamut of diverse reasons out there, some of which have practically no overlap with any of the others.

Some may want to "learn" Italian or German in order to be able to sing opera in those languages. Others want to be able to study chess publications in Russian. Others again want to read Homer in the original, and still others are ethnic Chinese Cantonese speakers who want to be able to understand Mandarin, or *pu tong hua*, the official language of the People's Republic. There are even those who simply see a language class as a way of meeting people and would have been just as happy signing on for Flower Arrangement or Gourmet Food Preparation if only those classes had met at a convenient time.

Reference is made to the Berlitz technique of "total immersion," whereby "students speak, listen to and read only the foreign language in the classroom." BUT in real life, which nearly always means multiple students with a single teacher, the following is true:

a. What students spend most of their time doing is either listening to their fellow students mangling the language in question by attempting to speak it or being inhibited from attempting to speak it by the presence of those same fellow students.

b. Alternatively, they may be spending most of their time listening to the teacher speaking it, something that leaves each of them with only a fraction of the remaining time available to practice speaking. As a corollary, that time tends to be monopolized by one or two students who are either more advanced or have a higher threshold of embarrassment than the rest.

c. They may be struggling with their own particular problems (pronunciation, grammar, understanding, etc.) which may not be those of the other students.

d. They will also have to spend much of their time listening to the teacher dealing precisely with those problems that, rightly or wrongly, may be irrelevant to their own, and precisely because of this irrelevance, they will find their attention straying, their irritation rising, and their motivation ebbing.

e. If the teacher is one who encourages a great deal of active student participation, the presence of only one other student in a class of two can reduce by almost half the useful return on the time invested by the other. The larger the class, the less time is available for individual students to be able to air their own problems, reveal their own weaknesses, and get useful feedback on them from the teacher.

    The nearest the article gets to recognizing these complex, counterproductive factors is to say, "If there are more than 15 students, individuals are likely to spend too much time silent."

f. The "group dynamics" of a class can become a counterproductive factor. Among other things, students who are, rightly or wrongly, sensitive to their own shortcomings, especially if they are comparing themselves unfavorably with their fellow students, are likely to be inhibited from participation. Other students, who feel, rightly or wrongly, that they can shine may claim a disproportionate share of class time and the teacher's attention. This urge, although it may be dismissed as infantile, can nevertheless be a seriously disruptive factor in a class full of adults, and it often takes the form of asking the teacher questions, thus drawing the attention of the teacher and indeed the whole class to the questioner. As often as not, these questions are designed to display knowledge rather than to elicit it.

The article goes on to state that "for some, total immersion is second best to learning a language while living in the foreign country in question," thus clearly implying or accepting the implication that living in a foreign country is the best way to learn a foreign language. Being immersed in water may be a *necessary* condition for learning to swim, but it is certainly not a *sufficient* one. In the realm of language learning—or rather *failing to* learn—the evidence abounds.

Throughout history, soldiers, such as Roman legionaries throughout the empire and GIs in Japan and Germany after World War II, have occupied or been stationed in foreign territory. There is little evidence to suggest that their mere physical presence, even for long periods of time, led to their learning the languages of the environment, for all the "fraternization" that may have taken place. In such cases, it is nearly always the "fraternizee," the native of the country in question, who has been the one motivated to make the effort to acquire the language of the "fraternizer."

Further evidence of the primacy of motivation over sheer territorial presence as a factor promoting language learning can be drawn from the experience of civilian expatriate communities, especially English-speaking ones.

The long-term presence on Turkish soil of an American professoriat at Robert College in Istanbul in the 1950s and 1960s did nothing to promote or motivate the learning of the language of the country.

Significantly, some of the Turkish students who were assigned to the writer for remedial coaching at that time were clearly suffering from the fact that their American teachers were unable to discuss with them in their language (Turkish) the problems they were having with the language they were being taught, and being taught *in!*—namely, English. If ever a virtue was made of necessity, it was the rationalization that it was good for the students to hear *nothing but* English in the classroom.

At best, those expatriates responsible for running households or shopping learned enough of the language to get by with servants and shopkeepers, but even here an acquaintance, however nodding, on the part of the latter with English, or on the part of both with a lingua franca such as French, would mean that not even that little Turkish was learned.

Another very powerful and common factor that militates against the acquisition of the language of a country in spite of presence in it is the company of relatives or friends who tend to constitute a kind of linguistic ghetto for the student. Friends who teach English to Hispanic immigrants in the United States are given to periodic bouts of breast beating and hair tearing over their inability to make significant progress with their students. They are constantly on the lookout for new *methods* and, like parents of problem children, are forever wringing their hands over where they went wrong. Both the parents and the teachers seem to forget that they are by no means the only game in town and that there are far more powerful factors at work elsewhere in the environment outside their classrooms and households, forming the characters of their children and thwarting the acquisition of English by their Latino students— namely, the influence of their respective peer groups.

Because of the snowballing, worldwide dominance of English, Anglophones are often deluded into thinking that the foreigners who are so eager to embrace their language are somehow especially gifted in language acquisition or that they themselves are congenitally poor language learners.

Teachers of foreign languages in English-speaking countries tend to be similarly deluded into thinking that what they see as a lack of success in their efforts can be remedied by adopting different—and especially *novel*— teaching methods.

What is not properly understood is that the reason why we can't learn their languages and they can learn ours has nothing to do with *mentality or methods*; it has all to do with *motivation*.

WILL THE TRANSIT PASS MAKE
NEW YORKERS FLABBY?

———◆———

WHY WALK FROM GRAND CENTRAL to Times Square in the open air for nothing when you can do it underground for two dollars and fifty cents?

In 1999, New York City, after phasing out the subway token, introduced the transit pass for travel on its buses and subway system.

On December 13, the headline on the *New York Times* letters page was "Will Transit Pass Make New Yorkers Flabby"?

Particular prominence was given to what the author of this first letter described as a potential side effect of the weekly or monthly subway pass. Only the inhabitant of a fairy tale where pumpkins turn into coaches at midnight, and who has absolutely no firsthand experience of it could so thoroughly misrepresent the realities of New York public transportation.

The image of casual and instantaneous effortlessness blithely conjured up by the expression "jump on the train" is a grotesque travesty of the actual tortuous, labyrinthine, and highly aerobic process, whereby subway riders carry an average body weight of some 150 pounds plus clothing and burdens from their point of departure to the actual strap from which they will hang for the duration of the first stage of their journey.

If they are lucky enough to have to change trains only once, all they will have to do at this point is fight their way through a mass of unyielding and impervious bodies, only to be met at the doorway by a barely resistible eruption of bodies struggling to get off, followed by the surge of other bodies fighting to get in. Then it's "upstairs, downstairs, and in my lady's chamber" all over again.

The writer of this letter has put the subway cart before the horsepower. The fact is that it is precisely rising to the challenge posed by the obstacle course presented by the subway system that keeps its riders, as they are so ruggedly termed in New York, so lean and mean—especially in comparison with their automobile-bound fellow citizens who inhabit the wide-open spaces between the big cities.

The aerobic benefits are derived from the sheer distance they have to cover on foot and the stairs they have to climb, and for upper body conditioning, there is nothing like the isometric tension of clinging for sheer equilibrium to strap or pole in a juddering, lurching bus or subway train.

One of the better-kept secrets of the system is the aerobic bonus so thoughtfully provided by the transit authorities in what is known as the "shuttle," whereby, for the modest fee of two dollars and fifty cents,* citizens are encouraged to walk half the distance from Grand Central to Times Square and onto a disused and immobile subway train, which is then quite convincingly caused to rattle and shake for two minutes. The riders are then disgorged to complete the other half of their journey on foot, as unaware as your correspondent seems to be of how much exercise they have taken.

---

* This is really not such a bad deal if you consider how much fancy midtown gyms charge you to use their treadmills and StairMasters.

WISHING LIFE AWAY

———◆———

"PLAYING TIME" VERSUS "ELAPSED TIME"

TAKE BASEBALL, FOR EXAMPLE. THE time it normally takes to complete a Major League Baseball game is about three hours. Years ago, in response—and in self-defense—to Americans I met soon after arriving in this country who would tell me how tedious and slow a game of cricket was, I timed a few baseball games. I found that of the "elapsed time" of approximately three hours, the ball was in play for only about twelve minutes, or one-fifteenth of the "elapsed time."

What proportion of your waking life have you "wished away" in the form of "elapsed time"—instead of keeping the ball in play, or actually "living" your life? Perhaps fortunately, it does not appear, from the literature on the subject, that when our "sell-by" date comes around, many of us are programmed to regret what must be an impressive total of time wished away in a "waiting mode."

On the surface, it seems that the complexities of modern—or rather, as we are learnedly advised, postmodern—life spawn far more waiting situations than that much-harked-back-to preindustrial life of such alluring simplicity.

Today, to pluck an example at random, I have telephoned several people I need to get in touch with. After waiting for their answering machines to answer and for the messages inscribed thereon to run their often needlessly elaborate course—sometimes in more than one language!—I can then either unburden myself or chip away further at my remaining life-span by trying again later.

I suppose that some people have the faculty of releasing their minds from the clamp that the fact of waiting seems to impose on mine so that they can simply go on living—mentally, at least—just as if they were not waiting, but I am not one of them. In the doctor's waiting room, others may actually be reading the magazines they are gazing at, but what I am doing is *waiting*, and simply placing the printed page within my line of sight is just another way of doing it.

In the plainest possible language, "wishing away our lives" is something we do when we are waiting impatiently for something to happen—that is, when we "can't wait" for something to happen.

The things we are waiting for vary enormously: to get out of prison, to see the doctor, for a train to arrive, for the journey to end, for your turn at Scrabble, for your turn at the bank or the checkout counter, for someone who is late for your appointment, for your toothache to go away, (for the insomniacs among us) for sleep to wrap us in oblivion (except for the bad dreams), for that letter you've been expecting, for the traffic to get moving again in a jam, and, on my Exercycle, for the end of my timed stint, watching the minutes ticking slowly away and wishing it were 10:27 a.m. instead of 10:21!

How often have you found yourself wishing that your consciousness could be suspended until the hoped- and waited-for second, minute, hour, or day actually arrived and you could resume living?

Would one consciously opt for a life from which all those "wished-away" seconds, minutes, hours, and even days and weeks had been subtracted? What if a fairy with a magic wand appeared and offered you ten years' less "elapsed time," leaving you only with the "playing time"—the time when you are in "living" rather than "waiting" mode? Would you accept? Or is the time we wish would go away just too valuable to give up?

Alternatively, what would you decide if that good fairy offered you the opportunity literally to "wish away" those bits of life that you wish were over and done with, that you were "wishing away"—but, of course, with the understanding that your "elapsed-time" life-span would be correspondingly reduced, leaving only "playing time"?

For an example of how profoundly subjective this distinction can be, take the business of flying long distances. Flying, for economy-class passengers at least, has become much more uncomfortable in recent years, but there are still friends of mine who actively welcome the prospect of sitting in a severely confined space for hours in an oxygen-deficient tube of metal hurtling through the skies, because it gives them a chance to "relax" and read. For myself, no matter what I might appear to be "doing," such as "reading" a book or "watching" a movie, what I am actually "doing" is waiting impatiently to land. Once my foot hits terra firma, I resume life, a satisfaction that is short lived and peters out when I am painfully reminded of how long the wait is going to be for immigration, customs, and the arrival of the luggage. In the abstract, I would be willing to be anesthetized from the moment I enter the airport until the moment I leave it at the other end of the journey. However, if that good fairy with the wand happened to be waiting for me at the entrance of the terminal on my arrival and offered me that choice, I have the feeling that something inside me would reject it—only to spend the rest of the journey regretting it, of course.

The distinction between our waiting and our living time is nothing like as clear-cut as the words suggest. When we get up in the morning, we have to go through all those same old motions we perform every day to get ourselves ready to begin it—the washing, the dressing, the grooming. Some of us, of course, may welcome, even relish, these preparations for their own sake, depending partly on what value we place on the way we look when we encounter the outside world. For the rest of us, these may simply be chores that have to be done, like emptying the garbage, chores that represent for us merely "elapsed time" between the innings of real living.

In childhood, the prospect of having to wait a whole hour—or worse, a whole day—before being given something you want feels like an eternity. Late in life, years, months, weeks, days, and hours whiz past you faster than you can snatch them.

Nowhere more than in prison—that is, the blue-collar version with no TV, golf course, pool, gym, or library—time must seem to inch by so slowly. It would be interesting to poll prisoners to find out whether any would accept the good fairy's first deal, and if so, whether there would be a tendency for prisoners serving longer sentences to be more, or less willing to accept the offer.

What if, in the hope of putting a brake on that "winged chariot hurrying near," one could volunteer for a prison sentence, provided one could take all one's toys and playthings along? Or would that very privilege destroy the whole point of the exercise because it would relieve boredom and tedium, which are precisely those elements that make time pass too slowly? Or would the sheer fact that you were being *forced to do, or confined to doing,* those things you used to do because you enjoyed doing them when you were free, spoil your appetite for them and turn what was once "living" time into "waiting" time, and "playing" time into "elapsed" time? It's worth recalling that while bricklayers all over the kingdom were only too keen to put down their tools when the working day ended, Winston Churchill used to lay bricks for fun at the weekend.

The ultimate acid test: What if you were breathing your last and that good fairy appeared at your bedside, offering you a bonus of a continuation of life, but life limited strictly to all and only that "elapsed" time you had "wished away" during it?

TALES AND THEIR EMBELLISHMENT

———

EVERYONE EMBELLISHES HIS OR HER tales. Even in the most casual conversation, to narrate is to embellish, to strive for effect (usually by exaggeration)—in a word, to create. One moment of reflection, one twinge of honesty is enough to tell us that this is true of ourselves and others, yet this knowledge seems to have little or no power to prevent our accepting uncritically and at face value what is narrated by our interlocutors in casual conversation, even when, as is so often the case, their stories cast them invariably (as our own stories cast us) as aggrieved parties, innocent victims, heroes, or sages in conflicts in which life pits them (as it pits us) against an ignoble succession of villains, bullies, and idiots.

One reason why we tend to respond with a "wow!" or an empathetic "tsk!" rather than a "bullshit!" is that with strangers and slight acquaintances we are restrained by the conventions of politeness, and with close friends, by the convention and, indeed, function of friendship that, at least for conversational purposes, we are our friends' automatic allies against the rest of the world—even when the adversary, over whom a friend has triumphed or by whom he or she has been worsted in his or her tale, happens to be one of our other friends!

But there is another reason why we are so ready to buy our friends' tales wholesale, and this is because of their resale value. Once heard, these tales become part of our own conversational stock, which we then purvey—with our own embellishments—basking at least in the moonlight of glory, sympathy, awe, or wonderment cast by their retelling.

Each retelling of our life's experiences adds one more layer of insulation or distance between the teller and the facts of the story, rather like the thirty layers of mattress between the princess and the pea in Hans Christian Andersen's story. However, that story serves to stress the supersensitivity, and hence the delicacy and refinement, of the princess. In the case of the teller and his or her tales, the effect of the "thirty mattresses" between the teller and his or her "pea" is such that, instead of actually recalling the events in question, what he or she ends up doing is repeating by rote the lines he or she has learned by heart, like a favorite joke or an actor replaying a part.

This process, of course, by no means precludes the gradual accretion of embellishments subconsciously designed to enhance the interest and melodrama of the tale.

In the end, the recounter of episodes and experiences from his or her own life has no more been present at the events retold than the teller of a favorite shaggy dog story has been there to witness the events he or she is recounting.

Sharing the Experience

Canned Laughter, Diana, and the Eclipse

How many Californians does it take to change a light bulb?
Seventeen. Why? One to fix the light bulb, and sixteen to share the
experience.

How much of the pleasure in, or reaction to events is due to the ricochet effect of "sharing the experience," and to what extent are the impact and the pleasure of an experience heightened and reinforced in proportion to the number of other people involved? How much difference does it make whether they can be seen and heard by each other?

The notion of "sharing the experience," however, needs to be refined. For example, a million people may be viewing the same show on TV, but separately, in the privacy and solitude of their own living rooms, while a mere three hundred people may be seeing the same show in the same theater at the same time, where the presence of the other 299 creates a qualitatively different experience. Undoubtedly, the ricochet effect makes an important difference in the reaction; whether admiration, laughter, tears, suspense, or excitement, the mood is bound to be sharpened, heightened, and reinforced by the collectiveness and mutuality of the experience.

There is also the element of anticipation—witness the well-nigh irresistible impulse on the part of the audience to titter and giggle at almost any gesture or remark by a character, especially at the beginning of a performance in a theater and especially if it has been billed as a comedy—a psychological effect unlikely to be reproduced in a lone viewer in the privacy of his or her living room.

This mutual reinforcement factor must be the reason why producers of TV sitcoms pipe canned or live audience laughter into the living rooms of the lone viewers—in the hope that they will find the show funnier than they would have if left to their own devices. Consider also the allied practice of actively prompting the "spontaneous" applause, laughter, and other kinds of "audience reactions," not to mention the shots of groups of the audience "spontaneously" screaming for "Jerry" on the Jerry Springer show.

This thought was prompted by a recent total eclipse. Everybody interviewed on TV, including and especially the mistress of ceremonies, kept telling us how "awesome" and "fantastic" the experience was. Allowance, of course, has to be made both for the powerful suggestive influence of the approved, desirable response emanating from the emcee and for the selectivity factor—interviews with sullen, unresponsive, and indifferent interviewees seldom make it to our TV screens, in the same way that game show contestants are clearly selected for their willingness and ability to "act up."

Left to ourselves (and that includes being free from the buildup effect of all the advance eclipse promos and publicity), how many of us would have felt like screaming—or even feeling—"awesome" and "fantastic" in response to the "darkness at noon" experience in the privacy of our living rooms, or our rooftops?

There is also another factor to be reckoned with when it comes to public performances of all kinds—a factor that, by definition, cannot apply to TV viewers. This is the impulse to justify to oneself—and perhaps to others—one's investment of money, time, effort, and ultimately even one's dignity and self-esteem. The larger the investment, the stronger the impulse is.

The loss of face in one's own eyes and, particularly, in the eyes of others at having made a bad bargain or "bought a lemon" is probably universal, but nowhere so strongly felt as among Americans. This, after all, is the country in which the most wounding, humiliating, and opprobrious epithet is "loser" and where one of the most venerable and oft-quoted slogans is "winning isn't every-thing—it's the only thing."

Those who occupy expensive seats at Broadway shows and take expensive foreign vacations feel subliminally under great pressure to persuade themselves, and especially to convince their friends, that they have had a good time and thus well and truly got their money, time, and trouble's worth.

A historic case of an experience being shared to the point of mass hysteria was the aftermath of the death of Diana, Princess of Wales, in August 1997. In a nutshell, if it hadn't been for the sight of all those others doing so on TV, who, left to their own devices, would even have had the spontaneous inclination to do what thousands upon thousands of their fellow citizens were setting out to do, actually forsaking their homes, responsibilities, and nearest and dearest at the drop of a hat and going to the trouble and expense of traveling hundreds of miles from the far reaches of the kingdom to throw bouquets onto a veritable flower mountain outside the gates of Kensington Palace in London?

It is noteworthy that for the most part, this mass displacement of the British population took place by bus and train, and that this mass compulsion "to share the experience" seemed to have a much weaker grip on the car-owning classes; otherwise, the north-south motorways would have been backed up for miles, with traffic at a standstill.

SHOULD CANCER RESEARCH REPLACE *MONDAY NIGHT FOOTBALL* ON TV (AND WHY IT WON'T)?

—————◆—————

THE US WOMEN'S NATIONAL SOCCER team was ranked by FIFA as number one in the world continuously from March 2008 to December 2014, having won its first world title in 1991. And in the 1980 Winter Olympics, the US women's ice hockey team won the gold medal after having beaten the USSR in the semifinal.

On February 20, 2008, in a letter to the editor ("Re: Olympian Heights for Women, Not for Viewers: Non Heroic Coverage"), a reader complained:

"The shoddy treatment from CBS reinforces in young women's minds that the sports they play are not as important as the sports men play."

Sports are shown on TV not because they are important but because they are entertaining. If importance were the criterion, sports might never be shown on TV at all, and *Monday Night Football* would be replaced by three hours of live coverage of cancer researchers at work in their labs.

In fact, the reversal of cause and effect that is at work here was succinctly stated in an episode of *Seinfeld*, in which Jerry Seinfeld and his friend George Costanza are shown pitching a show to NBC TV—namely, the one in which they are appearing in this scene. In it, his friend, George, in answer to the question put by the head of NBC, "What is the show about?" replies triumphantly, "Nothing!" To the next question, "Then, why would people watch it?" George replies equally triumphantly, laying down his ace card, "*because it's on TV*," only to be trumped by the riposte "Not yet!"

There are two things that make sports entertaining: excellence of performance and partisanship. It is no doubt politically incorrect to say so, but through no fault of their own—largely a matter of physique—women, all other things being equal, are simply not as good at certain sports as men. In the same way, short men, again for reasons of physique, are not, all other things being equal, as good as tall men at basketball.

If women were as good as men at ice hockey, there would be no reason for them not to be competing in the same leagues as men. However good two basketball teams of short men might be for their size, they are not the ones basketball fans want to watch on TV.

As for the other factor, partisanship, that is probably the only reason why American viewers have ever seen women's ice hockey—in the form of the victorious US women's team on TV—*at all.*

SPORTS TALK

———◆———

IN THE EARLY FIFTIES DURING the Wimbledon fortnight, in breach of a tangled web of prohibitions that summarily curtailed the human rights of British "public" schoolboys of the time in ways that would not be tolerated in the barrack room or even the prison today, I would exit clandestinely from school by way of a sloping bank at the far edge of the playing field and spend the afternoon crouched in front of the nearest television to which I was able to beg, crave, or cajole access. It would be monochrome and of minuscule proportions by today's standards.

What was just as much an archaic, historical relic by today's standards was the commentary, delivered by one Dan Maskell, and I mean "one." Alone and, to judge by his discreet and hushed undertone, crouched within earshot of the public and players on the Centre Court, he would offer a few well-chosen terse and laconic comments on the play as and when he felt it relevant. I don't believe it occurred to him, his audience, or his producers to think of the intervening silences as in any way untoward, undesirable, or unwelcome.

Just how bygone those days are can be judged by the equally archaic relics one saw on court: the aging, paunchy, and bespectacled Czech Jaroslav Drobny, 1954 Wimbledon champion, and the one-armed Austrian H. Redl, himself by no means in the first flush of youth, to name but two. Indeed, it had not been too long beforehand that the tournament had been graced by the beflannelled— white, of course—Duke of York, before he was forced to turn in his racket and sneakers for an orb and scepter.

Today, the commentators'—or "chatters'"—box cannot be manned, or personned, by fewer than a pair, often three of a kind, and from time to time a full house in what appears to be a desperate attempt to keep in thrall those viewers who are none too keen on sports in the first place long enough to be exposed to the next series of commercials.

It has been well said that power corrupts. Never in media history or practice has more unchecked power been placed in the hands of any individual performer than that currently accorded to sportscasters. One of the main reasons power corrupts is that the greater the power, the less likelihood there is of contradiction. The more absolute and the more lasting the power, the more apt is the dictator to believe in his own authority and infallibility. It is probably only the constant waves of dissent and contradiction breaking over our shores—in the home, at work, or in the pub—that cut most of us down to size and keep us more or less honest.

There is no other figure in the media to match the sportscaster in his command of vast audiences for hours at a time with the freedom, and indeed the professional obligation, to say practically anything that comes into his head without any meaningful risk of contradiction; the cheery banter among fellow commentators rarely takes the form of meaningful debate, rebuttal, or contradiction, although it certainly distracts attention from the event that viewers have tuned in to watch—perhaps it is even meant to! Even if there is occasional and intermittent feedback from producers, it comes after the event, too late to mitigate the effect of any wayward but authoritative assertion that may have been made, and with no visible chastening effect when the errant, unrepentant sportscaster is once again unleashed on the unsuspecting public.

It is an irony worth noting that as advancing video technology has made it ever easier for us to see exactly what is happening on the field of play, even if we missed it the first time around—from vantage points and in a proximity rarely enjoyed by spectators on the spot—so the "videocrats" have felt it necessary to accompany these images with an ever-increasing volume of talk, often in triplicate.

Over the years, I have taken considerable trouble to note and classify some of the more egregious liberties taken and offenses committed by those whom our generous and thoughtful TV networks have hired in order to help us watch, talk us through, or distract us from our favorite sporting events—help, by the way, that we seemed to be able to do very nicely without in those backward days when we actually went to watch them "live."

Here is a, by no means, exhaustive list of categories of offense repeatedly committed. Sometimes the categories overlap or shade into each other, and sometimes the examples fit into more than one category.

Probably the two most common and comprehensive categories are *Tautology* and *Wisdom after the Event*. Others include the *Hedged Bet* or the *Win-Win Expertise*, *Truism Masquerading as Analysis*, the *Disguised Tautology*, the *Solipsistic Fallacy*, and *Language Crimes*.

Most of the examples are drawn from tennis and some of the other sporting events, including specifically or predominantly American spectator sports that the author likes to watch. Because of his long residence in the United States, most of the culprits, or recidivists, named by the author, are those who perform on US television.

Probably the first example that drew my attention to the rich seam of Tautology to be mined out there in "them there TV hills" was uttered during the Collegiate National Invitation (basketball) Tournament in the 1970s in a game between Manhattan and Maryland Eastern Shore at Madison Square Garden:

"There's no place like here at the Garden for some of these young players to get a chance of playing here."

IT TAKES AN EXPERT

Rhoden, William C. "Sports of the Times." *New York Times*, quoting Bill Parcells, New York Jets coach, on the Jets's prospects for the playoffs (1997–1998):

"Whoever plays the best from here on wins…Four teams are still in contention for the AFC East…the team that's able to play the best in the last six games is going to win."

This is about as penetrating an insight as an anatomist who tells you that men over six feet are likely to be taller than men under five feet nine inches.

Sunday Times, London. World Athletics Championships, Stuttgart, August 29, 1993.

"Out of the Mouths of Daves"

David Coleman: "If Stevie Smith is going to get in with the medals, he has got to get ahead of his rivals."

New York Times, November 25, 2002. National Football League. After the New York Giants had lost to the Houston Texans 14–16 in an error-ridden game, their coach, Jim Fassel, explained:

"Like I said all week long, I said it to them a hundred times—the team that plays the best is going to win."

Too bad he stopped at a hundred; after the 101st time, they might have finally gotten it into their heads that it was a mistake for them to play worse—pardon me, the worst.

July 20, 2002. Athletes themselves are, of course, not immune to the virus, but then, no one ever said that golf champions were supposed to be champion analysts.

Before the British Open, someone asked Ernie Els what it would take for him to win.

"I have to play a lot better," said Els. "I haven't played that good the last couple of weeks."

March 17, 1992. Lipton International, Key Biscayne. Becker versus Mancini—one set all—Mancini leading 4–2 in the third.

Fred Stolle: "The match is reaching that point now where one of the players has got to win it; the other player is not just going to stand by and let you win it."

Let's give our presiding tautologist the benefit of the doubt and credit him with a tiny residue of meaning. It would have to be something like "only the player who plays aggressively and tries to hit winners will win."

Well, yes, if his "winners" go in, and no, if they don't. In that case, it is at least equally likely that the other player will win. One of the logical flaws in this "analysis" is that the alternatives offered by the speaker are nonexhaustive. There are several approaches open to either player that are neither "has got to win it" nor "stand by and let you win it." They could play a careful, low-risk, defensive game, to name but one.

Ibid. Becker has just won a point at the net.

F. Stolle: "If he'd just played this way from the beginning of the match, he (Becker at one set all, 2–4 down and 30 all in the third) would get it over with much more quickly."

If by "*this way*" F. S. means "playing at the net," nothing at all follows from that premise, since Becker might equally well have lost as many points as he actually lost by *not* playing at the net; but if he means. "playing *successfully* at the net," the result is sheer tautology, since playing in any shape or form *successfully*—including playing nothing but drop shots, or playing standing on one's head—is no longer a *manner* of playing but the *result* of playing.

At this point, I am wondering whether to introduce a subheading, "Rampant or Crass Tautology," in order to accommodate the gems of excruciating obviousness favored by Cliff Drysdale, known to an exclusive circle consisting largely of myself as the Sententious One. For years, no tennis tournament broadcast on US TV has been complete without the stichomythia provided by Drysdale and his partner Fred Stolle, on whom he conferred the Homeric epithet of "the Fiery One." I have felt impelled to make up for Stolle's spineless and quite unfiery acquiescence by conferring on C. D. in absentia this Homeric epithet of my own coining:

The Quintessential Drysdale: "You don't want to get too many points behind in the tiebreaker." And just in case any of you out there are wondering why, as quick as a whip, he's in there telling you "It's tough to recover from."

February 4, 1995. Davis Cup. France versus United States. Cedric Pioline leading Todd Martin in second set after winning the first.

C. Drysdale, unfortunately, not quite inimitably: "It looks even worse for the US now that he's down a set *and* a break."

To get a feel for the level of expertise demonstrated here, imagine you have summoned the plumber to fix the mess in your bathroom and he offers, "Well, it looks as if your toilet bowl has overflowed, and your floor looks even worse covered with all that stinking waste!"

January 1992. Australian Championships—Final. Edberg versus Courier; one set all; on service in third set; Courier down 0–40 to Edberg.

C. Drysdale: "It looks as if this could well be the first break in the third set."

He could, of course, have stuck his neck right out with "will be," but the "could well be" strikes a nicely judicious note suggestive of profounder lucubrations.

I include this gem under the general heading of Drysdaliana, since I cannot quite puzzle out to which particular category of sententious mindlessness it properly belongs.

February 21, 1993. US Indoor Championships—Semi Final. Rostagno versus Woodforde.

C. D.: "That's the key, Fred—enjoyment; if only you go out to enjoy it, you just play better."

First, who knows whether C. D. is even right in assuming or deducing that one or other of the players is in fact "enjoying it"? In any case, if the purpose— or even the effect—of enjoyment is "to play better," this is in total contradiction with the idea of "playing for enjoyment," which, if it means anything, must mean the enjoyment that comes from playing for its own sake.

Presumably, amateur, weekend painters enjoy their hobby; does that mean that they do or must get better every weekend? Just imagine the bedrooms that would be exploding in homes all over the land—at least in the younger and more active households—if people got better and better at sex *every time they enjoyed it*! The denouement of increasing expertise in eating is even harder to imagine. The logic of this dictum is akin to that of saying that the best way to trick or cheat someone is to be sincere.

I don't know what C. D. would say were the external manifestations of "enjoyment," but I doubt whether J. McEnroe or I. Nastase—not to mention the Fiery One himself—displayed many of them when they were at their best. Often, after a losing streak, leading players tell their interviewers that they haven't been "enjoying" their tennis lately. Could there possibly be a little reversal of cause and effect here? I certainly don't recall ever hearing a player on a winning streak saying that he *wasn't* "enjoying" his tennis, not to mention that winning is not in itself necessarily a measure of "playing better." What if your opponent is simply a "better" player or is also "playing better"—even if you are?

June 8, 1989. French Open. C. Drysdale, after S. Graf had just lost a set to M. Seles:

"Before this tournament, everybody would have said that Steffi Graf would have gone through this championship without losing a set. Well, that will certainly not happen."

Overblown claims are sometimes made on behalf of the French language; they say that it has the *mot juste* for just about everything. Well, for tautologies of these monumental proportions, what can you say except *ah, bon!*

September 25, 1998. Davis Cup, United States versus Italy. C. Drysdale, knowingly and significantly:

"I think the early games in this third set are important."

As distinct from which? The later ones, when, for example, you have just lost your service in the final set at 4–all and are now 5–4 down and need to break your opponent's serve to stay in the match?

March 5, 1994. Edberg serving at 5–3 in first set versus Sampras.

C. D.: "Sampras is thinking, 'it's got to be now, if I'm going to get back in this set.'"

Maybe, maybe not. Maybe he's thinking, "If I don't get back in this set now, I still have the next two or three sets to get back in the match," or "Oh God, I forgot to call my mother before I left the hotel like I promised," or "I should never have let my broker buy that stock for me!" Or maybe C. D. is simply instinctively trying to off-load responsibility for the staggering unoriginality of this insight.

July 4, 1972. Wimbledon Final. Monica Seles one set down and 1–4 down in second set. Bud Collins offers the following penetrating analysis:

"If Monica can only hold here and pull herself together, she's only a break down"—that is, "How little she has to do to win." Equally—or much more so—why not the following? "She's already a set and a break down; she's got an awful long way to go to get even, let alone win."

However, apart from the doubtful value or validity of this expertise, how come this type of "analysis" always leaves the opponent out of the equation?

All other things being equal, there might just be something in this kind of comment in events like the high jump or figure skating, where competitors' performances, although compared with their opponents', are not directly affected by or intricately intermeshed with that of their opponents.

If by "pull herself together" B. C. means "raise her game," then (a) what if her opponent doesn't let her (you can't improve your return of serve if your opponent is acing you), and (b) what if her opponent also "pulls herself together," or raises *her* game?

Or, conversely, what if Monica doesn't "pull herself together," but her opponent starts playing worse? Then Monica may well win anyway. So here we have the authoritative, uncontested expert "analysis" posing a condition—if she "pulls herself together"—that (whatever it is supposed to mean) turns out to be neither a necessary nor a sufficient condition for pulling a win out of a losing situation.

March 17, 1992. Lipton International, Key Biscayne. M. Chang versus P. Sampras, down 3–6, 4–6, 2–4.

C. D.: "Michael Chang is on the edge of a precipice here—he's just got to find a way of holding his service and breaking Pete Sampras's, or he's out of here."

Is this *analysis, information, prediction, deduction, diagnosis*—or what? A litmus test for armor-plated tautology—the **armadillo** or **the duck-billed platitude** of the sportscaster's menagerie—is whether there is any possible fact, evidence, or event that could possibly prove it false. Yes, "a rose is a rose is a rose," but why on earth does someone need to be paid to tell us so?

Ibid. C. D., after telling us that Chang had complained to the umpire about some calls: "But, as Mary Carillo pointed out, as hard as Pete Sampras hits the ball, anything can happen."

Yes, I suppose this at least possesses the virtue of reminding the dullards among us that "it ain't over till it's over."

Ibid. C. Drysdale: "When he's on, he can beat almost anyone in the world, but when he's off..."

Isn't it possible that, inter alia, he might be "on," but the particular "almost anyone in the world" he happens to be playing might choose that very day to be even more "on"?

Ibid. Becker versus Mancini, Mancini leading 4–2 and 30–all in the third set.

F. Stolle: "The next game or so will be absolutely crucial; the next two points are huge."

Inevitably, after rubbing shoulders with the Sententious One for so long, the Fiery One was bound to have siphoned off some of his magic.

And for an encore, as if in response to imaginary applause from his invisible audience, after Mancini has just lost two match points in succession, F. S. obliges with a further penetrating insight: "He knows he has let Becker off the hook now."

Some tournament or other. Stich versus Connors, one set all, tiebreaker in the third, Connors leading 5 points to 3.

Unknown (happily for him!) commentator, sticking his neck out about as far as the pope did when he addressed the United Nations and came out boldly and unequivocally against hunger: "He has to get the next two points to clinch the tiebreaker, if he is to have a chance of winning the match—and he knows it!"

THE HEDGED BET OR THE WIN-WIN PROPHECY
This "heads, I win; tails, you lose" prescience dates at least as far back as the Oracle of Delphi, and fortune tellers, astrologers, chiropractors, psychics, horserace tipsters, and stockbrokers are still making a living from it.

Mary-Jo Fernandez has just lost the first set to A. Sanchez, and we are advised by Mary Carrillo that "she (M. J. Fernandez) must either be more patient or go for the shots and end them earlier."

This duck-billed platitude doesn't even have the merits of a genuine tautology. It is also flawed by the Solipsistic Fallacy, which ignores the fact that the performance of the opponent on the other side of the net contributes in at least equal measure to the outcome and that this performance may equally well fluctuate in any direction in the course of play. Hence, *any given* adjustment in the play of M. J. Fernandez does not take place in a vacuum, and it therefore simply does not follow that such an adjustment, including either of the two antithetical ones with which Mary Carrillo has ringed her target and hedged her bets, even if it resulted in M. J. F.'s improving her play, would guarantee victory. After all, the improvement might not be great enough to make the difference, and in any case, her opponent is no less likely to improve *her* play.

ABC TV. Monday Night Football, January 11, 1992..

Dallas versus Philadelphia. John Madden: "The closer you get to the line, the tougher it is [to score]." That is to say that if you had offered J. Madden in his coaching days a choice between two starting field positions, he would always have chosen the one *further* from the opposing team's goal line! All commentators, without exception—including J. M.—always describe starting positions nearer the opponent's goal line as "good field position" and the opposite as bad!

LANGUAGE CRIMES—JARGON THAT STANDS LANGUAGE ON ITS HEAD

November 8, 1987. Green Bay versus Chicago Bears. Former coach and prominent football "analyst" John Madden: "The Packers have done a good job of *defending* the wide receivers."

At this point, Chicago had thrown fifteen passes to wide receivers, and three had been caught. This same "could go either way" logic can be found in all competitive "opponent" sports. Did they *defend* well, or was it poor passing by Chicago?

This particular kind of language crime is not peculiar to sports talk but is prevalent in many areas of contemporary American discourse. It involves appropriating perfectly good words that already have a perfectly serviceable meaning and twists them *gratuitously* into meanings that, as in this case, sometimes have to be understood as virtually the opposite of the standard accepted usage. The Packers have not been *defending* Chicago's wide receivers; they have actually been *attacking* them—and pretty aggressively, at that. This is the same jargonizing drive that has given us trains that *depart* stations and salesmen who *sell* the customer—or even whole cities!

LOGIC CRIMES

The game or sport I happen to be talking about is somehow different from—and thus mystically superior to—all other games and sports. In the same spirit, incidentally, language patriots will proudly tell you of words or expressions in their languages that "cannot be translated into any other language."

November 12, 1995. San Francisco 49ers versus Dallas Cowboys.

John Madden: "The great thing about *this game* (i.e., football) is that you don't know what is going to happen."

One wonders why people even bother to stage ping-pong or billiards tournaments. Where's the suspense?

Disguised Tautology

This is a much more slippery customer than the outright, in-your-face version (see above).

The Irish Times. February 28, 2000: "Darren Clarke…as a 66/1 outsider, he caused a sensation by beating Tiger Woods in the final of the $5 million Andersen Consulting Match Play Championship. His transformation this time is attributed to *'growing maturity'* for one of the game's underachievers."

In other words, he did it because he was now ready to do it, and to prove it, he did it. If he hadn't, then, of course, he wouldn't have (grown mature). If his victory had "been attributed" to his "growing beard," at least one would have had a chance of actually glimpsing a cause to which to attach an effect! This one is right up there with "*concentration*" (see below).

This offense also overlaps with the logical failure that afflicts comment on all "opponent" sports, a failure to reckon with the at least equal possibility that the winner may have won because of the poor play of the opponent, or that the loser lost because of the excellent play of the opponent—no matter how "mature" the player may have suddenly grown.

Wisdom After The Event—Masquerading As Insight

USA Channel. US Open Tennis Championships. September, 1989.

Ann White: "Smart play there by Evert."

After Evert had approached the net on an unpenetrating approach shot and Garrison had just missed passing her on the forehand.

Would it still have been "a smart shot" if Garrison had not missed?

Similarly, after a failed attempt at a drop volley by Garrison, Ann White tut-tutted:

"That was a real low percentage shot by Garrison."

Is that what she would have said if the shot had been successful, even though it would have been just as "low percentage"?

Ibid. After A. Sanchez had just successfully drop-shotted G. Sabatini across court, John Barrett sagely informed the public, "The perfect moment."

If the shot had missed, he would undoubtedly have told us as authoritatively that it was "a poor choice of shot" or "low percentage."

September 9, 1992. US Open. S. Graf versus A. Sanchez.

Tracy Austin, ex cathedra: "That was real smart of Arantxa—the change-up [Ameri-talk for an (allegedly) slower than usual service] made Steffi think about it, and she netted the return."

And even smarter of T. A. to get inside—and out of—the heads of both players in the batting of an eyelid. So much for all the difficulties the world's greatest thinkers have had down the ages in relating cause to effect.

If Steffi had not netted the return, what are the chances that we would have heard something like "you can't afford to ease up on your service when you're facing a great return like Steffi's"?

POSTMORTEM DIAGNOSTICS

This offense is akin to the wrangling postmortem pontification—four pontifices, all equally infallible—that used to go on around the bridge table in my playing days, and one of the reasons I gave up playing. This would ensue immediately after the cards had been gathered and all relevant material evidence removed.

Instant replay, of course, can now serve as a corrective to misstatements of fact, but not, alas, to profound and insightful *interpretations* of them.

July 2, 1997. Sampras versus Korda, J. McEnroe presiding. Whenever anyone, especially Sampras, missed a shot, one of the commentators would inevitably say:

"He tried to do too much with it."

This, inter alia, could equally well apply to balls that land on or near the line, or, for that matter, just scrape over the net. Indeed, all winning (in the sense that excludes "unforced errors" by the opponent) shots are, in a sense, calculated risks. Otherwise, all tennis matches would be decided by the balance of "unforced errors," as indeed they came close to being in a certain kind of ladies' match, especially in a previous era.

April 27, 1997. Monte Carlo Final. Fred Stolle, as Rios wins the point: "Good shoulder turn again."

Even if the reason for striking the ball well *is* "good shoulder turn," well-struck balls in theory can, and in practice do, go out or into the net, just as a ball on which the striker's "eye has been kept" may or may not go in. (See below, July 5, 1992, Wimbledon Men's Final.) This mindless mantra, which is a real favorite with the WATE (Wisdom after the Event) crowd, along with all the others of this type, was exploded once and for all by John Crowe, the coach at an NCPR tennis course at Bisham Abbey in England. For a live demonstration of the importance of "keeping your eye on the ball," he asked his assistant to toss a tennis ball toward him very gently while he studiously, ostentatiously, and unblinkingly watched the ball all the way past his outstretched racket.

The "can't lose" syllogism at work here goes something like this: if the point is won, the player must have done something right (forget for the moment, as the pundits do all the time, that it may well have been the opponent who did something *wrong*), and our "analyst" knows immediately and unerringly exactly what it was and cannot be gainsaid.

All these pundits of "analysis" should be made to stand up and be counted by being confronted with a series of replays showing players in the act of hitting the ball, but without showing its subsequent trajectory and fate. They would then have to tell us how good or how bad a shot it was (going to be), and why—without the benefit of hindsight!

March 17, 1992. Lipton International, Key Biscayne. Becker versus Mancini. Mancini serving for the match at 5–3.

F. Stolle: "The pressure is clearly behind the man from Argentina."

Why on earth? Surely, if anything, the pressure would be on the heavily favored player (Becker), who has to break service in order to stay in the tournament.

A little later, F. S. contrives to have it both ways when, with a little sleight of self-contradiction, he allows as how Mancini will probably now "take it to Becker," since "he has nothing to lose."

July 5, 1992. Wimbledon—Men's Final. Ivanisevic versus Agassi.

As Ivanisevic netted a volley:

Chris Evert: "He took his eye off the ball there."

Once again, this is pseudodiagnosis or "analysis" after the event. The replay showed no evidence of eye being taken off ball. This comment is about as mindless as saying that marksmen at a firing range only miss the bull's-eye when—and because—they are not *aiming* at it. We all know that many bull's-eyes are missed *in spite of the fact* that we are aiming at them. Surely it is equally possible to *aim* and *miss* in tennis—or any other ball game—although it could, of course, always be that pseudodiagnostician's favorite, a lapse of *concentration* q.v.

There is also the false implication that "keeping your eye on the ball" is (a) a sufficient and (b) a necessary condition of a successful volley—that is, a volley that lands inside the court. In this sense, a "successful" volley is not necessarily a winning one or a "good" one. Indeed, a "good" volley is not even necessarily a "winning" one (since the opponent may return it with an even better shot), and a "winning" one is not necessarily a "good" one (since the opponent may "muff" the return).

Part of the point that is chronically missed by the stock use of this mindless cliché is that the player, far from "taking his or her eye off the ball," is instinctively aware that it is not good enough just to get volley in court (a "successful" volley) but, depending on the state of the score and the player's estimate of the opponent's abilities, that it is also necessary to hit it well out of the opponent's reach, thus dangerously narrowing the available target to something far smaller than the whole court, which was our "analyst's" primitive assumption that the player was aiming at and somehow *missed* because the "eye was taken off the ball"! Yes, indeed, if you start from the assumption that someone is trying to hit the proverbial barn door from point-blank range and misses, it might not be totally idiotic to imagine that something pretty radical had gone drastically wrong.

Ibid. C. Evert, after Ivanisevic has just netted an attempted forehand drive: "He didn't get down low enough."

To show that "getting down low" is not a sufficient condition for getting a forehand drive into court, we have only to apply the J. Crowe test—that is, get down low, and blast the ball over the fence. As to whether "getting down low" is even a necessary condition, well, how many times do we see, inter alia, major players, far from "getting down low," actually striking extremely successful drives with both feet visibly off the ground, not to mention the number of times we have seen Ivanisevic himself hitting successful drives from equal or higher altitudes?

Among the host of other factors available to choose for this instant diagnosis, there was, for instance, the not uninteresting fact that it was set point, the first of the tiebreaker. Considering that, how about the tad more plausible "he choked under the pressure"?

May 25, 1992. French Open. Savchenko versus Pierce. Unidentified commentator (soprano) on Pierce: "It was really the way she played today that determined the score."

Well, as the philosopher replied to his friend who greeted him with the question, "How's your wife?" I suggest asking "Compared with what?"

M. J. Fernandez versus S. Graf. After M. J. F. has just hit a firm forehand winner down the line with the score at "ad out":

C. Evert: "It's easier to play this way when you're behind—you've nothing to lose. That's the way she should play when she's ahead."

This utterance puts paid to any notion that fuzzy logic is some breathtakingly novel invention dreamed up by supersmart, cutting-edge cybercrats and supersedes conventional logic. Not that C. Evert gets the credit for the invention—she is simply carrying on a fine old sportscasting tradition. She starts with some fuzzy language.

1. By "*this way*" does she mean hitting the ball (a) hard and uninhibitedly; (b) hard, uninhibitedly, and in court; or (c) hard, uninhibitedly, in court, and out of the reach of her opponent?

    If (a), it is certainly *easier* to hit a tennis ball as hard as you can without caring too much about where it lands, but if you're keeping the score, it is hardly a recommended winning strategy.

    If (b), then the trouble is that the harder you hit the ball in order to discomfit your opponent, the less likely you are to hit it in the court, so that the net return on your investment may be no greater than it was before you started "*playing this way.*"

    If (c), then the recommendation ceases to be a strategy and becomes a pure tautology, which is true by definition. We don't really need the higher expertise to realize that if we win all the points, we will defeat our opponents—any more than the World Food Programme could make a great deal of use of the papal solution to the hunger problem made in the course of His Holiness's address to the UN General Assembly: "Let the hungry eat at the table of mankind."

2. In any case, *"playing this way,"* (a) or (b), may very well have been the reason why she has fallen behind in the match in the first place, and she should therefore be doing precisely the opposite and switch to a more cautious, defensive style of play.

3. To the extent that there is any substance at all in this utterance, the fact is that the exact opposite is true. At "ad out," at any stage in the match, a risky shot that fails loses you the whole shebang, game, set, or match. At "ad in," you have a margin of error, so all is *not* lost if your risky shot fails.

Shibboleths And Mantras

Of all the shibboleths and mantras that are dished out as regularly and reverently as old ladies make the rounds of the temples in Katmandu to spin their favorite prayer wheels, pride of place must go to "the crucial seventh game."

1997. US Clay Court Final. Chang (the favorite) versus Stafford. In the first set, Chang *won* the "crucial" *seventh* game to hold his service but lost the set 4—6. So much for the "crucial" seventh! If anything at all can be usefully described as "significant," if not "crucial," in these circumstances, it is whether or not Chang won the seventh game by holding or by *breaking* service.

In the second set, Chang won the seventh game to reach 5—2 and went on to win the set 6—2. As to whether it was his winning of the seventh game that made the crucial difference—compared, say, with his winning the eighth and final game—your guess is as good as mine. After all, according to the piece of folk wisdom delivered immediately following, the eighth game won by Chang was "the hardest service game to hold" because "it was the one immediately after he had broken his opponent's service game."

In the third set, Chang won the seventh—and, it so happened, the final game of the set, winning 6—1. That game was certainly *decisive*, as indeed any set- and match-winning game would be, but it was undoubtedly a lot less "crucial" than, say, winning the final game of a 7—5 or a 6—4 set, or the nonmagical twelfth or tenth games, respectively.

It is surely no coincidence that the number 7 has been accorded mystical or magical status in many folklores and cultures, including the Bible.

Ibid. Commentator: "How important is this *first service* game to Stafford? A guy really wants to get his teeth into this match right away!"

Q.: Does Stafford want to win his first service game at all? Somewhat? A lot?

A.: How about "yes" to all three...and his second...and his third?

1992. Volvo International, San Francisco.

Tim Mayotte: "When you need a break, the **first point** is essential." Well, of course, who is going to worry about winning the game point, or last point, or even *losing* game point to your opponent when he is leading 40–30 once you've got the first point comfortably tucked away and once led 15–0 in the game?

Other favorites that have been treated under other rubrics include "shoulder turn," "getting down low," "keeping your eye on the ball," and drop shots that are inevitably "low-percentage shots"—unless they happen to win the point! This potent arch mantra once held all commentators in its thrall, but I have not been hearing it quite so much in recent years, although I hesitate to ascribe this to a sudden upsurge of good sense rather than the fluctuations of fashion. It seems to have given place to the closely related comment: "The hardest service game to hold is the one immediately after you have broken your opponent's service." To wit, consider the following.

February 29, 1992. MSG TV. Purex Tournament—semifinals. Washington versus Gilbert.

Tim Mayotte and Barry Mackay at the mike: "Absolutely, Barry, if you get broken, your opponent is much more vulnerable on the next game."

Apart from anything else, every time a player is the first one to lose his service in a set, it is, by definition, *not after* winning his opponent's service!

CONCENTRATION

Just as, according to no less an authority than Dr. Johnson, patriotism is the last resort of the scoundrel, so "concentration" is the last resort of the "analyst." When the toothpaste tube of disguised tautology and mindless cliché masquerading as exegesis is just about squeezed dry, commentators, whose understanding nothing passeth, can always contrive to extract one last drop. "Concentration," apart from being the arch mantra, is such a capacious garment for commentators, ever anxious to wrap themselves in the mantle of omni-science, that it spills over into several of the listed categories of offense.

One of its principal functions is that of "disguised tautology." One of the purest everyday examples of this device is that used by stores—and other commercial and bureaucratic institutions—that tell their hapless customers that they are afraid that they cannot accept returned goods *because it is not their policy.* The maximum mean-ing that can be squeezed out of this is that "they *never* do it" or "they have decided never to do it." In other words, they *won't* do it *because* they never *do,* or the *reason* why they *won't* is that they *don't.* The chances are that they rarely have to grapple with a bemused, baffled, and frustrated customer who is obstreperous enough to ask them the *reason* for their policy after being told that "the policy *is* the reason."

One test of whether a statement is a pure tautology is whether it can be shown to be false—or true, for that matter. With other mantras of the "instant diagnosis" category, like "good shoulder turn" or "the crucial seventh game," if you want to take the enormous trouble, you can look for evidence either way. With the former, you can carefully examine a slow-motion replay, and with the latter, you can painstakingly record the evolution of the score in a large number of matches and see how "crucial" the seventh game actually turns out to be. But what kind of replay or accumulation of statistics could possibly prove or dis-prove a claim that lack of "concentration" was the cause of a missed shot, a lost set, or a lost match? Much of the time, in fact, players are aiming at such small targets in their attempts to get the ball in court (*and* out of their opponent's reach at the same time) that a more useful question to try to answer might well be "how on earth did he or she get it *in?*"—a much rarer and more unlikely outcome—than "how on earth did he or she miss?"

One more feature of this mantra, which is shared by many of the others, is that whatever "concentration," or lack of it, may or may not be, it totally ignores the factor of the opponent in the equation, who may at any time be outconcentrating, or being outconcentrated by, *his or her* opponent. As a rule, lack of "concentration" seems to be attributed almost exclusively to lapses on the part of the "overdog." This is paralleled in locker-room post-mortems the world over, where loss of "concentration" is something that only ever happens to the speaker—never the opponent—and is somehow felt to make his or her lapses more respectable and the opponent's victory somehow less creditable.

MSG TV New York. February 1992. Finals of the Volvo (San Francisco) Tournament. Chang versus Courier. Chang leading 3–1, first set. Advantage Chang. Chang serves wide to Courier's backhand, drawing him out of court, and nets the straightforward volley off the return.

Commentator: "He overplayed it; he must have lost his concentration."

This kind of talk is just a "busy" way of telling us what we all know—namely, *the fact that* the player lost the point or made an error—under the guise of explaining *why*, something we, the untutored telly masses, do not know. In other words, as in the case of "it's not our policy," such statements pass off the fact *that* something happened as the *reason why* it happened. In any case, if the expression has any meaning at all, it is contradicted by "he overplayed it"; that is, "he was trying too hard to keep it out of his opponent's reach"—anything but a lapse of "concentration."

Ibid. After one of the players has put away a good attempted passing shot down the line:

Barry Mackay: "Great anticipation." Or did he just guess right?

B. Mackay again: "Against Chang, you go for far too much and lose your concentration."

Surely, against such a relentless and effective retriever, what you do is start to aim at an increasingly narrow target in an attempt to keep it out of his reach, thus increasing your chances of missing that target.

November 1992. Dallas Cowboys versus LA Rams. After Michael Irvin has just dropped an "easy" pass:

Verne Lundquist: "Well, there's a loss of concentration!"

Does this really explain *why* he dropped it? Or is it just a way of telling the audience *that* he dropped it, while feeding them the suggestion that because of some superior power of analysis, he has explained *why*? There are, after all, one or two other factors in the equation, such as the patter of four not so tiny feet in his immediate vicinity, belonging to two charging 250-pound opponents bent on causing him officially sanctioned grievous bodily harm the moment he makes contact with the ball. Again, the meaningful question here is, "How on earth does anyone *ever* actually catch the ball in such circumstances?"

December 12, 1992. New York Giants versus Phoenix Cardinals (National Football League). After the Giants had been drawn offside and penalized five yards:

Commentator: "That's a lack of concentration on the Giants' defense."

The same commentator, moments before, had said: "That's the third time the Cardinals' quarterback has used the 'hard count.'"

So which was it? Was it smart of the Cardinals to draw the Giants offside, or was it lack of "concentration" on the part of the Giants?

There are numerous areas of life, including games, where people are duped by deception. In the sidewalk con game "Spot the Lady," or the "Three-Card Game," victims, after the initial win they are allowed in order to suck them in, find that they then lose time after time, but the idea that they are doing anything but *concentrating* furiously in order to defend their investment is clearly ludicrous.

ABC TV. November 25, 1993. Georgia versus Georgia Tech (college football). After Georgia had just drawn a penalty for being offside:

Commentator: "Once again, Georgia are shooting themselves in the foot—it's just a lack of *concentration*."

Getting "offside" in football (American) is closely akin to making a "false start" in sprint events. If we must have an instant explanation, surely it is the exact opposite. Every nerve is strained and focused—or *concentrated*—precisely on not losing a split second after the starter's pistol is fired and on getting off to the best possible start. How about "*over*concentration"?

June 3, 1996. French Open. Monica Seles versus Jana Novotna. Seven–all in the first set tiebreaker. Seles hits Novotna's serve a little beyond the baseline—in an honest attempt to win a point against service.

Tracy Austin in the chatterbox: "Just a little lapse of *concentration*."

Maybe all these players—or better still, their diagnosticians—should be sent to the "deconcentration camp," which I would urge the Central Council for Physical Recreation to open for the treatment and rehabilitation of persistent "disguised tautologicians"!

November 29, 1992. New York Jets versus Kansas City Chiefs (National Football League).

Bill Parcells, commentating: "There's just no excuse for getting beat in that situation; that's just poor *concentration*—just a *concentration* lapse."

The Chiefs, on third and seventeen, had just completed a pass for fifty-five yards. Who exactly was not concentrating on what? In the same breath, Parcells was commending the call as "low risk, and even if it's intercepted, it's just the same as a punt, and the receiver [Willie Davis] has exceptional speed. It was a perfect pass and a great catch."

It was exactly the kind of play, in fact, of which, when they are in the mood, sportscasters, including Parcells, will say, "You just can't defend a play like that!"

If the play was that good, then *that* was the reason for its success, and lack of *concentration* on the part of the defense had nothing to do with it. Who, exactly, on the defense was not concentrating on what when the quarterback lofted a "perfectly thrown pass" over their heads that resulted in a "great catch" by a receiver who could run faster than any of them?

New York Times. October 11, 2002.

"Manchester City earned a 3–1 victory over Manchester United yesterday...A furious Ferguson blamed 'a lack of "*concentration*"' for the goals." I wasn't there to see the game, and maybe some key United defenders were simply moping around the goalmouth waiting for their Chinese takeout orders to be delivered, but isn't it just possible that Manchester City earned some or all of their goals by good play?

April 30, 2001. "'It was a real, real lousy day for Agbayani [outfielder who made three fielding errors]," Mets manager Bobby Valentine said. "I think he had a little lapse of *concentration*."

All three errors came on hits that bounced past or off Agbayani. What if he misjudged the bounce? It's hard to imagine that after Agbayani had seriously embarrassed himself in front of the crowd, the media, and his teammates by twice missing the ball, his mind would somehow be wandering the third time the ball came his way. High anxiety? Maybe.

This is the same kind of facile, instant "wisdom after the event" explanatory logic that was used by the media when they jumped all over George H. W. Bush's electoral campaign *after* he lost to Clinton in 1992—"a terrible campaign," "total disarray," and the like.

It used to be that *omnia vincit amor*. In the competitive feeding frenzy of today's "info-media," it is *immediacy* that trumps all, and if something, however complex and intricate, succeeds or fails, the media pundits are ready to step up and tell us exactly why. One can't help wondering why they always wait until the precise moment when their retrospective but somehow prophetic wisdom ceases to be of any use to us. It is the same kind of infallibility a racehorse tip-ster would enjoy if the grateful beneficiaries of his postrace tip were somehow allowed back to the betting windows to put their money on the winner of the last race.

Modern-Languages Department

"Liberté, Egalité, Fraternité"

It is easy to understand why the French Revolution chopped off people's heads in the name of freedom (brotherhood is a little harder to reconcile with wholesale decapitation), but why on earth did it make such a big thing of "deuce" (known in French as *egalité*)?

Ignorance is fine, but when it is flaunted and betrayed by pretentiousness, the combination is harder to forgive. In mitigation—if not defense—it should be said that this syndrome is not unique to the sportscaster fraternity but is common throughout the media, where reach is always exceeding grasp.

CNN. Pat McEnroe, February 22, 2002. "He [Sampras] needs to put a little mustard on that one…Yes, and there wasn't much *moutar* [for *moutarde*] on that one."

Clearly, P. McEnroe and other offenders, notably, the "Effervescent One," Bud Collins, have heard somewhere that you don't pronounce the last conso-nants in French words—or indeed, maybe in "European" words in general—hence the all-too-frequent *Steffi Gra* (for *Graff*) as in *Mardi Gras*, not to mention another favorite, *couPe de gra* (for *coup de grace*).

The American Foreign Legion

Commenting on the French Open in 1993, Chris Evert remarked:

"Mary Jo [Fernandez] is the first *American* in the final since *Martina*" (née Navratilova—and Czech).

Well, it depends what you mean by American. Not too many Roman gladi-ators started life as Romans, and a good many of their latter-day American *con-freres/soeurs* did not start life as American and probably would not have ended up as American were it not for the athletic scholarships and the special and acceler-ated naturalization privileges accorded to foreign-born athletes, among others, who are, or are likely to become, jewels in the American crown. On this basis, Monaco could probably field a Davis Cup championship team!

And now I give you the last, but not, alas, final, word in unbridled, self-indulgent, but above all, plausible-sounding fatuity. As is the case for all momentous historical events, it is important to register the precise time when it occurred. Do you remember what you were doing at 11:50 a.m. on August 24, 1985? Well, just in case you didn't happen to be listening to CNN, here is what you missed:

"All baseball managers stress fundamentals—it's the most important part of the game."

And there we all were, thinking it was the peripherals!

The prosecution despairs.

22808880R00149

Printed in Great Britain
by Amazon